PCI Compliance

Second Edition

PCI Compliance

Understand and Implement Effective PCI Data Security Standard Compliance

Second Edition

Dr. Anton A. Chuvakin
Branden R. Williams

Technical Editor
Ward Spangenberg

AMSTERDAM • BOSTON • HEIDELBERG • LONDON
NEW YORK • OXFORD • PARIS • SAN DIEGO
SAN FRANCISCO • SINGAPORE • SYDNEY • TOKYO
Syngress is an imprint of Elsevier

SYNGRESS®

Syngress is an imprint of Elsevier
30 Corporate Drive, Suite 400, Burlington, MA 01803, USA

This book is printed on acid-free paper.

Copyright © 2010 by Elsevier Inc. All rights reserved.

Notices

Knowledge and best practice in this field are constantly changing. As new research and experience broaden our understanding, changes in research methods, professional practices, or medical treatment may become necessary.

Practitioners and researchers must always rely on their own experience and knowledge in evaluating and using any information, methods, compounds, or experiments described herein. In using such information or methods they should be mindful of their own safety and the safety of others, including parties for whom they have a professional responsibility.

To the fullest extent of the law, neither the Publisher nor the authors, contributors, or editors, assume any liability for any injury and/or damage to persons or property as a matter of products liability, negligence or otherwise, or from any use or operation of any methods, products, instructions, or ideas contained in the material herein.

Library of Congress Cataloging-in-Publication Data
Application submitted

British Library Cataloguing-in-Publication Data
A catalogue record for this book is available from the British Library.

ISBN: 978-1-59749-499-1

Printed in the United States of America
09 10 11 12 13   5 4 3 2 1

Elsevier Inc., the author(s), and any person or firm involved in the writing, editing, or production (collectively "Makers") of this book ("the Work") do not guarantee or warrant the results to be obtained from the Work.

For information on rights, translations, and bulk sales, contact Matt Pedersen, Commercial Sales Director and Rights; email: *m.pedersen@elsevier.com*

For information on all Syngress publications
visit our website at *www.syngress.com*

Typeset by: diacriTech, Chennai, India

Working together to grow
libraries in developing countries

www.elsevier.com | www.bookaid.org | www.sabre.org

ELSEVIER   BOOK AID
International   Sabre Foundation

Contents

Foreword

From my perspective as one of its original authors, the history of PCI – although short – has certainly been a tortured one and one with too many conflicting interpretations, or should I say misinterpretations? It is this conflict that currently inhibits the widespread "correct" adoption and use of PCI. Instead, we often see PCI interpreted as a proscriptive check list that, if applied, will magically make an organization secure.

Clearly, that is not the case as is evidenced by the different disclosures of customer confidential information we have seen of late from organizations that passed their PCI assessments with flying colors.

Finally, we have a solid and comprehensive reference for PCI. This book explains in great detail not only how to apply PCI in a practical and cost-effective way but more importantly why. From what I have witnessed in the last several years, answering why PCI, and more importantly, why information security, is probably the single most important question one should ask, especially if you're in a regulated industry and in particular, if PCI applies to your organization.

In short, this book explains very clearly that we use PCI as a risk-based framework for implementing security architecture because a proscriptive approach cannot work for the multivarious types of organizations to which it applies. Thus, it must be tailored to fit their specific processing environment as well as business and technical requirements.

When PCI was originally promulgated it was envisioned to be implemented within the context of a comprehensive and holistic security architecture. Such an approach functions to support an overall (corporate security) risk-based governance schema, which is ultimately the goal of PCI. Given the tools presented here, an organization should be able to address PCI within the context of a comprehensive and holistic security architecture. Further, the book goes beyond explaining the primary requirements of PCI and looks at how to create a strategy for applying technology to those requirements. Of particular note and a topic often debated by security practitioners is how to use compensating controls. (Surprise, those are not intended to be a safe harbor one can use instead of a comprehensive security solution.) This is the first book that takes a realistic look at compensating control and should enable organizations to use these only when appropriate.

Developing a solid security architecture of course does not necessarily imply compliance. For that reason, this book also discusses the means for managing a PCI project to achieve compliance as well as what the considerations are for the ongoing management of the security and governance infrastructure designed and implemented with the security architecture.

There is a wealth of information here that anyone involved in a PCI assessment or remediation efforts should know. It will certainly make those efforts less painful and, in fact, quite useful and instructive. If there is a single point to take away from this book, it is this: develop a "security and risk" mindset and not a "compliance and audit" one.

Such an approach to PCI, not to mention the many requirements and regulations that organizations face today, will serve them well.

—Joel Weise
Information Systems Security Association (ISSA) founder and
chairman of the ISSA Journal Editorial Advisory Board
Burlingame, CA

Acknowledgments

First and foremost, the most important part: I'd like to thank my wife Olga for being my eternal inspiration for all my writing, for providing invaluable economic advice, and for tolerating (well, almost always…) my work on the book during those evening hours that we could have spent together.

Next, I'd like to specially thank Derek Milroy for his exclusive material used in Chapter 8, "Vulnerability Management," and also for reviewing the book contents.

Also, I'd like to personally thank the following people for their contributions to the book:

- Walt Conway from 403 Labs for his insightful example used in Chapter 3, "Why Is PCI Here?"

- John Kindervag from Forrester Research for inventing the concept of customer data security as part of corporate social responsibility (mentioned in Chapter 15, "Myths and Misconceptions of PCI DSS").

- Nicolas Lidzborski from Qualys for reviewing book chapters and providing useful feedback on the book. Also, I'd like to thank Qualys for the examples used in Chapter 8, "Vulnerability Management."

- Angelina Ward, our illustrious Senior Acquisitions Editor, for believing that a book's second edition can be that much better than the first.

- Matthew Cater, our Developmental Editor, for putting up with us as authors and in particular for putting up with my quirks in regards to references.

—Dr. Anton A. Chuvakin

I would first like to thank Anton for having the confidence in giving an author his first big break! Thank you for believing in me! And thank you to all of my customers, from whom I learned so much!

I'd like to dedicate this book to the fantastic staff at VeriSign that supported me before we divested:

- Especially the PCI Practice (Steve, Rob, Matt, Gina, Greg, Jeff, JD, Christopher, Joe, Bill, Sherri, Frank, Susan, and James) for keeping the dream alive! Of course, Todd for approving my PTO requests to work on the book.

- The Marketing, Communications, and Events teams (Ben, Melissa, Christina, Karen K., and Alex) for believing in what we do, and Karen S. for helping me to become a better blogger!

- The Ops folks (Deb, Darlene, Alice, Channing, and Brad) who make our lives OH so much easier!

- My homeboys (and girl) on the D-Sales team (Debbi, Amir, and Tracey)!

To Matthew Cater, our Developmental Editor, whose patience is an amazing virtue.

To my extended family (Mimi, Papa, Izzie, Tia, Uncle, Abigail, Sydney, Hank, Nono, Pop, Just Pearl, Ashy, Wade, and Tinker) for putting up with my writing schedule.

To my children, Garrett and Payton (and kitties Scooter and Vasco), for whom I live, despite missing a few of your firsts while helping someone conquer PCI DSS.

Finally to Chris, my love, my inspiration, the reason why I work so hard, so the day may come where our biggest decision is which park bench we will enjoy our lunch.

—Branden R. Williams

About the Authors

AUTHORS

Dr. Anton A. Chuvakin is a recognized information security expert and book author. His information security experience covers PCI DSS, log management, intrusion detection, network forensics, honeypots, etc.

Anton is the co-author of *Security Warrior* (ISBN: 978-0-596-00545-0) and a contributing author to *Know Your Enemy: Learning About Security Threats*, Second Edition (ISBN: 978-0-321-16646-3); *Information Security Management Handbook*, Sixth Edition (ISBN: 978-0-8493-7495-1); *Hacker's Challenge 3: 20 Brand-New Forensic Scenarios & Solutions* (ISBN: 978-0-072-26304-6); *OSSEC Host-Based Intrusion Detection Guide (Syngress,* ISBN: 978-1-59749-240-9); and others.

Anton has published dozens of papers on log management, correlation, data analysis, PCI DSS, security management, and other security subjects. His blog, www.securitywarrior.org, is one of the most popular in the industry. In addition, Anton teaches classes and presents at many security conferences across the world; He recently addressed audiences in the United States, United Kingdom, Singapore, Spain, Russia, and other countries. He works on emerging security standards and serves on the advisory boards of several security start-ups.

Currently, Anton is developing his security consulting practice, focusing on logging and PCI DSS compliance for security vendors and Fortune 500 organizations. Dr. Anton Chuvakin was formerly a Director of PCI Compliance Solutions at Qualys. Previously, Anton worked at LogLogic as a Chief Logging Evangelist, tasked with educating the world about the importance of logging for security, compliance, and operations. Before LogLogic, Anton was employed by a security vendor in a strategic product management role. Anton earned his Ph.D. degree from Stony Brook University.

Branden R. Williams (CISSP, CISM, CPISA, CPISM) is the director of the Security Consulting Practice at RSA, the security division of EMC. He has been involved in information technology since 1994 and has focused on information security since 1996. He started consulting on payment security in 2004, assessing companies against the Visa CISP and MasterCard SDP programs. He has a Bachelors of Business Administration in Marketing from the University of Texas, Arlington, and a Masters of Business Administration in Supply Chain Management and Market Logistics from the University of Dallas.

Branden is also an Adjunct Professor at the University of Dallas, Graduate School of Management. He publishes a monthly column in the ISSA Journal entitled "Herding Cats" and authors a blog at www.brandenwilliams.com/.

TECHNICAL EDITOR

Ward Spangenberg (CISSP, CISA) is the Director of PCI Services for IOActive, Inc. Ward has been a security professional for more than 15 years, using his knowledge of system and network penetration, Web-application analysis, and security auditing to provide clients with the requisite tools for meeting federal, industry, and PCI compliance requirements. Ward has authored original works on Cisco devices, IBM Services, and he is a recognized speaker on Cloud Computing Security as well as PCI DSS.

FOREWORD CONTRIBUTOR

Joel Weise has worked in the field of data security for more than 30 years, designing and architecting security solutions.

Joel is a founder of the Information Systems Security Association and the chairman of the ISSA Journal's editorial board.

Joel is a leading expert on legal and regulatory issues as they relate to security and how various solutions should address governmental and other mandates such as PCI, Sarbanes–Oxley, Gramm–Leach Bliley, and HIPAA. He specializes in security policy, cryptography, smart card multi-application systems, and public key infrastructures.

Joel's current work is focused on adaptive security, maturity modeling and the convergence of data security, governance, and standards.

About PCI and This Book

If you are like most information technology (IT) and information security professionals, the idea of becoming compliant with Payment Card Industry Data Security Standard (PCI DSS) or countless other regulations does not sound like much fun. It is much more common to associate compliance efforts with the other extreme, and that is PAIN. Whether it is the pain of not knowing what to do, pain of failing the assessment, or pain of "doing compliance" on a $0 budget, there are plenty of challenges that earned compliance – PCI DSS compliance in particular – have in common with pain.

Thus, we face the seemingly impossible challenge to write a fun and insightful book about PCI DSS. We realize all the difficulties of achieving this, and we are committed to the challenge. We'd like to invite you, our reader, to travel with us in the hopes that when you turn the last page, you would come to realize that PCI DSS compliance can indeed be (YES) fun!

There are many standards and regulations out there. If your company's stock is publicly traded in the United States, you must adhere to the Sarbanes–Oxley (SOX) mandates. Financial companies fall under the Gramm–Leach–Bliley Act (GLBA). Those in the energy sector work toward

North American Electric Reliability Corporation (NERC), Federal Energy Regulatory Commission (FERC), or Critical Infrastructure Protection (CIP) standards. If you are in the health care industry, your network must comply with the Health Insurance Portability and Accountability Act (HIPAA) standards and may be subject to assessment under the new HITRUST Common Security Framework. Other countries have their own "alphabet soup" of standards such as British BSI, Russian GOST (Russian for "gosudarstvennyy standart" or "state standard"), worldwide International Organization for Standardization (ISO)/International Electrotechnical Commission (IEC), and so on. However, the PCI DSS occupies a special place among the standards due to two reasons: broad, worldwide applicability and the presence of enforcement mechanism that is seen as imminent and unavoidable, unlike for some other mentioned regulations.

The overarching theme of all these standards, laws, and regulations is that organizations need to secure their data and protect their networks to keep citizens' data safe. In some cases, weak information security may only affect the company. However, when the data on the corporate network contains personal information about patients, customers, or employees, a breach of security can have implications far beyond the company. A breach of a company dealing with hundreds of millions of customers, such as a card payment processor, will have implications touching nearly the entire society and, thus, decreasing such occurrences is in the public interest.

Visa, MasterCard, American Express, Discover, and JCB banded together to develop PCI DSS to ensure that credit-card customer information is adequately protected and to protect the card industry. Breaches of customer information lead to money loss and damaged reputations, and the credit-card industry wants to protect itself from financial loss or eroded consumer confidence in credit cards as a means of transacting money.

We will use its experience with PCI DSS, both from the PCI Qualified Security Assessor (QSA) side and from information security side, to explain the most up-to-date PCI DSS guidelines to you. However, we will do so in a broader, more holistic approach. The objective of this book is not only to teach you about the PCI DSS requirements but to help you understand how the PCI DSS requirements fit into an organization's information security framework, and how to effectively implement information security controls so that you can be both compliant and secure. In addition, we will focus on how to do this in the easiest and most painless way, but without compromising security in the process.

This book will make constant reference to the PCI DSS. PCI DSS, and its related standards, is owned by the PCI Security Standards Council (PCI SSC), sometimes known in the industry as PCI Co. Before you start reading this book, you should go to the Council's Web site at www.pcisecuritystandards.org and download PCI DSS version 1.2.1 under the Security Standards/PCI DSS heading.

As of this publication, PCI DSS is at version 1.2.1. The changes between versions 1.2 and 1.2.1 are not enough to differentiate in this book, so when we refer to PCI DSS version 1.2, assume that includes version 1.2.1.

WHO SHOULD READ THIS BOOK?

Every company that accepts card payments, processes credit- or debit-card transactions, stores payment card data, or in any other way touches personal or sensitive data associated with payment card processing is affected by the PCI DSS. Nowadays, it means that virtually all businesses, no matter how big or small, need to understand their scope of PCI DSS and how to implement PCI controls to work toward reducing their risk, or face penalties or even the possibility of having their merchant status revoked.

Even with such a broad audience compelled to comply with the PCI DSS, this book had to be written for a specific technical level. This book could have been written in very simple terms to educate the general population about PCI DSS. We could have written an in-depth technical tome providing every bit of detail a network engineer or security administrator might need to configure and implement all controls mandated by PCI DSS. This book aims in the middle and is more of a strategic guide to help executive management understand the implications of PCI DSS and what it takes to be compliant. Overall, the book would be useful for everybody in IT and in management of the organization that deal with credit cards. This would include executive management, IT and IT security management, network, server, application developers, database managers, as well as everyone interested in payment security.

As a result, this book is for the IT managers and company managers who need to understand how PCI DSS applies to their organizations. This book is for the small- and medium-size businesses that don't have an IT department to delegate to. The book is also for large organizations whose PCI DSS project scope is immense. It is for all organizations that need to grasp the concepts of PCI DSS and how to implement an effective security framework that is also compliant. This book is intended as an introduction to PCI DSS, but with a deeper and more technical understanding of how to put it into action. Finally, even PCI "literati" will benefit from the stories and case studies presented by us!

HOW TO USE THE BOOK IN YOUR DAILY JOB

You can use the book during the entire lifecycle from complete PCI unawareness to ultimate security and compliance enlightenment. Specifically, you can use it as provided in the following:

- Learn what PCI DSS is and why it is here to stay

- Figure out how it applies to you and your organization

- Learn what to do about each of the 12 main requirements

- Gain knowledge about dealing with PCI assessors

- Learn how to plan and manage PCI DSS project

- Understand all the technologies referenced by PCI DSS

- Get the best experience out of what can be seen as a painful assessment process

WHAT THIS BOOK IS NOT

While reading the book, it is useful to remember that this is not the book that will unambiguously answer every PCI DSS esoteric question. Also, there is simply no way to create a book that will answer PCI DSS questions as the regulation applies to your own environment. Indeed, there are a lot of similarity in how networks and systems are deployed, but given broad applicability of PCI DSS – from small e-commerce sites to huge worldwide retailers – there is no way to have a book "customized" for your networks, systems, and applications. It is not meant to be the final authority for all issues related to PCI DSS, and it is not the unabridged guide to all things of PCI DSS. Finally, even though the book is written using one of the authors' QSA[1] experience, your QSA is the ultimate judge of most PCI "puzzles" you will face on your journey to compliance.

ORGANIZATION OF THE BOOK

Each chapter of the book is designed to provide you the information you need to know in a way that you can easily understand and apply. To aid in that goal, the chapters follow a common structure which, wherever possible, includes

---

[1] The term *QSA* and the role of QSAs in PCI DSS assessments will be explained in Chapter 3, "Why Is PCI Here?"

the description of the PCI DSS requirement, the value of the requirement for PCI DSS and security, common tips and select tools useful for satisfying the requirement, as well as common mistakes and pitfalls.

Specifically, we are trying to first explain what is the control or a concept we are talking about, whether it is log management or compensating controls. Then, we explain where in PCI DSS this concept sits and why it is needed for information security – how it reduces risk. Next, we explain what you should do with this concept to be secure and compliant using examples, common practices, etc. Most chapters have a detailed and entertaining case study. When we said that we will make PCI fun, we really mean it! Most chapters have a summary that provides a brief recap of the concepts discussed to reinforce what you read or to help you identify areas that you may need to re-read if you feel you don't understand them yet. Where possible, we also try to highlight common mistakes and pitfalls with these requirements or PCI concepts.

SUMMARY

This section provides a brief description of the information covered in each chapter:

- Chapter 1: About PCI and This Book – This chapter explains why PCI DSS is special and what this book is about.

- Chapter 2: Introduction to Fraud, ID Theft, and Regulatory Mandates – This chapter explains cybercrime and regulations and is a brief look at payment card fraud, cybercrime, ID theft, and other things around PCI DSS.

- Chapter 3: Why Is PCI Here? – This chapter gives an overview of PCI DSS and why the card industry was compelled to create it. This chapter also includes some discussion about the benefits of PCI DSS compliance and the risks of noncompliance.

- Chapter 4: Building and Maintaining a Secure Network – This chapter explains the necessary steps in protecting data for PCI DSS compliance and other reasons: to have a secure network in the first place. This chapter discusses the basic components of a secure network and lays the foundation for building the rest of your PCI DSS compliance.

- Chapter 5: Strong Access Controls – This chapter covers one of the most important aspects of PCI DSS compliance access control. The information in this chapter includes the need to restrict access to only those individuals that need it, as well as restricting physical access to computer systems.

■ Chapter 6: Protecting Cardholder Data – This chapter explains how to protect card data that is stored on your systems, as well as how to protect data while it is in transit on your network.

■ Chapter 7: Using Wireless Networking – This chapter covers wireless security issues and wireless security controls and safeguards managed by PCI DSS.

■ Chapter 8: Vulnerability Management – This chapter explains performing vulnerability assessments to identify weaknesses in systems and applications, and how to mitigate or remediate the vulnerabilities to protect and secure your data.

■ Chapter 9: Logging Events and Monitoring the Cardholder Data Environment – This chapter discusses how to configure logging and event assessment to capture the information you need to be able to show and maintain PCI compliance, as well as how to perform other security monitoring tasks.

■ Chapter 10: Managing a PCI DSS Project to Achieve Compliance – This chapter gives an overview of the steps involved and tasks necessary to implement a successful PCI compliance project. This chapter includes a discussion of the basic elements that should be included in future projects and to proactively ensure they are PCI compliant.

■ Chapter 11: Don't Fear the Assessor – This chapter makes you understand that an assessor is there to work with you to validate your compliance and help you with security. They are not the enemy. This chapter explains how to use the findings from a failed assessment to build ongoing compliance and security.

■ Chapter 12: The Art of Compensating Control – This chapter explains how compensating controls are often talked about and misunderstood. This chapter will help build understanding and confidence in the reader when dealing with this tricky and often ambiguous component of PCI DSS.

■ Chapter 13: You're Compliant, Now What? – This chapter covers the details you need to keep in mind once you have achieved compliance. Security is not as simple as just getting it implemented. You have to monitor and maintain it. This chapter contains information about ongoing training and periodic reviews, as well as how to conduct a self-assessment to ensure continued compliance.

- Chapter 14: PCI and Other Laws, Mandates, and Frameworks – This chapter covers how PCI DSS relates to other regulatory "beasts": laws, frameworks, and regulations.

- Chapter 15: Myths and Misconceptions of PCI DSS – This final chapter explains common but damaging PCI myths and misconceptions, as well as explains the reality behind them.

CHAPTER 2

Introduction to Fraud, ID Theft, and Regulatory Mandates

Credit card fraud and identity theft are problems that plague our information-dependent society and predate the age of the Internet. Ironically, the things that make your life easier and more convenient also make crime easier and more convenient. Moreover, the Internet allowed some crime that only happened on a small scale to grow and spread globally, and the Internet's scalability turned electronic-based crimes into a global concern. Some crime was automated and changed from rare to widespread, for example, Nigerian e-mail scams. Gone are the days where criminals need to be in the same location, country, or even continent to scam you out of your hard-earned dollars. Nigerian e-mail scams started many years ago and are profitable for the scammers. They send out millions of e-mails claiming to be a relative of a Nigerian dignitary with frozen assets and want you to transfer the money for them. You give them your bank account information and/or send them "seed money" to get things moving and end up with nothing.

Criminals have gone high-tech and have discovered that there is a significant amount of money to be had with very little risk. Hacking a company database or orchestrating a phishing attack while sitting in your pajamas and eating chocolate ice cream in the living room of your house has much more appeal than robbing banks or convenience stores. Add to that the lower risk of a confrontation with firearms and electronic crime becomes even more attractive! Depending on the company being targeted, the sophistication of the attack, and sheer luck sometimes, the high-tech crime may also be significantly more lucrative than traditional armed robbery. Sadly, cross-border prosecution issues significantly fuel a cybercriminal's activity.

Malicious software (malware) and cyber-criminals are not the only threat. Sadly, the very companies and organizations that are entrusted with sensitive information are often to blame. Consumers and businesses are faced with a wide variety of threats to their data and personal information on any given day. Spyware, phishing attacks, and botnets (the name derived from "robot" or "bot" and "network") are all computer attacks that are on the rise and pose a significant threat to corporate and home users, as they connect to the Internet from their computers. However, those threats pale in comparison with the amount of personally identifiable information and sensitive data compromised through carelessness or negligence by individuals and corporations.

TOOLS

Did you know that the Privacy Rights Clearinghouse has tracked all reported breaches since the Choice-Point breach on February 15, 2005? To see all these breaches with an explanation and amount of records lost, point your browser here at www.privacyrights.org/ar/ChronDataBreaches.htm. As of this writing, they estimate that over 340 million records have been compromised.

DatalossDB at http://datalossdb.org/ is another useful site for tracking the impact of data breaches. Despite its name, most of the recorded and analyzed data "loss" incidents are really data theft and abuse incidents. DatalossDB crew makes an awesome job of tracking all publicly reported incidents and digs out the details on them.

According to some sources, more than 50 million individual records were exposed as far back as in 2005 through the loss of mobile devices or portable storage media or by attackers gaining access to the corporate network and extracting the data themselves. A security breach at CardSystems in June 2005 was responsible for 40 of the 50 million total. Every year since then, we've seen major companies fall victim to Payment Card Industry (PCI)-related security breaches. DSW Retail in 2005, The U.S. Department of Veteran's Affairs in 2006, The TJX Companies in 2007, Hannaford Brothers in 2008, and now Heartland Payment Systems in 2009 continue to demonstrate both the poor state of security and increasing sophistication of the bad guys, as well bloating the ranks of the bad guys (as more and more countries have growing populations on the Internet) who want this data and know how to profit from it.

In an "Information is King" era, when more consumers are using computers and the Internet to conduct business and make purchases, taking the proper steps to secure and protect personally identifiable information and other sensitive data has never been more important. It is bad for companies, individuals, and the economy at large if consumer confidence is eroded by having personal information exposed or compromised.

NOTE

Change your mindset and think of yourself as a consumer, Internet user, or citizen not as a security or payment professional. What data do you hold dear? Think through the following list of scenarios:

1. What data or information about me can be considered sensitive and should not be disclosed, be corrupted, or be made permanently or temporarily unavailable? Think of a broad range of types of information – from a rare photo that only sits on a hard drive of one PC to your bank account number, medical history, or information about anything you've done that you are not proud of.

2. Think whether this information exists in any electronic form, on your computers or anywhere else? Is that picture on your "private" Facebook page or present in an e-mail spool somewhere?

3. Next, think whether this information exists on some system connected to the Internet. Sadly, the answer today would be "yes" for almost all (!!!) information people consider sensitive. For example:

   a. Credit card information – check
   b. Bank account information – check
   c. Personal financial records – check
   d. Sensitive personal files – check
   e. Health records – check (most likely)

4. Think what will happen if this information is seen, modified, or deleted by other people. Will it be an annoyance, a real problem, or a disaster for you?

5. Now, think about what protects that information from harm. Admittedly, in many cases, you don't know for sure. We can assure you that sometimes your assumption that the information is secure will be just that – an assumption – with no basis.

Going through this list helps you not only understand data security rationally but also feel it in your "gut."

Information technologists are affected by a number of laws and regulations designed to coax businesses into addressing their security problems. Depending on what industry a company does business in, they may fall under Sarbanes–Oxley (SOX), the Gramm–Leach–Bliley Act of 1999 (GLBA), the Health Insurance Portability and Accountability Act (HIPAA), Federal Information Security Management Act (FISMA), and other regulatory mandates that we mentioned in the very beginning of Chapter 1, "About PCI and This Book," that are being drafted and revised as our book goes to production. Maybe this confusing hodgepodge of alphabet soup makes for a tough job understanding how to comply with all these measures, as many organizations still fail to enforce adequate security.

NOTE

If you feel lost and out of control, don't. Remember, all these crazy compliance initiatives are trying to minimize the risk associated with an underlying problem – poor security. Taking a step back and looking at a standard security framework, like ISO27002, would do more to boost your global compliance efforts than attacking any one of these by themselves. A mature ISO27002 program would be able to adapt to future compliance initiatives or changes in a way that would minimize the overall impact compliance has on your organization.

Breaches often target consumer credit card information because of the revenue this type of data can generate on the black market. Card companies recognized the rising threat to their brands and the large payment systems they invested in, and eventually they came together to develop the PCI Data Security Standards (DSS). In essence, the credit card industry has taken proactive steps to assure the integrity and security of credit card data and transactions and maintains the public trust in credit cards as a primary means of transacting money. If you want to accept credit cards as payment or take part in any step of the processing of the credit card transaction, you must comply with the PCI DSS or face stiff penalties.

NOTE

Most of the above regulations focus on the issues of data protection from theft or confidentiality of sensitive data. When we think about fraud and abuse of somebody's identity, we think about people stealing data, as if it were a thing to stash in the pocket. Indeed, to assume an identity and apply for credit under that name, a thief needs that identity's most sensitive personal information. In the United States, the typical combination needed for ID theft ("ID theft bundle") is as follows:

- Social security number (SSN)
- Your mother's maiden name
- Your full name
- Your current and past addresses and phone numbers
- Your employer name and address

From this pack, only the first two are not truly public and require work to obtain, and the rest of the bundle can be assembled later after the most sensitive information is in the possession of the attacker.

However, think what happens after your identity has been stolen and assumed by the attacker, who now lives "your" life and applies for credit cards, loans, and bank accounts using your name.

He now *modifies* or *corrupts* your data by harming your stellar credit score, reputation, standing with financial institutions, employers, government agencies (for example, if he commits crime and then shows fake ID with your name).

Thus, remember that ID theft is not only about information theft; the damage comes from actual changes to your critical information!

And while the attacker (excluding the most "special" cases which we are not prepared to discuss here…) cannot "erase" your life from the systems, the damage done to your future life can be significant, especially if the case of ID theft is detected late in the game.

Unlike SOX or HIPAA, the PCI DSS is not a law; however, in many ways, it is more effective. Noncompliance won't land you in jail, but on the rare and extreme side, it can mean having your merchant status revoked. For some organizations, losing the ability to process credit card payments would drastically affect their ability to do business and possibly even bring about the death of the company. Earlier this year, we saw a congressional hearing on the effectiveness of PCI DSS. Representatives from the PCI Security Standards Council and Visa faced tough questions in prepared statements from the committee. Although PCI DSS can be effective in stopping security breaches, companies still seem to struggle with its implementation. Entire blogs have been dedicated to the subject from Anton's Security Warrior Blog (www.securitywarrior.org/) to Branden's Security Convergence Blog (www.pciblog.info/) and Chris Mark's PCI Answers blog (www.pcianswers.com/).

WARNING

Although PCI DSS itself is not a law, at the time of this writing, both Nevada and Minnesota have enacted laws requiring that companies serving their residents comply with PCI DSS.

NOTE

By the way, credit card theft and ID theft are not the same. In fact, they have literally nothing to do with each other. You might not care much if your personal credit card information is stolen due to legally-mandated card liability limits, but you *must* and, in fact, *will be made* to care if your identity is stolen.

There is nothing extraordinary or magical about the PCI DSS requirements. The guidelines spelled out are all, essentially, common sense security practices that any organization should follow without being told. Companies with mature information security programs have had few problems adding unique PCI DSS requirements to their programs. Even so, some of the requirements leave room for interpretation and complying with PCI DSS can be tricky. Here's a hint: if one particular requirement for PCI DSS seems too hard to comply with, you might be approaching it all wrong. Think less about how to get out of complying, and think more about how to incorporate and build upon the baseline of security provided by PCI DSS.

As with any information security regulation or guideline, you need to keep your eye on the ultimate goal. When executing a compliance program, some organizations follow the letter rather than the spirit or intent of the requirements. The end result may be that they were able to check off all the compliance boxes, declaring their network compliant, but not really be secure. Remember, if you follow the requirements and seek to make your network as secure as possible, you are almost guaranteed to be compliant. But, if you gloss over the requirements and seek to make your network compliant, there is a fair chance that your network could still be insecure. It could even happen as soon as a few minutes after your assessors leave!

Major retailers and larger enterprises are well aware of the PCI DSS. They have dedicated teams that focus on security and on PCI DSS compliance. They have the resources and the budget (even in the economic recession we find ourselves in) to bring in third-parties to assess and remediate issues. The scope of PCI DSS affects almost every business, from the largest retail megastores down to a self-employed single mother working from her home computer. If the business accepts, processes, transmits, or in any other way handles credit card transactions, they must comply with PCI DSS.

SUMMARY

The purpose of this book is to provide an overview of the components that make up the PCI DSS and to provide you with the information you need to know in order to get your network PCI DSS compliant and keep it that way. We've discussed how larger Compliance-Driven Alphabet Soup Initiatives can really confuse the business side of operations. Security is a business issue, and a good security program puts a framework in place to address issues like compliance before they become a problem.

Each major area of security covered by the PCI DSS is discussed in some detail along with the steps you can take to implement the security measures on your network to protect your data. Anton and Branden, your humble authors for the next 13 chapters, are established information security professionals. We've been there and done that, and we have acquired wisdom through trial and error. We hope our experience will help you implement effective solutions that are both secure and compliant.

Why Is PCI Here?

Chances are if you picked up this book, you already know something about the Payment Card Industry Data Security Standard (PCI DSS); however, you might not have a full and clear picture of PCI DSS – both the standards and its regulatory regime – and why they are here. This chapter covers everything from the conception of the cardholder protection programs by the individual card brands to the founding of the PCI Security Standards Council (PCI SSC) and PCI DSS development. It also explains the reasons for PCI DSS arrival that are critical in understanding how to implement PCI DSS controls in your organization. Also, many of the questions people ask about PCI DSS and many of the misconceptions and myths about PCI have their origins in the history of the program, so it only makes sense that we start at the beginning.

WHAT IS PCI AND WHO MUST COMPLY?

First, "PCI" is not a government regulation or a law.[1] As you know, when people say "PCI," they are actually referring to the PCI DSS, at the time of this writing, of version 1.2.1. However, to make things easy, we will continue to use the term *PCI* to identify the payment industry standard for card data security.

Unlike many other regulations, PCI DSS has a very simple and direct answer to a question "who must comply?" Despite its apparent simplicity, a lot of people have attempted to misunderstand it, which leads the authors to believe that most of such people had their own agenda. This always reminds us of a quote from Upton Sinclair, a noted American novelist, who said "It is difficult to get a man to understand something when his job depends on not understanding it" [1]. So, PCI's answer to "who must comply?" is any organization that accepts payment cards or stores, processes, or transmits credit or debit card data must comply with the PCI DSS.

NOTE

PCI applies if your organization accepts, processes, stores, and transmits credit or debit card data.

It is very easy to understand the motivations for such broad applicability. It is clearly pointless to protect the card data only in a few select places; it needs to happen wherever and whenever the card data is present. This is where a thought might cross your mind as to why the data is present in so many places. A recent MasterCard presentation at a payment security conference presented a curious statistic that there are more than 200,000 locations where payment card data is stored in large amounts. Please hold that thought as it is a very important one to keep while reading this book. Without jumping too much ahead in our story, we'd say that in many cases, adjusting your business process to not touch the card data directly will save you from a lot of security and compliance (and not just PCI DSS compliance!) challenges!

In this book, we are primarily concerned with merchants and service providers. The merchants are pretty easy to identify – they are the companies that accept credit cards in exchange for goods or services. The PCI official

---

[1] PCI DSS or the elements of it have been adopted as actual law in at least two US states at the time of this writing. The State of Nevada explicitly called PCI DSS by reference and made it mandatory for some businesses operating in this state. The State of Minnesota has adopted select provisions of PCI DSS as a state law.

definition of a merchant [2] states: "a merchant is defined as any entity that accepts payment cards bearing the logos of any five members of PCI SSC (American Express, Discover, JCB, MasterCard, or Visa) as payment for goods and services." For example, a retail store that sells groceries for cash or credit cards is a merchant. An e-commerce site that sells electronic books is also a merchant.

However, when it comes to service providers, things get a bit trickier. PCI Council Glossary [3] states: "Business entity that is not a payment card brand member or a merchant directly involved in the processing, storage, transmission, and switching or transaction data and cardholder information or both. This also includes companies that provide services to merchants, services providers or members that control or could impact the security of cardholder data. Examples include managed service providers that provide managed firewalls, IDS and other services as well as hosting providers and other entities. Entities such as telecommunications companies that only provide communication links without access to the application layer of the communication link are excluded."

A merchant can also be a service provider at the same time: "…a merchant that accepts payment cards as payment for goods and/or services can also be a service provider, if the services sold result in storing, processing, or transmitting cardholder data on behalf of other merchants or service providers" [2]. A more esoteric situation arises if a company accepts credit cards as a payment for services it provides to other merchants who also accept credit cards. In this case, such an entity is both a merchant and a service provider. For example, if you provide hosted shopping cart and processing services to merchants and accept payment cards, you would be both.

After those initial definitions, we will describe the whole payment ecosystem for the purposes of PCI DSS.

Electronic Card Payment Ecosystem

Before we go into detail on PCI compliance, we'd like to paint a quick picture of an entire payment card "ecosystem" (see Fig. 3.1).

FIGURE 3.1 *PCI Payment Ecosystem*

Figure 3.1 shows all the entities in payment card "game":

- Cardholder, a person holding a credit or debit card

- Merchant, who sells goods and services and accepts cards

- Service provider (sometimes Merchant Service Provider (MSP) or Independent Sales Organization (ISO), who provides all or some of the payment services for the merchant

- Payment processor, which is a particular example of an MSP

- Acquiring bank, which actually connects to a card brand network for payment processing and also has a contract for payment services with a merchant

- Issues bank, which issues payment cards to consumers (who then become "card holders")

- Card brand, which is a particular payment "ecosystem" (called "association network") with its own processors, acquirers, such as Visa, MasterCard, and Amex

The primary focus of PCI DSS requirements is on merchants and MSPs. This is understandable since this is exactly where most of the data is lost to malicious hackers. Whether TJX in 2005 to 2007 (45 or 90 million cards stolen, depending on the source) or Heartland Payment Systems in 2008 to 2009 (more than 100 million cards stolen), merchants, and service providers have let cards be stolen from them without incurring any of the costs to themselves and without having a motivation to improve their security even to low levels prescribed by PCI DSS. While the merchants were letting the card data "run away," the issuing banks were replacing them at their own cost and incurring other costs as well. Thus, PCI DSS was born to restore the balance to the system by making sure that merchants and service providers took care of protecting the card data.

Goal of PCI DSS

In light of what is mentioned above, PCI DSS is here to reduce the risk of payment card transactions by motivating merchants and service providers to protect the card data. Whether this goal is worthy, whether there are other secondary goals, or even whether this goal is being achieved by a current version of the data security standard is irrelevant. What matters is that PCI is aimed at reducing the risk of transaction and it seeks to accomplish that by making merchants and service providers to pay attention to many key aspects of data security, from network security to system security, application security, and security awareness and policy. What is even more important, it encourages merchants to drop the data and conduct their business in a way that eliminates costly and risky data storage and on-site processing, whenever possible. Reduction of fraud is expected to be a natural result of such focus on security practices and technologies. One of the original PCI creators has also described PCI as the following: "the original intent was to design, implement, and manage a comprehensive, cost effective and reliable security effort" [4] and not a patchwork of security controls.

It is interesting to note that the "Ten Common Myths of PCI DSS" document from the PCI Council presents the six domains of PCI DSS as its goals [5]:

1. Build and maintain a secure network

2. Protect cardholder data

3. Maintain a vulnerability management program

4. Implement strong access control measures

5. Regularly monitor and test networks

6. Maintain an information security policy

While the above six domains can be seen as tactical goals while implementing PCI DSS, the strategic focus of PCI DSS is card data security, payment card risk reduction, and ultimately the reduction of fraud losses for merchants, banks, and card brands.

Overall, while motivating security improvements and reducing the risk of card fraud, PCI DSS serves an even higher goal of boosting consumer confidence in what is currently the predominant payment system – credit and debit cards. While we can debate whether cash is truly on the way out, the volume of card transactions is still increasing at an impressive 20 to 40 percent rate annually. If anything – whether malicious hackers, insiders, or any other threat – can hinder it, major implications to today's economy may be incurred. Thus, PCI DSS defends something even bigger than "bits and bytes" in computer systems, but the functioning of the economic system itself.

Applicability of PCI DSS

It is likely that the statements about accepting card data or processing, storing, and transmitting payment card data will likely sound tiresome by the time you are finished reading our book; it is worthwhile to remind you that

PCI DSS applies to all organizations that do just that, and there are no exceptions. Our Chapter 15, "Myths and Misconceptions of PCI DSS" covers some of the common delusions and clarifies that the above PCI applicability is indeed the reality and not the myth.

While the applicability of PCI DSS to organizations that deal with card data is certain and all the DSS requirements apply, the question of validating or proving PCI compliance is a bit different. It differs for merchants and service providers; it also differs by card brand and by transaction volume.

First, there are different levels of merchants and service providers. Tables 3.1 and 3.2 show the breakdown.

Table 3.1 Merchant Levels

Merchant Level	Description
Level 1	Any merchant that processes more than 6 million Visa or MasterCard transactions annually
	2.5 million American Express Card transactions or more per year, or any merchant that has had a data incident; or any merchant that American Express otherwise deems a level
	Merchants processing over 1 million JCB transactions annually, or compromised merchants
Level 2	Any merchant that processes between 1 and 6 million Visa transactions annually
	Any merchant with greater than 1 million but less than or equal to 6 million total combined MasterCard and Maestro transactions annually
	Any merchant that processes between 50 thousand and 2.5 million American Express transactions annually
	Merchants processing less than 1 million JCB transactions annually
Level 3	Any merchant that processes between 20 thousand and 1 million Visa e-commerce transactions annually
	Any merchant with greater than 20,000 combined MasterCard and Maestro e-commerce transactions annually but less than or equal to 1 million total combined MasterCard and Maestro e-commerce transactions annually
	Any merchant that processes less than 50 thousand American Express transactions annually
Level 4	All other Visa and MasterCard merchants

NOTE

Visa Canada levels may differ. Visa Europe is also a separate organization that has different rules. Discover and JCB do not classify merchants based on transaction volume. Contact your payment brand for more information while paying attention to your location.

Table 3.2 Service Provider Levels

Level	MasterCard	Visa Inc
Level 1	All third-party providers (TPPs), all data storage entities (DSEs) that store, transmit, or process greater than 300,000 total combined MasterCard and Maestro transactions annually	VisaNet processors or any service provider that stores, processes, or transmits over 300,000 transactions per year
Level 2	Includes all DSEs that store, transmit, or process less than 300,000 total combined MasterCard and Maestro transactions annually	Any service provider that stores, processes, or transmits less than 300,000 transactions per year

NOTE

Visa Canada levels may differ. Visa Europe is also a separate organization that has different rules. Discover and JCB do not classify merchants based on transaction volume. Contact your payment brand for more information while paying attention to your location.

As we mentioned above, these levels exist for determining compliance validation that is discussed in the next section. The levels are also sometimes used by the card brands to determine which fines to impose upon the merchant for noncompliance.

PCI DSS IN DEPTH

In the next section, we take a detailed look at PCI DSS standard, its entire regulatory regime, deadlines, as well as related security vendor certification programs.

Compliance Deadlines

Now that we touched upon the compliance basics, it is time to face the painful fact: all the PCI DSS compliance deadlines are *in the past* (See Table 3.3).

Table 3.3	Compliance Dates for Merchants: All Passed		
Level	**American Express**	**MasterCard**	**Visa Inc**
Level 1	October 31, 2006	June 30, 2005 or December 31, 2010 for merchants that are self-certified previously	June 30, 2004
Level 2	March 31, 2007	June 30, 2004	June 30, 2007
Level 3	N/A	June 30, 2005	June 30, 2005
Level 4	N/A	N/A	N/A

This means that now is the time to be compliant. There are additional dates for various other related requirements (such as card brand dates for Payment Application Data Security Standard [PA-DSS] compliance), but all core PCI DSS dates have indeed passed.

Some of you recall receiving a letter from your company's bank or a business partner many years ago that had a target compliance date. Such letters are rare since the dates for PCI DSS compliances have actually passed. This date may or may not be aligned with the card brands' official dates. This is because the card brands may not have a direct relationship with you and are working through the business chain of acquiring banks. When in doubt, always follow the guidance of your legal department that has reviewed your contracts.

Thus, barring unusual circumstances, the effective compliance deadlines have long passed. Various predecessor versions of the PCI 1.2 standard had unique dates associated with them, so if your compliance efforts have not been aligned to the card brand programs, you are way behind the curve and will not likely get any sympathy from your bank.

As far as additional dates by card brands, please refer to the following resources:

- Visa: http://usa.visa.com/merchants/risk_management/cisp_key_dates.html. This page includes dates such as "U.S. Level 1 Merchants Full PCI DSS Compliance Validation Deadline" (September 30, 2010 applies to new merchants) and "U.S. Level 2 Merchants Full PCI DSS Compliance Validation Deadline" (December 12, 2010 applies to new merchants as well).

- MasterCard: www.mastercard.com/us/sdp/merchants/merchant_levels. html. This page includes recent change for merchant compliance validation for Level 2 merchants with an associated deadline of December 2010.

■ Discover: www.discovernetwork.com/fraudsecurity/disc.html. This page contains no additional deadlines but simply refers to the PCI Council site. All PCI requirements currently apply to all merchants.

■ American Express: www209.americanexpress.com/merchant/single-voice/dsw/FrontServlet?request_type=dsw&pg_nm=home. This page also does not contain any additional deadlines; all PCI requirements currently apply to all merchants.

■ JCB: www.jcb-global.com/english/jdsp/index.html.

Compliance and Validation

As we mentioned before, depending on your company's merchant or service provider level, you will either need to go through an annual on-site PCI assessment by a Qualified Security Assessor (QSA), or complete a Self-Assessment Questionnaire (SAQ) to validate compliance. In addition to this, you will have to present the results of the quarterly network perimeter scans that had to be performed by an approved scanning vendor (ASV).

In particular, while SAQ validates PCI compliance, there needs to be evidence that validates that the questions in the SAQ are answered truthfully.

When submitting a SAQ, it will have to be physically signed by an officer of your company.[2] At the present time, there is no court precedent for officer liability as a result of false attestation. However, industry speculation is that this person may be held accountable in a civil court, especially if he or she commits an act of perjury while certifying.

If you are planning on submitting a Report on Compliance (ROC) instead of the SAQ, you will need to follow the document template outlined in the PCI DSS Security Audit Procedures document. After the SAQ has been filled out or the ROC has been completed, it must be sent along with all the necessary evidence and validation documentation to the acquirer, to the business partner, or to the card brand directly. It depends on who requested the compliance validation in the first place.

It is a common misconception that the compliance requirements vary among the different levels. Both merchants and service providers must comply with the entire DSS, regardless of the level. Only verification processes and reporting vary. Visa Web site explains it like this: "In addition

---

[2] Electronic attestation of a full digital copy has also been considered acceptable.

Table 3.4   PCI DSS Validation Requirements

Merchant or Service Provider Level	Visa USA		MasterCard	
Level 1	ASV scan	QSA on-site assessment	ASV scan	QSA on-site assessment
Level 2	ASV scan	SAQ self-assessment	ASV scan	QSA on-site assessment (after 2010)
Level 3	ASV scan	SAQ self-assessment	ASV scan	SAQ self-assessment
Level 4	ASV scan if requested by the acquirer	SAQ self-assessment	ASV scan if requested by the acquirer	SAQ self-assessment

NOTE

Discover and JCB handle merchant PCI compliance validation differently. Contact the payment brand for more information.

to adhering to the PCI DSS, compliance validation is required for all service providers" [6].

The validation mechanisms, as of the time of this writing, are given in Table 3.4.

Further, the exact scope of PCI DSS validation differs based on the exact way the organization interfaces with card data. Specifically, quoting from the PCI Council Web site, the circumstances that affect what sections of the SAQ the merchant should complete for validation are provided in Table 3.5.

So, to summarize, the exact scope of any one's PCI DSS validation depends on the following:

- Merchant or service provider status

- Transaction volume

- Card brand

- The method of accepting cards and interacting with card data

Table 3.5 Validation Types Based on Card Acceptance Methods

Card Processing	Self-Assessment Validation
Card-not-present merchants, all cardholder data functions outsourced. This would never apply to face-to-face merchants	SAQ type A, which is the smallest. It only includes parts of 2 out of 12 requirements, about 15 out of 224 questions
Imprint-only merchants with no electronic cardholder data storage	SAQ type B, which covers sections of 5 out of 12 requirements
Stand-alone terminal merchants, no electronic cardholder data storage	SAQ type B, which covers sections of 5 out of 12 requirements
Merchants with point-of-sale (POS) systems connected to the Internet, no electronic cardholder data storage	SAQ type B, which covers sections of 11 out of 12 requirements; curiously, it does not include the logging requirement (Req 10)
All other merchants (not included in Types 1 through 4 above) and all service providers defined by a payment brand as eligible to complete an SAQ	SAQ type D, which includes all the 12 requirements and a full set of 224 questions

NOTE

Although American Express and Visa allow Level 1 merchants to have their PCI compliance validated by the merchant's internal audit group, MasterCard does not explicitly allow this. If this affects your company, contact MasterCard for clarification.

WARNING

Don't let yourself become complacent. If you are a Level 4 merchant across the board and are not required to do anything to validate your compliance with PCI DSS, remember, by accepting even one card per year, you are required to *comply* with PCI DSS. Many Level 4 merchants end up in big trouble when they realize they had to comply with PCI DSS regardless of their validation requirements. In addition, due to different validation levels across major card brands, their situation in regards to PCI compliance may be much worse.

Also, it is important to note that the specifics of validation requirement might change. For example, in June 2009, MasterCard announced that Level 2 merchant will not need to be validated via an on-site assessment. Expect validation requirements to become stricter in the future.

It is worthwhile to note that it is possible for a company to be a merchant and a service provider at the same time. If this is the case, the circumstances should be noted, and the compliance must be validated at the highest level. In other words, if a company is a Level 3 merchant and a Level 2 service provider, the compliance verification activities should adhere to the requirements for a Level 2 service provider.

One of the notable PCI assessors, Walt Conway, relates the following educational story about merchant and provider validation:

> *"My favorite is when the vendor replies that they are compliant as a Level 3 (or 2 or whatever) merchant. That response is completely irrelevant and inexcusably misleading. That they are compliant as a merchant is meaningless to you when you use them as a service provider. They can self-assess as a merchant – they cannot as a Level 1 service provider. That extra step is meant to protect you. If you get that kind of reply, you are likely dealing with an over-eager and/or ill-informed sales rep…ask to talk to an adult" [7].*

History of PCI DSS

To better understand the PCI DSS role, its motivation and its future, it is useful to look at its origins and history.

PCI DSS has evolved from the efforts of several card brands. In the 1990s, the card brands developed various standards to improve the security of sensitive information. In the case of Visa, different regions came up with different standards since European countries and Canada were subject to different standards than the US. In June 2001, Visa launched the Cardholder Information Security Program (CISP). The CISP Security Audit Procedures document version 1.0 was the granddaddy of PCI DSS. These audit procedures went through several iterations and made it to version 2.3 in March 2004. At this time, Visa was already collaborating with MasterCard. Their agreement was that merchants and service providers would undergo annual compliance validation according to Visa's CISP Security Audit Procedures and would follow MasterCard's rules for vulnerability scanning. Visa maintained the list of approved assessors and MasterCard maintained the list of ASVs.

This collaborative relationship had a number of problems. The lists of approved vendors were not well-maintained, and there was no clear way for security vendors to get added to the list of each particular card brand. Also, the program was not endorsed by all card brand divisions. Other brands such as Discover, American Express, and JCB were running their own programs as well. The merchants and service providers in many cases had to undergo several independent assessments by different "certified" assessors just to prove compliance to each brand, which was clearly costing too much and not resulting in quality assessments either. For that and many other reasons, all card brands came together and created the PCI DSS 1.0, which gave us the concept of PCI compliance.

Unfortunately, the issue of ownership still was not fully addressed, and a year later, the PCI Security Standards Council was founded, and its Web site www.pcisecuritystandards.org was created. Comprised of American Express, Discover Financial Services, JCB, MasterCard Worldwide, and Visa International, PCI Council (as it came to be known) maintains the ownership of the DSS, most of the approved vendor lists, training programs, and so on. There are still exceptions, as the list of approved payment application assessors only recently has been transferred from Visa PABP to PCI Councils' PA-DSS. Also, incident forensics is still handled by the card brands themselves and not by the PCI Council. For example, Visa still runs its Qualified Incident Response Assessor (QIRA) certification.

NOTE

Visa QIRA can be found on Visa Web site at http://usa.visa.com/download/merchants/cisp_qualified_cisp_ incident_response_assessors_list.pdf.

Even today, each card brand/region still maintains its own security program beyond PCI. These programs go beyond the data protection charter of PCI and include activities such as fraud prevention. The information on such programs can be found in Table 3.6. In certain cases, PCI ROC needs to be submitted to each card brand's program office separately.

Table 3.6 Brand Security Programs

Card Brand	Additional Program Information
American Express	Web site: www.americanexpress.com/datasecurity. E-mail: American.Express.Data.Security@aexp.com
Discover	Web site: www.discovernetwork.com/resources/data/data_security. html. E-mail: askdatasecurity@discoverfinancial.com
JCB	Web site: www.jcb-global.com/english/pci/index.html. E-mail: riskmanagement@jcbati.com
MasterCard	Web site: www.mastercard.com/sdp. E-mail: sdp@mastercard.com
Visa USA	Web site: www.visa.com/cisp. E-mail: cisp@visa.com
Visa Canada	Web site: www.visa.ca/ais

PCI Council

PCI Council or, fully, PCI Security Standards Council or PCI SSC, describes itself as "an open global forum for the ongoing development, enhancement, storage, dissemination, and implementation of security standards for account data protection" [8].

PCI Council charter provides oversight to the development of PCI security standards (including PCI DSS, PA-DSS, and PIN Entry Devices [PED]) on a global basis. It formalizes many processes that existed informally within the card brands. PCI Council published the updated DSS, at the time of this writing at version 1.2.1, which is accepted by all brands and international regions; it also updates the supporting documents such as "PCI Quick Reference Guide" and recent "Prioritized Approach for DSS 1.2" (March 2009) and "PCI SSC Wireless Guidelines" (July 2009) documents.

Version 1.2.1

The Council mission also includes maintaining two vendor certification programs for on-site assessments (QSA) and network scanning (ASV), which are covered in the next section. The lists of current QSAs and ASVs are located at the council Web site: www.pcisecuritystandards.org/qsa_asv/find_one.shtml. In addition, the Council also runs the so-called "QA programs" (quality assurance programs) for QSAs and ASVs. which are aimed at maintaining the integrity of site assessments and vulnerability scans.

PCI Council is technically an independent industry standards body, and its exact organizational chart is published on its Web site (www.pcisecuritystandards.org/about/organization.shtml). Yet, it remains a relatively small organization, primarily comprised of the employees of the brand members.

The industry immediately felt the positive impact of PCI Council. The merchants and service providers can now play a more active role in the compliance program and the evolution of the standard, whereas the QSA and the ASVs find it much easier to train their personnel.

TOOLS

At the time of this writing, PCI Council provides a few useful tools to help track PCI DSS compliance. These are explained in the following:

- "Prioritized Approach for DSS 1.2" tracking spreadsheet allows for easy compliance program tracking and reporting, whether internal or to the card brands or acquirers. The sheet can be downloaded at www.pcisecuritystandards.org/education/prioritized.shtml.

- "PCI SSC New SAQ Summary" documents are not just helpful, they are actually mandatory for those validating PCI compliance via an SAQ. The PCI Council provides the fillable documents that can be used for tracking compliance at a small organization. All the SAQs can be obtained for free at www.pcisecuritystandards.org/saq/instructions_dss.shtml

To summarize, the most important things to know about PCI Council are as follows:

- The Council maintains and updates the PCI DSS, and now a PA-DSS and a PED, as well as a set of supporting documents.

- The Council does *not* deal with PCI validation process and, specifically, with enforcement via fines or other means. These responsibilities are retained by the card brands.

- PCI Council also certified security vendors as QSAs and ASVs and maintains current lists of certified vendors, as well as polices the vendors to maintain the integrity of PCI validation. The industry immediately felt the positive impact of PCI Co. The merchants and service providers can now play a more active role in the compliance program and the evolution of the standard, whereas the QSA and the ASVs find it much easier to train their personnel.

Let's look at the QSAs and ASVs in more detail.

QSAs

PCI Council now controls the companies that are allowed to conduct on-site DSS compliance assessments. These companies, known as QSAs,[3] have gone through the application and qualification process, having had to show compliance with tough business, capability, and administrative requirements.

NOTE

QSAs are only permitted to conduct on-site DSS assessments. They are not automatically granted the right to perform perimeter vulnerability scans, unless they also certify as an ASV. Many companies today can be found on both lists (QSAs and ASVs) to be able to provide complete PCI validation services to merchants and service providers.

---

[3] In the past, there was a different name for a company (QSAC or Qualified Security Assessor Company) and an individual professional employed by such company (QSA or Qualified Security Assessor).

QSAs also had to invest in personnel training and certification to build up a team of assessors, also called QSAs.

QSAs have to recertify annually and have to retrain their internal personnel. The exact qualification process and the requirements are outlined on PCI Council Web site; however, of particular interest are the insurance requirements. QSAs are required to carry high coverage policies, much higher than typical policies for the professional service firms, which becomes important later. A recent lawsuit ("Merrick Bank v. Savvis," see more details in [9]) presents an example risk that QSA faces; in this suit, the bank is suing the assessor who validated CardSystems, a target of a massive card data breach, as PCI compliant. Please use Google to find out how the lawsuit progressed and who won; the results will not be known before the book goes to print.

NOTE

The QSAs are approved to provide services in particular markets: US, Asia Pacific, CEMEA (Central Europe, Middle East, and Africa), Latin America and the Caribbean, and Canada. The qualification to service a particular market depends on QSA's capabilities, geographic footprint, and payment of appropriate fees.

The QSA is a certification established by PCI Co. Individuals desiring this certification must first and foremost work for a QSA or for a company in the process of applying to become a QSA. Then, they must attend official training administered by PCI Council and pass the test. They must also undergo annual requalification training to maintain their status. An individual may not be a

TOOLS

Anybody can look up the individuals with current QSA certification by using QSA Employee Lookup at www.pcisecuritystandards.org/qsa_lookup/index.html.
    See Fig. 3.2 for an example.

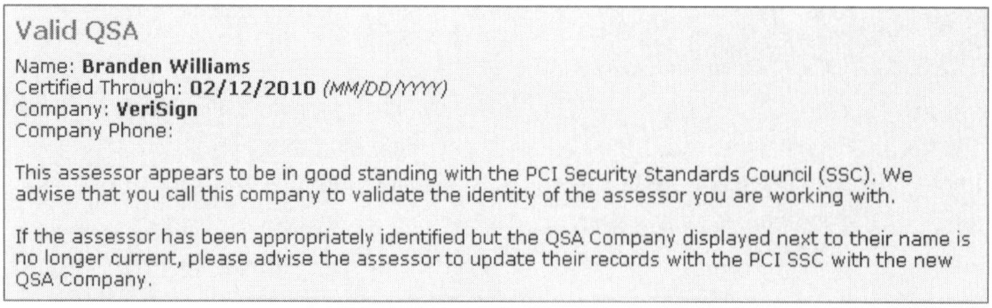

Valid QSA

Name: **Branden Williams**
Certified Through: **02/12/2010** (MM/DD/YYYY)
Company: **VeriSign**
Company Phone:

This assessor appears to be in good standing with the PCI Security Standards Council (SSC). We advise that you call this company to validate the identity of the assessor you are working with.

If the assessor has been appropriately identified but the QSA Company displayed next to their name is no longer current, please advise the assessor to update their records with the PCI SSC with the new QSA Company.

FIGURE 3.2   *QSA Employee Lookup Tools*

QSA, unless he or she is presently employed by a QSA company; however, a QSA can carry the certification between QSA companies when changing jobs.

We cover the tips on working with your QSA in Chapter 11, "Don't Fear the Assessor." If there is one thing to remember when engaging a QSA, the QSA should be your partner. Treating your QSA like an auditor will only lead to a painful process whereby both parties end up frustrated and disillusioned.

ASVs

As you know, PCI DSS validation also includes network vulnerability scanning by an ASV.

To become an ASV, companies must undergo a process similar to QSA qualification. The difference is that in the case of QSACs, the individual assessors attend classroom training on an annual basis, whereas ASVs submit a scan conducted against a test network perimeter. An organization can choose to become both QSA and ASV, which allows the merchants and service providers to select a single vendor for PCI compliance validation.

It is important to note that ASVs are authorized to perform external vulnerability scans from the Internet, but PCI DSS also mandates internal vulnerability scans (performed from inside the company network), which can be performed by anybody – internal security team or consultant.

We cover all the tips on working with your ASV in Chapter 8, "Vulnerability Management."

QUICK OVERVIEW OF PCI REQUIREMENTS

Now it is time to briefly run through all PCI DSS requirements, which we cover in detail in the rest of this book.

PCI DSS version 1.2 is comprised of six control objectives that contain one or more requirements:

- Build and maintain a secure network
  - Requirement 1: Install and maintain a firewall configuration to protect cardholder data
  - Requirement 2: Do not use vendor-supplied defaults for system passwords and other security parameters
- Protect cardholder data
  - Requirement 3: Protect stored cardholder data
  - Requirement 4: Encrypt transmission of cardholder data across open, public networks

- Maintain a vulnerability management program
    - Requirement 5: Use and regularly update antivirus software
    - Requirement 6: Develop and maintain secure systems and applications
- Implement strong access control measures
    - Requirement 7: Restrict access to cardholder data by business need to know
    - Requirement 8: Assign a unique ID to each person with computer access
    - Requirement 9: Restrict physical access to cardholder data
- Regularly monitor and test networks
    - Requirement 10: Track and monitor all access to network resources and cardholder data
    - Requirement 11: Regularly test security systems and processes
- Maintain an information security policy
    - Requirement 12: Maintain a policy that addresses information security

The above-mentioned 12 requirements cover the whole spectrum of information technology (IT) areas as well as venture outside of IT in Requirement 12. Some requirements are very technical in nature (e.g., Requirement 1 calls for specific settings on the firewalls), and some are process and policy-oriented (e.g., Requirement 12) and even go into contract law (some of the subrequirement in Requirement 12 cover the interactions with MSPs.

The detailed coverage of controls makes things easier for both the companies that have to comply with the standards, the auditors (in case of Sarbanes–Oxley [SOX] or other laws and standards), or the assessors (in case of PCI DSS). For example, when compared to the SOX Act 2002, companies do not have to invent or pay for somebody to invent the controls for them; they are already provided.

What is interesting is that almost every time there is a discussion about PCI DSS, someone would claim that PCI is too prescriptive. In reality, PCI being prescriptive is the best thing since antivirus solutions invented automated updates (hopefully, you can detect humor here). PCI DSS prescriptive nature simply means that there is some specific guidance for people to follow and be more secure as a result (if they follow the spirit and not only the letter of PCI standards)! Sadly, in many cases, the merchants who have to comply with PCI DSS and who still think it is "too fuzzy" and "not specific enough" are the ones basically asking for a compliance and security *to do* list or a task list; and no external document that guarantees that your organization will be secure can ever be created.

In particular, when people say "PCI is too prescriptive," they actually mean that it engenders "checklist mentality" and leads to following the letter of the mandate blindly, without thinking about why it was put in place – to protect cardholder data, to reduce, or to share risk/responsibility. For example, it says "use a firewall," so they deploy a shiny firewall with a simple "ALLOW ALL<->ALL" rule – an obvious exaggeration that clarifies the message here. Or, they have a firewall with a default password unchanged. In addition, the proponents of "PCI is too prescriptive" tend to think that fuzzier guidance (and, especially, prescribing the desired end state *and* not the tools to be installed) will lead to people actually think about the best way to do it.

So, the choices to write security-motivated regulatory guidance are as follows:

1. Mandate the tools (e.g., "must use a firewall") and risk "checklist mentality," resulting in both insecurity and "false sense" of security.

2. Mandate the results (e.g., "must be secure") and risk people saying "yes, but I don't know how" and then not acting at all, again leading to insecurity.

The author team is of the opinion that in today's reality #1 works better than over pill #2 (and that is why I like PCI more), but with some pause to think, for sure. Although the organizations with less mature security programs will benefit at least a bit from #1, organizations with more mature programs might be able to operate better under #2. However, data security today has to cover the less-enlightened organizations, which makes #1 choices – embodies by PCI DSS – the preferred one.

As a far as scope of PCI DSS within the organization is concerned, PCI compliance validation may affect more than what you consider the "cardholder environment." According to PCI DSS 1.2, the scope can include the cardholder data environment only if adequate network segmentation is in place. In most cases, this implies the use of dedicated firewalls and non-routable virtual local area networks (VLANs). If you do not have such controls in place, the scope of PCI compliance validation will cover your entire network. Think about it: if you cannot ensure that your cardholder data is confined to a particular area, then you cannot focus on this area alone, and you have to look everywhere.

NOTE

Just because a POS system is on the list of compliant payment applications (PA-DSS), it does not mean that your particular implementation is compliant. Also, it definitely does not mean that your entire organization is PCI compliant. You should work with the application vendor and with your QSA to verify this.

In order for the device to be added to the PA-DSS list, the payment application, online shopping cart, or POS vendor has to show and document the secure method for their application deployment. However, it is ultimately the merchant responsibility to follow the secure and compliant deployment guidance.

For the benefit of consumers who may be more familiar with a brand name rather than a parent company, PCI compliance is validated for every brand name. Thus, if a company has several divisions or "doing business as" (DBA) names, each entity has to be validated separately. For reporting simplicity, the ROCs or SAQs may note that they include validation of multiple brand names.

You may discover that sometimes you are unable to comply with the letter of PCI DSS while still striving for its spirit. For example, you may need to temporarily store cardholder data unencrypted for troubleshooting purposes or to use a password of less than mandate minimum length on a legacy system. As long as you follow reasonable precautions, card brands understand this need. Another example may include recording certain call-center conversations for customer service purposes. Again, card brands understand that these recordings may contain cardholder data, so accommodations are made accordingly.

In many cases, compensating controls have to be used to achieve compliance when your company cannot exactly meet a given requirement. The important thing to remember about compensating controls is that they have to go beyond the requirements of PCI to provide the same or higher assurance of cardholder data protection. When compensating controls are claimed, additional documentation must be completed. Please see Chapter 12, "The Art of Compensating Control" for detailed coverage of compensating controls.

Changes to PCI DSS

One of the key challenges for any security standard is to change fast enough to follow the threat changes (and those change literally every day since criminal computer underground has to evolve to stay in business) and to change slow enough to still be considered a technical standard (and not simply advise to "do the right thing"). For prescriptive technical standards that directly call out security controls, such as firewalls, network intrusion prevention, and vulnerability scanning, the challenge is even more extreme.

In fact, today PCI DSS is sometimes criticized for being "constantly in flux" and for "not moving fast enough" at the same time, but by different people.

The changes are that the PCI standards are guided by the PCI Council document called "Lifecycle Process for Changes to PCI DSS" [10]. The document describes the following stages for each standard revision:

1. Market Implementation (9 months)

2. Feedback Begins (3 months)

3. Feedback Review and Decision (8 months)

4. New Version/Revision and Final Review (3 months)

5. Discuss New Version/Revision (1 month)

The overall process takes 24 months for each DSS revision (whether major from 1 to 2, which has not happened yet, or minor such as from 1.0 to 1.1) and always includes extensive public commenting and review periods to incorporate the input from all stakeholders.

PCI DSS AND RISK

The relationship between PCI DSS and risk management has been an unstable one. It was mentioned previously in the context of PCI's goal for reducing the risk of card transaction and for preventing the merchants from accepting the risk of someone's loss. On the other hand, many people point out that PCI DSS presents a list of control with no regard to organization's own risk assessment. Let's explore the relationship of PCI and risk a bit further.

First, a common question: can one claim that PCI increases the merchant's overall risk? When people ask that question they usually imply that PCI added the risk of loss via noncompliance fines and raised fees to the risk of direct losses due to card theft from a merchant's environment (such as reputation damage, cost of new security measures, and monitoring)? The answer is clearly a "no," since before PCI, most of the negative consequences of a card theft, even a massive one, were not falling upon the merchant shoulders but on others such as card-issuing banks. PCI, on the other hand, creates a powerful motivation for protecting the data on the merchant side.

Still, despite that reality about PCI, many CEOs or CFOs are asking the question, "Why would I need to spend the money on PCI?" And, no, the answer is not "Because there are fines" (even though there are fines indeed). The answer is that the list of negative consequences due to neglecting data security and PCI DSS is much longer than fines.

Your company's contract with the acquiring bank probably has a clause in it that any fines from the card brand will be "passed through" to you. With all compliance deadlines passed, the fines could start tomorrow. Visa USA has announced that it will start fining acquirers (which will pass on the costs to the merchant) between $5000 and $25,000 per month if their Level 1 merchants have not shown compliance. In addition, the fines $10,000 per month may already be imposed today for prohibited data storage by a Level 1 or Level 2 merchant.

On top of that, if both noncompliant and compromised, higher fines are imposed as well. However, believe it or not, if compromised, this will be the least of your concerns. Possible civil liabilities will dwarf the fines from the card brands. Some estimates place the cost of compromise at $50 to $250 per stolen account (per stolen, and not per one used for fraud, which will likely be a subset of the whole stolen card pool). It is known that some companies that have been compromised have been forced to close their doors or sold to competition for nominal amount. According to PCI Council study, the per capita cost of a data breach has gone up more than 30 percent in the past year.

Let's use The TJX Companies, which operates stores like TJ Maxx, Marshalls, and so on, as a case study. On January 17, 2007, TJX announced that they were compromised. Because they did not have robust monitoring capabilities such as those mandated by PCI, it took them a very long time to discover the compromise. The first breach actually occurred in July 2005. TJX also announced that more than 90 million credit-card numbers were compromised. In addition to the fines, lost stock price, and direct costs of dealing with the compromise, over 20 separate law suits have already been filed against TJX; some have been converted to class-action status.

Whether you believe your company to be the target or not, the fact is that if you have cardholder data, you are a target because you are someone's "ticket to a better life" via criminal business. You and your organization are simply someone's sheep to be fleeced, and your losses are their gains. Cardholder data is a valuable commodity that is traded and sold illegally worldwide. Organized crime units profit greatly from credit-card fraud, so your company is definitely on their list if you deal with card data. International, federal, and state law enforcement agencies are working hard to bring perpetrators to justice and shut down the infrastructure used to aid in credit-card-related crimes; however, thousands of forum sites, Internet chat channels, and news groups still exist, where the buyers can meet the sellers. Data breaches like the one at TJX are not the work of simple hackers looking for glory; well-run organizations from the Eastern European block [11] and selected Asian countries [12] sponsor such activity and earn a great living from various illegal hacking activities.

The Web site http://datalossdb.org maintains the history of the compromises and impacts in terms of lost card numbers and other records. Since 2005, over 1 billion personal records (a mix of cards, identities, etc.) have been compromised. This includes companies of all sizes and lines of business. If the industry does not get this trend under control, the US Congress will give it a try.

Finally, and few people actually know it, but PCI DSS does mandate a formal risk assessment, not just a list of controls to implement! The Requirement 12.1.2 states that the information security policy must "include an annual process that identifies threats, and vulnerabilities, and results in a formal risk assessment."

BENEFITS OF COMPLIANCE

While the inclusion of benefits is redundant – after all PCI DSS compliance is *mandatory* for the organizations that deal with payment cards! – it is worthwhile to highlight the fact that PCI DSS has important benefits for the merchants, acquiring banks, issuing banks, as well as for the public at large.

If we are to mention one benefit, PCI DSS has motivated the security improvements like nothing else before it. Many organizations lived through the virus-infested 1980s, then worm-infested and spammy 1990s, and then through heavy data loss early 2000s without doing anything on security. PCI DSS had a huge impact on the laggards to get better.

CASE STUDY

Much of this book focuses on case studies where a company makes a mistake, or fails to do something that result in a breach. This case study is a nice change of pace where we examine someone doing something right!

The Case of the Developing Security Program

Yvette's Evangelical Emporium is a small chain of 50 stores supplying religious supplies to local churches and individuals. Yvette started her business in 1990 with a single store. Throughout the 1990s, she was able to open several new stores in neighboring counties and states, eventually building a 10 retail location business by 2000. In 2002, she took advantage of a depressed economy, and using some capital from investors and a significant trust that matured, she expanded her operation to 25 stores in 3 years and continued to expand over the next 4 years to double her size.

In 2005, Yvette realized that she needed to formalize her IT division and hired Erin, a progressive and security-minded IT executive, as her chief information officer. Erin presented a plan to standardize and build out her infrastructure so that future growth could be done in a cookie-cutter fashion; thus, saving millions in deployment and maintenance costs.

By 2006, they crossed the threshold from a Level 2 Visa merchant to a Level 1 Visa merchant and knew they would quickly need to put a solid PCI compliance program in place. Erin knew from her previous experience that small companies struggled with information security and made it a point to build in basic information security fundamentals into her IT operations, but they did not meet the baseline PCI DSS requirements and needed to be reworked.

Because of her new reporting levels for PCI, Yvette hired Steve to serve as the chief information security officer, reporting directly to her. Steve's task was to build an information security program that addressed PCI immediately, but would expand to be more applicable to information security such that future regulation would only require minor tweaks to the program.

Steve and Erin worked closely together to build a common set of controls to be rolled out to the entire company. Steve knew that PCI was a priority but considered everything he did in light of the ISO security framework (ISO17799 at the time). In some cases, he found that ISO far exceeded specific PCI requirements like in Business Continuity and Risk Assessments, and he found unique parts of PCI that were much more granular than ISO, like the treatment of sensitive authentication data (PCI Requirement 3.2). Steve's efforts ultimately paid off in spades as his information security program matured. Recent changes and additions to restrictions on healthcare data (which Yvette housed as part of an employee self-insurance program) and state data breach notification laws were already addressed by the program as it matured, and Yvette's cost associated with protecting data was much less than her competitors who only chased standards with immediate noncompliance repercussions.

NOTE

It is well-known that initial PCI DSS creators were well aware of ISO 17799 and other security standards. This awareness leads to the fact that if your organization has a solid security management program based on ISO/IEC 27002 (a modern descendant of ISO/IEC 17799 and BS7799), your PCI effort will be relatively easy and you will gain both solid security and compliance as a result. It is also likely that compliance with other regulations will not be overly onerous. PCI is more granular, whereas ISO is more broad, but they are largely in sync!

The Case of the Confusing Validation Requirements

Garrett's Gas Guzzling Garage operates 800 car repair locations across the United States. Garrett's recently opened 20 locations in Mexico City to help maintain and upgrade the fuel efficiency of old cars. Garrett is considered a Level 1 merchant in the United States but set up a different entity in Mexico City, and processes and settles locally with Bancomer. Although Garrett authorizes and settles locally in Mexico City at his small regional headquarters, he shares the data with the US-based parent for backup and analysis purposes.

His business is booming in Mexico City, and that business quickly became a Level 2 merchant. According to MasterCard's new validation requirements, this would mean that Garrett must have a QSA perform an on-site assessment of compliance for both locations. He was already doing this in the United States based on his Level 1 status, but now faces additional costs for doing this locally in Mexico City.

"But wait," some of you are saying, "What about Visa's rules?" Certainly glad you asked that! According to Visa, if a smaller, wholly owned subsidiary shares infrastructure and data with a parent company considered a Level 1, then that smaller subsidiary should also be viewed as a Level 1 and perform the same level of validation.

Back to Garrett, even though the 20 Mexico locations process through Bancomer, the data is shared with the US headquarters for backup and analysis. According to Visa's rules, the Mexican entity is considered Level 1 based on its relationship with the parent, and a Level 1 assessment must be performed.

As always, when in doubt, ask your acquirer what is expected of you. Your mileage may vary when it comes to some of these intricate rules. Some acquiring institutions may still treat certain subsidiaries as lower levels depending on the circumstances.

SUMMARY

PCI refers to the PCI DSS established by the credit-card brands. Any company that stores, processes, or transmits cardholder data has to comply with this data-protection standard. Effectively, all the target compliance dates have already passed, so if your company has not validated compliance, you are at risk of fines and other negative consequences of insecurity and noncompliance. The PCI is composed of 12 requirements that cover a wide array of business areas. All companies, regardless of their respective level, have to comply with the entire standard as it is written. The actual mechanism for compliance validation varies based on the company classification, driven by the individual card brand, transaction volume, exact method of accepting cards, etc. The cost of dealing with data breaches keeps rising, as does their number; noncompliance exacerbates the loss in case of a breach. Companies that do not take data security and compliance efforts seriously may soon find themselves out of business.

Now is the time to start the journey toward data security and compliance: get an endorsement from the company's senior management and business stakeholders, and start fulfilling your obligations and protecting the data.

REFERENCES

[1] Sinclair Jr UB. I, Candidate for governor: and how i got licked (1935), ISBN 0-520-08198-6; repr. University of California Press; 1994, P. 109.

[2] PCI Council Website, Article # 5410. http://selfservice.talisma.com/article.asp x?article=5410&p=81 [accessed 31.08.2009].

[3] PCI Council Glossary, Entry Service Provider. http://selfservice.talisma.com/display/2n/index.aspx?c=58&cpc=MSdA03B2IfY15uvLEKtr40R5a5pV2lnC Ub4i1Qj2q2g&cid=81&cat=&catURL=&r=0.73831444978714[accessed 17.07.2009].

[4] Joel Weise, private communication, e-mail dated July 1, 2009.

[5] Ten Common Myths of PCI DSS. www.pcisecuritystandards.org/pdfs/pciscc_ ten_common_myths.pdf [accessed 17.07.2009].

[6] Visa Cardholder Information Security Program for Service Providers web page. http://usa.visa.com/merchants/risk_management/cisp_service_providers. html [accessed 02.08.2009].

[7] PCI and Your Third-Party Service Providers – First, the Bad News. http://trea-suryinstitutepcidss.blogspot.com/2009/07/pci-and-your-third-party-service. html [accessed 10.08.2009].

[8] PCI Security Standards Council website. www.pcisecuritystandards. org/ [accessed 17.07.2009].

[9] Merrick Bank v. Savvis Update: Savvis Files Motion to Dismiss. http:// infoseccompliance.com/2009/06/23/merrick-bank-v-savvis-update-savvis-files-motion-to-dismiss [accessed 17.07.2009].

[10] Lifecycle Process for Changes to PCI DSS. www.pcisecuritystandards.org/pdfs/ OS_PCI_Lifecycle.pdf [accessed 17.07.2009].

[11] Black Hat: Fighting Russian Cybercrime Mobsters. www.informationweek. com/blog/main/archives/2009/07/black_hat_fight.html [accessed 11.08.2009].

[12] Chinese Hackers Attack Web Site Over Uighur Film. www.bloomberg.com/ apps/news?pid=20601081 [accessed 11.08.2009].

CHAPTER 4

Building and Maintaining a Secure Network

Information in this chapter

The concepts of defense-in-depth and layered security best represent the idea of building and maintaining a secure network. It would be great if users could rely on one type of technology or a single device to provide all of our security but that's not realistic, as history proves there are no silver security bullets. Some professionals use the analogy that security is like an onion – it has layers. Alone, each layer is weak and translucent, but together they're tough and solid.

A firewall is one layer but not necessarily the first layer. Figure 4.1 shows examples of different layers. The packet-filtering router that connects your company to the Internet may be the first layer, or there could be layers even further upstream at the Internet Service Provider (ISP). There you might configure a small rule set to filter out basic unwanted traffic like Internet Control Message Protocol (ICMP), finger, r-services, and anything else that you can live without crossing into your network space. The next layer contains the devices that make up your internal network infrastructure. Firewalls, intrusion detection systems (IDSs), intrusion prevention systems (IPSs), and switches all contribute to this layer of security. Next is the host-based

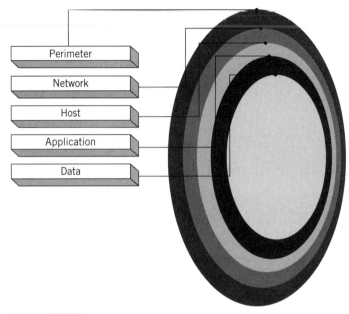

FIGURE 4.1 *Layers of Security*

security that you might have installed on specific machines. Host-based intrusion detection and prevention, anti-malware software, and other protective controls may include hardening of the operating system itself. The next layer covers the application. Any hardening of the application, access controls, and file or library permissions fall into this layer. The final layer covers protecting the data. Encrypting the data stored on the system is one of the easiest ways to protect it.

WHICH PCI DSS REQUIREMENTS ARE IN THIS DOMAIN?

This chapter assumes that the reader has a working knowledge of firewalls and firewall technologies. Luckily, these devices have been documented and explored by bloggers and sites all over the Internet. If you find yourself lost on a certain term, try punching it into a search engine! From time to time, I'll refer back to the Payment Card Industry (PCI) Self-Assessment Questionnaire (SAQ) and/or the Security Assessment Procedures (SAP) to clarify.

There are literally dozens of firewall manufacturers in the world but only a few different types of firewalls. The PCI standard does not specify what brand of firewall to use, but it does dictate functionality it needs to provide.

There are two main requirements that make up this domain.

1. Install and maintain a firewall configuration to protect cardholder data (Requirement 1).

2. Do not use vendor-supplied defaults for system passwords and other security parameters (Requirement 2).

Establish Firewall Configuration Standards

Requirement 1.1 of the PCI Data Security Standard (DSS) guides you through the process of configuring and maintaining your firewalls and routers. There is no real science to deciding on what type of device and configuration to use, just some forethought. PCI requirements make it easy for you by telling you what type of firewall to use, how it must be configured, how to maintain it, and what to protect against.

PCI DSS doesn't waste any time getting into change management. Requirement 1.1.1 details a formal process for approving and testing all external network connections and changes to the firewall configuration. There are a couple of things going on here. First, all external connections must be approved and tested. Approval implies that management, or relevant delegates, must know and agree to the connection. Once the connection is made, it must be tested. Testing can range from full on penetration testing to simple port scans to verify that the connection is opened as designed. If this is your first time through PCI DSS, the firewall should be baselined (as a best practice), and any changes to the configuration thereafter must be approved. Each stakeholder should have a say in whether or not the changes actually get implemented.

It's much easier to understand what needs to be secured if you can see it on paper. Requirement 1.1.2 needs a current network diagram. All connections to the cardholder data should be clearly documented, including any wireless networks. This diagram needs to remain current at all times. With a good change management process, keeping the network diagram up-to-date is a simple task.

The flow of data throughout the enterprise is often forgotten when putting together an accurate diagram. In fact, network diagrams in general are poor canvases for graphically depicting the flow of data. Most diagrams are created in Visio® or a similar tool. Although the tools are quite powerful in what they can do, most engineers think in different ways, thus creating different looking diagrams that may represent the same underlying theme. A method for creating data flows published in an article entitled *Data Flows Made Easy* illustrates a way you can simplify this process (www.brandenwilliams.com/brwpubs/DataFlowsMadeEasy.pdf). These flow matrices are useful to Qualified Security Assessors (QSAs) and are much easier to maintain than graphical depictions of the same thing.

Requirements 1.1.5 to 1.1.7 were combined, simplified, and expanded in scope in PCI DSS v1.2. All ports and services allowed through the firewall must now be documented – secure or not – and insecure protocols must have additional documentation about their use, business justification, and potentially a risk assessment performed against them in the environment. Requirement 1.1.4 may also be of use here. The administrator needs accurate documentation of all groups, roles, and responsibilities for logical management of network components. This is especially helpful when implementing the rule sets.

WARNING

The only services, ports, and protocols that are allowed are those that are required for business purposes. These must be secured and documented appropriately. The easiest way to document these is to add the justification to the actual rule base in a comment field for each rule. More formal methods of documenting these items could be through an assembly of change control tickets, a firewall rule set review by a third party qualified to perform such a review (which could be a new engineer or a third-party provider), or a formal corporate standards or requirements document. Remember that all documentation must be cross-checked against the current firewall ruleset, thus making documentation inline the most efficient way to handle this. Documentation is key, and if someone says "I need that port open because I said so," ask more questions.

Now that you have all your Internet connections documented and your network and data flows clearly defined, Requirement 1.1.3 states that firewalls need to be implemented at each connection point and between any De-Militarized Zone (DMZ) and the internal network. Finally, Requirement 1.1.8 is less stringent in PCI DSS v1.2 firewall, and router rule sets must be reviewed every 6 months instead of quarterly. Be sure to take your review process seriously. Going through the motions on any of the periodic PCI DSS maintenance tasks will quickly land you in autopilot on track for a breach. Your engineers should scrutinize every rule and ensure it needs to be there. One good way to check a rule's use is to log it. If you find rules that are listed in your policy but never actually hit during a 6-month period, chances are the rule is out of date and should be removed.

Denying Traffic from Untrusted Networks and Hosts

Confidentiality, integrity, and availability of cardholder data are at the heart of Requirement 1.2. Your firewall configuration has to accomplish several things. The rule of thumb here is to deny nearly all traffic. Only the minimum traffic required to conduct business should be allowed through the firewall – both inbound and outbound. It is much easier to filter everything initially and only open the required ports and protocols on those ports. This is where a good network diagram with data flows, coupled with an accurate list of required services, ports, and protocols (with business justification), is worth its weight in gold.

Denying all traffic from "untrusted" networks and hosts is easy to accomplish. Many firewall solutions do this right out of the box. If not, there is usually a rule that can be configured to do this. It all boils down to failing safe. After processing all the traffic permitting rules in the firewall policy, all firewalls should deny everything else. For example, a common deny-all rule is called the "stealth rule," whereby all traffic, inbound or outbound, specifically targeting the firewall device itself is dropped. Before that rule goes into play, you must have a rule that allows an administrator to access the management function of the firewall to make changes.

With the traffic being denied for all inbound and outbound traffic, specific rules need to be applied to enable your business to function. Verify the business need against your list of ports, protocols, and services first. To add even more security, if the source of traffic can be narrowed down to specific networks or hosts, make your rule more specific and only allow those through.

Restricting Connections

Requirement 1.3 in the DSS gets pretty granular with restricting connections between publicly accessible servers and any system component in scope for PCI. What does this mean to you? The database containing cardholder data cannot be in a DMZ that is publicly accessible. Stateful inspection firewalls must be used. If traffic is not explicitly allowed in the rule set, it should be denied. Any Request For Comment (RFC) 1918 addresses are not allowed from the Internet, and Internet Protocol (IP) Masquerading should be used where appropriate with Network Address Translation (NAT) or Port Address Translation (PAT).

NOTE

The PCI DSS states in Section 1.3.3 that the firewall solution must provide stateful inspection. Most commercial and open-source firewalls have expanded beyond basic port blocking techniques and have stateful inspection capabilities. Cisco provides this capability on top of basic access lists (ACLs) in a feature new to IOS 12.0 called Reflexive Access Lists (or RACLs), which can be useful when extending firewall capabilities to satellite locations such as retail locations and distribution centers.

RFC 1918, originally submitted in February 1996, addresses two major challenges with the Internet. One is the concern within the Internet community that all the globally unique address space (routable IP addresses) will be exhausted. Additionally, routing overhead could grow beyond the capabilities of the ISPs because of the sheer numbers of small blocks announced to core Internet routers. The term "private network" is a network that uses the RFC 1918 IP address space. Companies can allocate addresses from this address space for their internal systems. This alleviates the need for assigning a globally routable IP address for every computer, printer, and other device that an organization uses, and this provides an easy way for these devices to remain sheltered from the Internet.

TOOLS

RFC 1918 space is often quoted and misunderstood. According to the original RFC, which can be downloaded at www.faqs.org/rfcs/rfc1918.html, there are three blocks of IP addresses that are considered private and non-routable over the Internet. Those are 10.0.0.0-10.255.255.255 (10.0.0.0/8), 172.16.0.0-172.31.255.255 (172.16.0.0/12), and 192.168.0.0-192.168.255.255 (192.168.0.0/16). Any private networks in your corporation should be numbered within those allocations, or in rare cases, on non-RFC1918 space that is owned by the company and not advertised to the Internet. This can be dangerous, however, as a fat-fingered change could cause the space to be publicly routable. Using IP space that is publicly routable but does not belong to you is also very dangerous and should be avoided.

Requirement 1.3.8 dictates preventing RFC 1918 address space from accessing DMZ or internal network addresses. Some devices call this "Anti-Spoofing" technology, mainly because an old trick to get around firewalls is to spoof internal IP addresses from external hosts. RFC 1918 addresses originating from the external port trying to come in to the DMZ or internal network should raise a red flag in the logs for the device. The firewall rule set should only allow valid Internet traffic access to the DMZ. Requirements 1.3.2 to 1.3.3 add more color on restricting traffic from the Internet to only those addresses that are in the DMZ and restricting direct inbound routes from untrusted networks into the cardholder environment. Why can't Internet traffic pass to the internal network? Because Requirement 1.3.7 requires the in-scope database to be on the internal network segregated from the DMZ. The cardholder database should never be able to connect directly to the Internet. Front-end servers or services should only be accessible by the public. These servers and services access the database and return the required information on behalf of the requester just like a proxy. This prevents direct access to the database.

WARNING

There is no reason whatsoever to allow a database or other application to directly access the Internet, bypassing the DMZ. This could cause cardholder information to be vulnerable to unauthorized access.

It is just as risky to allow a database server to have two network interfaces: one on DMZ and one on the internal network, even if no actual routing takes place.

Personal Firewalls

Finally, rounding out Requirement 1, Requirement 1.4 mandates personal firewall software on devices that are used to access the organization's network. The devices in question can be employee-owned (maybe a home PC with a VPN Client on it), mobile (such as a laptop or Wi-Fi phone), or both. The firewall must be present on the device, must be active, and cannot be disabled by the user. The built-in Windows Firewall can be used, provided that an appropriate group policy removes the capability to disable it.

Other Considerations for Requirement 1

PCI DSS v1.2 added more granularity to the requirements around routers, specifically taking Requirements 1.1–1.3 and extending them to routers. The one requirement that seemed specifically targeted at Cisco routers and firewalls has been enhanced is Requirement 1.2.2, even though it specifically only mentions routers. If any network device in scope for PCI has the capability to have a different running and startup configuration, this requirement applies and you need something to check to make sure they are actually in sync. No changes should be made to the running configuration without first going through the appropriate change management procedures.

Additional firewall considerations should be taken with regard to wireless networks and mobile or personal computers. Systems with cardholder information must be segregated from wireless networks for Requirement 1.2.3, and those firewall rules limited only to what is necessary for business. Chapter 7, "Using Wireless Networking," has more information for you on how to get your wired and wireless networks working securely. These units may not always get critical patches in a timely manner, and the personal firewall provides some assurance.

The Oddball Requirement 11.4

Requirement 11.4, although not grouped in with Requirements 1 or 2, is part of building and maintaining a secure network.

IDSs detect unwanted activity on networks and systems, mainly from the Internet, but increasingly on hosts (host-based intrusion detection) and Wi-Fi networks (wireless intrusion detection). This activity is usually the product of a hacker executing an attack. IDS can detect malicious activity not normally prevented by firewalls including Trojan horses, worms, viruses, attacks against vulnerable services, unauthorized logins, escalation of privileges, and attacks on applications.

There are many types of intrusion detection or prevention systems that can be used to satisfy this requirement. This is an example of a requirement that companies can leverage to build solid intelligence around their network and produce real-time threat analysis data that can be exported to various risk management software. Below, you will find many types of IDSs that could be used to demonstrate compliance with PCI DSS. For those that you are unfamiliar with, try a couple of Internet searches for more information.

- Network intrusion detection system (NIDS) is an independent platform that examines network traffic patterns to identify intrusions for an entire network. It needs to be placed at a choke point where all traffic traverses. A good location for this is in the DMZ.

- Host-based intrusion detection system (HIDS) analyzes system state, system calls, file-system modifications, application logs, and other system activity.

- Protocol-based intrusion detection system (PIDS) monitors and analyzes the communication protocol between a server and the connected device (another system or end user).

- Application protocol-based intrusion detection system (APIDS) monitors and analyzes application-specific protocols.

- Hybrid intrusion detection system (Hybrid IDS) combines one or more of the approaches above. In most networks, an IDS is placed in one of three configurations:
  - Network Test Access Port (TAP) allows passive monitoring on a network segment. TAPs are more reliable than hubs or switches and relatively inexpensive to implement. Hubs have a potential for bottlenecks and packet collisions. Switches can also cause bottlenecks depending on the amount of traffic being mirrored to the SPAN port and have a tendency to not receive error packets. Handling virtual local area network (VLAN) can be complex or impossible.

❑ Host-based intrusion prevention system (HIPS) protects work-stations and servers through software that resides on the system. It catches suspect activity on the system and then either allows or disallows the event to happen, depending on the rules. Finally, it can also monitor data requests and read or write attempts and network connection attempts, potentially allowing it to be used as a compensating control for other requirements.

❑ Network-based intrusion prevention system (NIPS) is a network security solution, although HIPS protects hosts. It monitors all network traffic for suspect activity and either allows or disallows the traffic to pass. For a NIPS to work properly, it needs to be positioned in-line on the network segment so that all traffic traverses through the NIPS. The implementation of a NIPS is similar to a NIDS with one exception: because a NIPS has two NICS, a network TAP, switch, or hub is not required. The network only needs to be architected with the NIPS in a position where it can monitor all the network traffic inbound and outbound.

NOTE

An IDS is reactive in nature. It only monitors and sends alerts of suspect activity. In contrast, an IPS will not only alert but can also take action to mitigate the problem. So, if the functionality of an IPS to take corrective actions is not required, why spend the money to implement an IPS? The answer to this stems from the concept of palatable risk. An IPS solution provides the capability for corrective actions to be taken before a system administrator has the opportunity to respond, which can be desirable during an active attack against systems. Without human intervention, it is possible to cause a Type I error (or false positive) and block legitimate traffic from legitimate customers. Certain types of attack are clearly articulated and can easily be effectively blocked with an IPS.

Again, PCI DSS does not dictate which solution should be used. In many cases, this may come down to cost – cost to purchase and cost to maintain. Both the IDS and IPS have their advantages and disadvantages and should be weighed accordingly.

Requirement 2: Defaults and Other Security Parameters

A lot of thought goes into securing a network. You have to think not only about the network devices (e.g., routers, firewalls, IDS) but also about system defaults, configuration management, and encrypting nonconsole administrative access, to name a few.

Default Passwords

Default passwords exist with almost every operating system and application. Requirement 2.1 states that all vendor-supplied passwords must be changed before deploying a system on the network. Requirement 2.1.1 imposes the same mandate for wireless environments. Password policies and procedures are usually dictated by the organization. Although there are several alternatives for authentication like biometrics, smart cards, and tokens, most of us use the traditional user ID and password.

Additionally, if your organization has a procedure for adding new users and granting them access to systems, there may be some default passwords that you haven't thought about. If you can remember back to when you first received your user ID and password, you might recall that it was a preset generic password (does Password123 or Welcome1 sound familiar?) Before PCI DSS required otherwise, many system administrators used the same generic password for all new users. If your company has not changed its new user process globally to reflect the more stringent requirements for users with access to cardholder data, you may end up with some users that have generic passwords. For more information on this, see Chapter 5, "Strong Access Controls."

Simple Network Management Protocol Defaults

Requirements 2.1 and 2.1.1 mandate all system defaults be changed before deploying a system into production. Simple Network Management Protocol (SNMP) is associated with several known vulnerabilities – specifically, versions of the protocol before version 3 – and default strings can allow someone to learn nearly everything about a device and potentially change its configuration. SNMP is a good network management tool for administrators of large infrastructures, but if it is improperly configured, it can allow hackers to do significant damage on a mass scale. Make sure SNMP defaults are changed.

NOTE

The SNMP protocol has many versions. Most modern devices now support SNMPv3 that allows for individual user authentication and encryption of the SNMP channel. Avoid prior versions of the SNMP protocol.

The most basic form of SNMP security is the community string. There is a public community string that allows read-only access to network devices, and a private community string that allows read-write access. The default values for these community strings are "public" and "private," respectively. Remember, community strings are not unlike passwords, and any SNMP armed with those defaults can gain access to an SNMP aware network device.

WARNING

The only thing worse than having "public" as your community string is to have no community string at all. This would give anyone at least read access to your network devices. A hacker can find out a lot of information about a device through SNMP.

Delete Unnecessary Accounts

Systems and applications come with a variety of accounts built-in. Some are system accounts, and others are administrative accounts allowing vendors to support their products. All support accounts should be disabled or deleted immediately. These accounts are essentially backdoors into your system, and if not controlled closely, they can cause a compromise to easily occur. All guest accounts should be deleted or at least disabled. The passwords should be set to something no one knows, and you should consider renaming the account if it can't be deleted. The same goes for default administrator accounts. Rename them to something inconspicuous. Name them something that conforms to your organization's naming standards, and change the description of the account as well. It adds a layer of difficulty for an attacker looking for the account.

NOTE

Here are some common accounts to disable that are typically available on new installations with a basic password or no password at all.

- Root account on UNIX systems
- Administrator account on Windows systems

- SA account for Microsoft SQL
- qsecofr account on AS/400
- "Enable" passwords on Cisco routers

Develop Configuration Standards

All organizations should adopt a baseline that is considered to be a minimally acceptable configuration for all systems. It is a key element of security and aids a security team's efforts in reducing the vulnerabilities on their systems from the minute they are deployed, and this reduces the overall security risk to the organization. Requirement 2.2 mandates that all known security weaknesses are addressed and are consistent with industry-accepted system hardening standards. If a particular vulnerability is not addressed with specific hardening techniques, workaround solutions may need to be applied to mitigate the risk. Once you have adopted a standard, the systems should be baselined to ensure all systems are built and hardened the same every time. Creating security baselines on computers and your networks is no trivial task. It takes time and effort, but the end result is priceless. A security baseline is a standard set of security settings that are established for each type of computer or network component in your organization. The baseline configuration is a "point-in-time" configuration and should be updated regularly as new settings are applied. Your organization's security policy should drive what security features are applied to your systems. A well-defined security policy lays the foundation for security elements that must be put in place.

TOOLS

If you are not sure where to start, the National Institute of Standards and Technology (NIST) provides checklists for almost all platforms in use today that are freely available on their Web site, http://checklists.nist.gov/repository/index. html. These need to be modified and adapted for your organization. The Center for Internet Security (cisecurity. org) is another great site for checklists, such as their CIS Benchmark tools for tons of common operating systems.

Implement Single Purpose Servers

Requirement 2.2.1 mandates that critical servers provide a single service (e.g., Domain name system (DNS), database, e-mail, Web) to the organization. All too often, organizations try to save money by hosting multiple services on the same host. Each service brings its own vulnerabilities and risks to the table and provides a hacker with multiple choices for attack. If too many services are provided by a single server, an exploited vulnerability on one service (i.e., DNS) can bring down or cause a denial of service to the entire server. The integrity of all the services and data is questionable at that point. As a rule of thumb, increasing the number of services provided by a single host degrades the overall security of the server and the organization.

NOTE

If you are running a Web server that is interacting with a database, that Web server should always reside on its own host separated from the database server by a firewall. If the environment is virtualized, the Web server and database server can physically be on the same host but should be separated on individual guests.

This particular requirement is hotly debated among virtualization enthusiasts as well as small businesses with limited resources and multifunction servers. The use of virtualization in conjunction with this requirement is perfectly acceptable for PCI DSS. The main trick is to remember the host operating system (or the hypervisor if you are running a minimalist host installation) is in scope for PCI, but guest operating systems (or virtual machines) can be scoped out, depending on what they have access to and what they are doing. Remember, any guest host that can see into another guest host with PCI data in it may be deemed in scope.

The other side of this is multifunction servers for small businesses. This is a gray area without a ton of guidance. Depending on how you want to read the literal language, you could read it as broadly as a server with multiple services on it serving a single function; thus, it is compliant with the requirement. If you wanted to overdo it on the narrow side, then every server type service should have its own hardware or virtual machine to run on. The true answer is somewhere in between. Black box solutions are typically viewed as compliant with this requirement, where homegrown ones may not be.

The answer here is to use common sense. You probably don't need to have your cardholder database on a machine that also acts as your Primary Domain Controller and external e-mail server.

Configure System Security Parameters

You might think this is a "no-brainer," but not all system administrators know exactly which services are enabled and disabled on their systems and how the system itself is secured. Requirements 2.2.2 to 2.2.4 describe how system administrators must handle the services that are available and running on their servers. Requirement 2.2.2 is standard system hardening whereby all unneeded services are removed, which couples nicely with Requirement 2.2.4 that mandates the same for removing unnecessary scripts, drivers, features, etc. Any service, piece of software, and operating system feature that does not have business justification for running must be disabled or removed.

WARNING

Don't forget about your network appliances and peripherals. These should also have appropriate security features applied.

Requirement 2.2.3 mandates the configuration of all system security parameters to prevent misuse. This particular control includes both a question and answer session with the system and security administrators as well as verification that common security parameter settings are included in the standard configuration. This can be accomplished by reviewing internal vulnerability scan data, as well as interacting directly with the machines. You can expect your assessor to ask things such as "What is your security knowledge?", "How would you verify secure configurations on your particular equipment?", and "What kinds of services would you disable immediately after installing a new server?"

NOTE

Remember, in most cases, default installations have numerous vulnerabilities. A lot of these services, features, ports, protocols, and so forth were put there by the vendor, and it is well-known information that is freely available on the Internet.

Encrypt Nonconsole Administrative Access

System and network administrators, by design, have access to everything. They "own" the network and are responsible for keeping it functioning. However, some of the tools they use are a little less than secure. Many of the tools are antiquated and actually pass user IDs and passwords in the clear (such as Telnet and Rlogin). To accommodate Requirement 2.3, encryption solutions must be used for all nonconsole administrative access. Most modern platforms have open-source solutions for this such as OpenSSH as a replacement for Telnet and "R-Services" (see www.openssh.org for more information). Mainframes will usually require licensed software to enable encryption, so other compensating controls may be considered here.

NOTE

Compensating controls can be used for anything but Requirement 3.2, so in rare cases, you may be able to run services such as Telnet or rsh on your internal network. If you have a valid business case and have taken the appropriate steps to design and implement an acceptable compensating control, you may be able to use these services. From a security perspective, allocate resources to upgrade those systems as soon as possible. Services such as Telnet and rsh allow users to easily capture sensitive data and even modify data in flight. Virtually every maintained platform in use today has an encrypted nonconsole administrative option. For more information on compensating controls, see Chapter 12, "The Art of Compensating Control."

Hosting Providers Must Protect Shared Hosted Environment

PCI compliance goes further than just the commercial entity providing the goods and services. Far too often your favorite store is nothing more than a "store front" with no back office, just a building or a Web site that pushes goods. Typically, Web site hosting for these operations is done through a service provider. Requirement 2.4 mandates that hosting providers protect each entity's hosted environment and their data.

WHAT ELSE CAN YOU DO TO BE SECURE?

Secure networks are often dismissed as too hard to enforce. Why spend precious cycles chasing our tails with a locked-down configuration when we can get by fine without it?

Here is a dirty little secret that many professionals don't want you to know: security and functionality don't have to be mutually exclusive. In fact, when they are set up properly, companies can achieve both a substantial amount of flexibility and speed to market with a solid security posture.

Expanding on this requirement, go back to basics when reviewing your firewall rules. Make them start from a deny-all in both directions, and then before adding any exceptions, ask yourself if this rule is really needed. Don't just stop at the PCI environment; go throughout your entire enterprise with this same methodical review.

After you have your final set of rules, go back again and examine the network protocols and traffic that you are permitting. Can you change the software to use encrypted streams? Can you go a step further and force mutual authentication with SSL certificates (or some other means) between network hosts? If this is possible, perhaps you can further limit the types of traffic permitted through your firewall.

Finally, the best thing you can do is separate the people from the machines. No, I don't mean electrifying computer keyboards everywhere in your enterprise (but that could be a fun experiment). I mean put access controls and firewalls between your server farms and "userland." Users are creative little monkeys that learn how to take the keys from a tired zookeeper and let all the animals out at night. Even with massive investment into technologies to secure laptops and desktops, all it takes is one creative act to introduce unwanted software into the environment, potentially targeted at server platforms. Separating those environments will go a long way to build resilience and security into your network.

TOOLS AND BEST PRACTICES

Firewall and network administration are easy when you have only one or two devices like many small merchants. Larger companies have hundreds or thousands of devices to maintain and must use tools to automate portions of the administration.

Firewalls that accept plain text configuration such as Cisco PIX and Linux IPTables can easily have scripted solutions that allow one change in one file to propagate to a virtually unlimited number of sources. If all store configurations are the same, or at least can be grouped, you can input the baseline configuration into a database and then have a script that generates the appropriate configuration for each store based on variable data such as store IP addresses, special store cases/rules, and other custom configurations.

The database structure could be as simple as three tables: a store definition table that has custom elements such as IP address space, possibly other boolean configuration switches, a baseline store configuration that all stores should conform to, and a table for supplemental rules for local customization. However, these basic setup scripts could easily dump a working firewall configuration for each store, and then normal distribution methods could retrieve and install them. Adding a new device to all stores or changing a global configuration could now be done with minimal effort and cost.

Both of these firewall technologies, as well as a slew of other open-source or free options, can be graphically administered through an open-source tool called FWBuilder (www.fwbuilder.org). FWBuilder is free to individuals on certain platforms and available for a nominal fee for commercial licensors. If you've ever been scared of running a UNIX-based firewall or a Cisco PIX because of its command-line feel, try FWBuilder on for size.

Most enterprise class firewalls that use a graphical user interface to administer them, such as Checkpoint, have the capability to administer multiple enforcement points in one central location. Many of these can be scripted as well such that you could accomplish something similar to the above but through commercially available means.

Firewalls and routers can be assessed through automated tools that review their configuration and match them up against several security standards, including PCI DSS. Commercial examples of these tools include Redseal's Network Advisor (www.redseal.net) or Skybox's Network Compliance tool (www.skyboxsecurity.com). Depending on your particular firewall, you may be able to find open-source variants in their respective user communities.

COMMON MISTAKES AND PITFALLS

These requirements normally bite companies in a few specific ways. The companies requiring the most remediation under this requirement typically are companies going through PCI DSS for the first time. Documentation tends to be one of the biggest deficiencies companies face when assessing against this domain. Your best bet is to make sure that you have documented all your firewall rules as required by PCI DSS. Simply going through that process will force several issues that will help you meet your end goal of compliance with PCI DSS. Those issues are outlined below.

Egress Filtering

Firewall policies tend to forget that outbound traffic should not get a free pass. For firewalls to comply with PCI DSS (and be effective security devices), they must only permit traffic that is necessary for business – both inbound and outbound. To successfully enhance your firewall policies without interrupting your business, consider adding new rules to your firewall that "permit" certain types of traffic and then log any hits to those rules. This will allows you to quickly determine which rules will work and which ones will not.

Documentation

Without fail, documentation is one of the most tedious aspects of attaining and maintaining PCI compliance. Before your assessor comes on-site, make sure that all in-scope firewall rules are documented and have all the necessary approvals. The expanded scope of Requirement 1.1.5 now requires that all ports and services allowed in and out must have documentation associated with them. Consider performing a risk assessment on those rules and including that documentation as well.

System Defaults

Good internal vulnerability scanning finds most instances of default passwords or configuration on in-scope systems. Many breaches that happen today start with a default or blank password or default to an insecure configuration. Ensure that a vulnerability management program correctly identifies these mistakes and that the management process designed to take findings through to resolution (including the all-important feedback loop!) correctly reports progress on remediation activities.

CASE STUDY

For this section, we will explore two different cases to show how the requirements can be applied in both small and large companies.

The Case of the Small, Flat Store Network

Before PCI, the notion of a firewall anywhere except for the border of a network didn't exist. In fact, wasn't the old joke about security "Hey, I'm all about security! I have a firewall!"?

Unfortunately for most companies, big or small, rapid growth and pressure to meet financial expectations have stifled security such that compliance initiatives like PCI become challenging. In nearly every company, network segmentation had to be addressed at some level.

Joe's Jumping Jerky Joint, a small company given to Todd by his father Joe 10 years ago, has four stores and an e-commerce Web site that accepts credit cards for payment. Todd was notified by one of his acquirers that he is now a Level 3 merchant and must submit a SAQ to demonstrate his compliance with the PCI DSS. As a former Level 4 merchant, his knowledge of PCI DSS was limited; thus, his stores or online site have not been validated against the controls.

The physical stores use IP-based Point of Sale (POS) terminals that he purchased off of eBay, and they share infrastructure with some nonpayment related machines. There are two PCs that are used by the manager and assistant manager of each store to browse the Web, check e-mail, and access the order fulfillment screens from the online store. There is also one kiosk in the store that allows customers to sign up for e-mail updates. The stores also have a small cafe and tasting area where you can sample some of the jerky and have a light lunch or coffee. Todd provides free Wi-Fi to customers who come to the cafe.

Each store connects to the Internet via a business class Digital Subscriber Line (DSL) for his Internet service, allowing Todd to ensure certain minimum levels of bandwidth and favorable pricing when bundling other services. The business class DSL came with an upgraded router that provides the capability to create a DMZ, but he has not used this functionality to date.

Todd knows that the PCs and the kiosk are not fully up to date with PCI standards and that the wireless network is a problem for PCI, as there is currently no segmentation between it and the wired infrastructure. In order to meet PCI DSS, some changes must be made. Todd does not want to invest thousands of dollars into added infrastructure to comply with PCI DSS. What options are out there?

Luckily for Todd, he upgraded to the business class DSL! The DMZ functionality on the device allows Todd to segment the POS devices onto their own network with relative ease. He needs to purchase a small managed Ethernet switch to accommodate the few POS devices per store. Finally, he needs to review the configuration of his DSL router to ensure that the firewall settings are done appropriately according to PCI DSS. He will not be able to access the POS devices or the POS controller (if applicable) from the PCs on the network, so he may have to adjust some process to go to those machines directly for end of day batch processing.

For the Web site, Todd must work with his hosting facility to ensure that they are providing a PCI compliant solution. He should either ask for their completed Appendix A for his environment (too meet PCI Requirement 2.4 if applicable) or see by checking if they are on the CISP Compliant Service Provider list (www.visa.com/cisp). Regardless, his contract with his hosting company should comply with Requirement 12.8. See Chapter 6, "Protecting Cardholder Data," for more information. If they are a compliant hosting facility or service provider, he knows he can provide documentation to satisfy his internal assessment requirements for demonstrating compliance to PCI DSS. If not, he must work with them to ensure they take the appropriate steps to become compliant. If he decided to in source his Web site, he would need to document all his firewall rules and make sure he had sufficient ingress and egress filtering. Oftentimes, firewalls will default to a minimal inbound ruleset without restricting outbound traffic at all.

For examples of what Todd's network looked like before and after segmentation, refer to Figs. 12.1 and 12.2 in Chapter 12, "The Art of the Compensating Control."

The Case of the Large, Flat Corporate Network

Flat networks don't only appear at small retailers' store locations, they appear in the corporate offices too – oftentimes with much higher remediation costs.

Consider the case of Christine's Car Commissary, a large retailer with 2000 stores. Christine's company has recently become a Level 1 merchant and is facing fines of $25,000 per month under the VISA Compliance Acceleration Program. She hired a QSA, and among other findings, she discovers that her internal assessors have underestimated the scope of PCI due to their flat corporate network. The store locations have large enough IT installations to make segmentation as easy (if not easier) as James's Jumping Jerky Joint. Instead, she is faced with massive costs associated with upgrading legacy systems not involved in card processing on her corporate network, and many of which are no longer maintained and cannot meet PCI DSS.

Christine knows that she needs to get as many systems out of scope as possible to keep her remediation costs under control. Two years ago, Christine had to upgrade several of the core switches that run her corporate infrastructure simply due to capacity limitations. She smartly purchased for growth and has both CPU cycles and bandwidth to spare. Her IT staff have several VLANs defined in the core switching infrastructure, and with the recent upgrades, they have the ability to place ACLs on some of the switching interfaces (or in some cases, directly on VLANs).

Christine must quickly deploy ACLs to isolate the cardholder environment such that her legacy computing systems are not included in the scope of the assessment. After consulting with her vendors and IT staff, she decides to take a two-prong approach. Several of her distribution switches have empty slots available. She will purchase firewall blades to boost the security and efficiency of her switching network, allowing her to accomplish several things.

1. The cardholder environment will be segmented from the rest of the core network, thus significantly reducing the scope of the PCI assessment, saving both remediation and assessment costs. She uses her new firewall blades to handle this at the network core.

2. IT and Management staff requiring access to those systems (both internally and remotely) are provided two-factor authentication tokens and have VPN software installed on their laptops. When they are in the office, they must use that two-factor token to access the environment just like if they were at home. This can effectively change the perimeter of her corporate network (as it relates to PCI), thus further reducing scope.

3. Like Todd does in the previous example, Christine creates segmented areas inside her store locations. Christine accomplishes this differently but with the same level of effectiveness. She directs her IT staff to place RACLs in the stores to segment her POS environment from the administrative and wireless areas in the stores.

4. She also puts additional controls on the wireless network with more stringent RACLs and deploys wireless intrusion prevention systems (WIPSs) to further bolster the security around her wireless network.

5. Finally, Christine has her security staff review the overall architecture of her network and design additional enclaves to boost the

security of the network and increase its overall resistance to worms, viruses, and other malware that propagates via weak network access controls.

Christine is able to focus her IT and Security staff on the above five items, saving both time and money and successfully passes her PCI assessment by concentrating her resources on the in-scope sections of her network.

SUMMARY

All systems must be protected from unauthorized access, whether it's from the Internet or any other source. Seemingly insignificant Internet paths such as employee e-mail, browsers, or e-commerce services such as Web servers can prove to be disastrous if not secured properly. Throughout this chapter, we have discussed Requirements 1 and 2 of PCI DSS. Understanding these two requirements is fairly easy; complying with them and actually implementing the required security features can be somewhat overwhelming.

We discussed the types of firewalls that may be effective from both an internal and external standpoint, how to update your documentation, and the best ways to manage the enormous amount of data associated with them. We also discussed administrative access to systems and components and how to handle remote or non-console administrative access.

Configuration standards must take into consideration all network devices (i.e., firewall, router, switch, IDS) and your computers, servers, services, and applications. Default configurations and passwords are almost always published on the Internet. For this reason alone, take precautions and change all default settings so as not to make the attacker's job easy. If an attacker makes attempts to exploit your environment and finds it difficult, chances are he'll move on to someone easier.

Finally, baseline your standards. Once the different types of systems and components have been hardened, establish a baseline security configuration. This takes the guesswork out of building and configuring the next similar system. It will have the same configuration as the previous one if the baseline configuration is followed. The baseline security configuration should be updated on a periodic basis to include new changes to the system and should always follow what is stated in the configuration standards and required by your organization's security policy.

Strong Access Controls

Access controls are fundamental to good security in almost any situation. We put locks on our cars and homes to protect access to them. We put passwords on computer accounts to protect them. In this chapter, we describe some basic security principles that should be understood any time access control systems are implemented. By understanding these basic principles, you will find it easier to make decisions on implementing each proposed access control. After earning a general understanding of access controls, you learn how Payment Card Industry Data Security Standard (PCI DSS) addresses access controls and the requirements you must meet. Then, you learn about procedures that should be in place and how systems should be configured to enforce PCI compliance. Once you learn about logical access controls, as in locking down access on your systems themselves, you learn about the requirements to physically secure systems and media that contain sensitive information.

NOTE

Many times the easiest way to protect data is not to store it at all. It's a good idea to review the data you're keeping and verify that you really need to keep it.

WHICH PCI DSS REQUIREMENTS ARE IN THIS DOMAIN?

You will find references and inferences to access controls littered throughout PCI DSS. Implementing strong access controls is important enough to PCI DSS to have a toplevel heading dedicated to them, as well as three rather beefy requirements (Requirements 7, 8, and 9). Requirement 7 is the shortest of the three but is probably the most important from a policy and procedure aspect. Requirement 8 delves into many of the technical controls in-scope systems must enforce, and Requirement 9 concentrates on physical security. Before we go into Requirement 7, let's walk through some of the basic principles of access controls as defined by information security professionals worldwide.

Principles of Access Control

To understand the goals of access controls, it's important to understand the three pillars of security: confidentiality, integrity, and availability, or sometimes commonly known as the CIA Triad. As you implement access control in your organization, you should always consider how you are meeting or violating these three pillars.

NOTE

In the last decade, much criticism has come upon the CIA Triad. Opponents of the triad cite that the three pillars do not fully address the basic requirements of the expanding responsibility of information assurance. One of the most notable is the "Parkerian hexad" proposed by noted information security legend Donn Parker (term coined by M. E. Kabay). Parker argues that the CIA Triad only covers half of the information security pillars. The other three proposed are Possession or Control, Authenticity, and Utility. For the sake of argument, only the basic CIA Triad pillars will be covered here, though other philosophies of information security may be relevant to your organization.

Confidentiality

The principle of confidentiality means to prevent disclosure of information to parties not authorized to receive it. This means that if Abigail in accounting should not be able to read prerelease earnings statements prior to their communication to the street, access controls should prevent her ability to do so. For PCI DSS, we want to ensure that unauthorized users cannot access cardholder data. This data is defined as the primary account number (PAN), sensitive authentication data, and full track data, but it also includes other information about a cardholder or credit card account that is stored near the PAN. This means that an expiration date stored by itself is not considered cardholder data, but the expiration date stored next to the PAN would. Aside from PAN data, there are many other types of information we need to block from unauthorized eyes. Employee passwords or encryption keys are not considered cardholder data but may be used to grant access to such data and should be kept confidential.

Integrity

The principle of integrity is an assurance that data has not been altered or destroyed in an unauthorized manner. Going back to Abigail in accounting, her level and responsibilities in her job do not dictate that she needs to be able to modify financial reports before they are announced to the street. In this case, she should not have access to modify those reports, and management must be assured that the integrity of the financial statements they approved is in fact intact. You must put measures in place to ensure that data cannot be altered while it's being stored or while it's in transit. For example, logging data that is considered in-scope for PCI DSS should be stored in a manner that an administrator would know if it had been altered from its original form. Log files are not the only data with integrity requirements. Other data includes files that contain cardholder data, system files, logs, and other critical application files that would be covered under Requirement 11.5.

Availability

The principle of availability means that the data will be accessible to those who need it when they need it. Abigail in accounting is responsible for collecting credit card settlement data and assembling all the information into one format for submission to her acquiring bank. When she arrives at work in the morning, the last daily batch of data must be available for her to work on, and when she receives clearing information back from the acquirer, she must be able to access the previous daily batch for reconciliation. Although the first two pillars are concerned with locking down access, this one is concerned with allowing enough access that those who need the data can get to it. For PCI compliance, this means that employees needing access to cardholder data and other critical information to perform their jobs are granted the necessary access as part of Requirement 7.

Requirement 7: How Much Access Should a User Have?

Let's put the principles of confidentiality, integrity, and availability into practice. Remember, we want to balance integrity and confidentiality (which both restrict access) with availability (which allows access). To do this, we use the principle of least privilege. This means that we want to give an individual enough access, so they can do their work but no more.

Requirement 7 mandates that all access to cardholder data be restricted by business need-to-know. "Need-to-know" is used by governments to help define what access an individual should be given. Lee is an FBI agent and has Top Secret clearance. He gained this clearance by proving he was trustworthy through extensive background checks and several years of service. Lee is at the end of his career and has been given a boring desk job. Because his case load is fairly light, he decides to look for other Top Secret cases the FBI is investigating. Because of need-to-know, Lee is prevented from browsing through files unrelated to his cases even though he has Top Secret clearance. Unless Lee can convince his superiors that he needs access to such information, he will not be given access.

The same rules should apply in your organization. Just because Abigail works in accounting doesn't necessarily mean she needs access to all of your organization's financial information. For example, Sydney's job as a purchaser is to buy inventory to sell at her company's store locations. Because her job does not dictate that she should work with customer data, she does not need access to cardholder data and should, therefore, be denied access to it.

Your company must determine exactly what access each user needs. You need to make sure they can access things for their jobs, and they should be automatically locked out of everything else (Requirements 7.1.1 and 7.2.3). Companies typically do this by defining roles and assigning employees to those roles (Requirements 7.1.2 and 7.2.2). The first thing you need to do is determine what access the role needs to do its job. Management must be involved in this process, and a manager should sign off on the access granted (Requirement 7.1.3). The easiest way to accomplish this is to assume that no access is granted, and list the areas or resources that the role must be able to access to perform its job as exceptions. Once the roles are defined, the permissions should be input into the automated access control system (Requirements 7.1.4 and 7.2.1) built into the system where the data transits or is stored.

As you are looking at what access a role needs to complete its job, make a note of any information it will need read access to but not write access. For example, Abigail may need read access to cardholder information to be able to process it for settlement, but she would never need write access to change it. In this case, we would set permissions that would protect the integrity of the information. You should also determine if certain data can be retrieved via other employees when needed. For example, Abigail's manager may need access to certain financial data only once per quarter. Because Abigail works with this data every day, she could provide a quarterly report to her manager as needed.

Requirement 8: Authentication Basics

Requirement 8 mandates specific controls for individuals who have access to cardholder data as a part of their normal job. This largely sets systems up to be able to comply with Requirement 10, which we cover in Chapter 9, "Logging Events and Monitoring the Cardholder Data Environment." Each user of the system must be held accountable for his or her actions, and it's virtually impossible to hold an individual accountable for his or her actions when he or she shares his or her username and password with dozens of coworkers. Without shoulder surfing, screen scraping, other monitoring technology, or high-definition cameras installed on each person's workspace, we must rely on our systems to help us properly authenticate users.

This starts with Requirement 8.1, giving every user a unique ID before they may access systems in-scope for PCI DSS. Most companies provide unique accounts for things such as network resource access and e-mail, but things fall apart when administrator-level accounts get introduced into the mix. Nearly every system comes with a common administrator or root level account for administrative purposes. Most security best practices instruct administrators to rename and disable that account before the server is placed into production. This is relatively easy when you have infrastructure such as Lightweight Directory Access Protocol (LDAP) or Active Directory deployed, but it can be a challenge when you have machines that stand alone.

NOTE

Why do operating system manufacturers insist on continuing the trend of providing a root or administrator user account that has access to the whole system for whatever it wants to do? Poorly developed software with global administrator privileges will surely lead to a root-level compromise, whereby a system is then "pwned" by a hacker. Software that needs elevated privileges must be limited to sandboxes on the servers and should never require administrators to run it under the root-level administrator account. If your vendor tells you it is a requirement, tell them you will be taking your business elsewhere.

Once you have all users working off of unique, individual IDs, you must add some kind of password (or password-like) authentication to it to meet Requirement 8.2! Many security administrators look at this requirement and think, "Well DUH, guys...." The intent of this requirement is to both define acceptable methods of authentication and prod companies to think about more than just a password for their authentication needs. The most common way companies meet Requirement 8.2 is by assigning a password to the unique account. The makeup of the password is described in the section "Password Design for PCI DSS," later in this chapter. Alternatively, you could use some component of a multifactor authentication solution to access in-scope systems. Multifactor authentication might include a fingerprint reader embedded into your laptop or a certificate installed on your machine. Your assessor asks you to provide documentation on the authentication methods used, as well as performs the authentication for each method documented to ensure design matches reality. We'll discuss some of those exact settings in the "Windows and PCI Compliance" section of this chapter.

Two-Factor Authentication and Requirement 8.3

Requirement 8.3 mandates at least two-factor authentication for remote users accessing in-scope systems. As of this writing, it is rare to see a company without remote access technologies deployed into its environment. Administrators need remote access to machines in break-fix situations, and general corporate users may need remote access for tasks like responding to e-mail or uploading documents to collaboration products. Not all users need a two-factor solution to comply with this requirement. Remember your scope! Most companies only have a small subset of employees that need this type of authentication. Network and user segmentation is an excellent way to reduce the scope of this requirement, dramatically decreasing the cost and effort required to deploy a solution. Any user (be it an employee, contractor, or other third-party company's employee or contractor) who is accessing the cardholder data environment must perform a successful two-factor authentication before being granted access to the cardholder environment.

NOTE

Multifactor authentication does not need to consume your Information Technology (IT) budget! A cost-effective solution would be to set up a certificate authority inside your company, and issue user-based (*not* machine-based!) certificates that require a password to be used to "unlock" the certificate. As long as both the certificate and password are uniquely assigned (and not group-based), this is a perfectly acceptable solution to meet Requirement 8.3.

Rendering Passwords Unreadable in Transit and Storage

Requirement 8.4 has far reaching impact to most organizations. Companies sometimes get confused on exactly what is required here and struggle with the interpretation, especially as it relates to Requirement 2.3 (described in Chapter 4, "Building and Maintaining a Secure Network"). All passwords for in-scope systems and users must be transmitted encrypted to the system in question to prevent someone from capturing the password with simple network sniffing technology, and all passwords stored on a system must be encrypted at rest. The easiest way to delineate which users and systems this requirement applies to is to ask the following question: Does this system process, store, or transmit cardholder data, meaning is it in scope for PCI? If so, then all users with administrative privileges or access to cardholder data must use some kind of encrypted channel for their authentication like Secure Shell (SSH) or Secure Sockets Layer (SSL).

NOTE

There is some gray area with this requirement. What if a user's authentication credential could also be used for access to systems *not* in scope for PCI? For example, let's say that Rob is a UNIX administrator and is responsible for both in- and out-of-scope systems. Some of the out-of-scope systems do not have SSH deployed on them, and Rob must use Telnet to administer them. For ease of management, both types of systems authenticate to the same LDAP server. Would that mean that all systems must be upgraded to support SSH because credentials captured while Rob authenticates to an out-of-scope server could be used to authenticate to an in-scope server?

By reading the requirement alone and considering the scope, you might think you don't have to deploy SSH everywhere. If you read the *Navigating PCI DSS Document* (www.pcisecuritystandards.org/saq/instructions_dss.shtml#navigating), it seems to suggest that those systems *would* need to be upgraded to require SSH. The best thing you can do is err on the side of common sense. Why protect a credential in one place and not another? You should deploy some kind of encryption for anything using that credential.

Authentication and Requirements 8.5.1 to 8.5.7

Requirement 8.5 describes much of the technical and procedural aspects for handling usernames and passwords for PCI DSS. Because Requirement 8.5 is grayed out as far as a compliance requirement (and is really a roll-up requirement for everything below), we will start off with Requirement 8.5.1. For 8.5.1, your assessor selects a sample of user IDs from your entire population, asks you to supply the form authorizing the access, and then validates that the access on the system is set up exactly as authorized. Before your assessment begins, you should go through this process with your own sample. If you find that your authorization forms do not match the access granted, your assessor will probably find the same.

Requirement 8.5.2 is another one of those "Duh, guys" moments, but you would be surprised how easily companies are compromised because they didn't check to make sure that the person on the other end of the phone asking for a password reset was the actual owner of the account! One tactic used in penetration testing is to obtain the name of an actual employee, and then call the help desk posing as that employee and request a password reset. It works more often than you imagine. Requirement 8.5.2 aims to prevent that by making sure that if Steve requests a password reset that the help desk person on the other side of the phone or e-mail request, or the process on the other side of the browser verifies Steve's identity before doing it. Your help desk may need access to pertinent employee data such as an employee number, last four of a national ID (Social Security Numbers in the United States are essentially that), address, home phone, or other types of information known only to the employee. Help desk personnel should be trained on social engineering tactics and be prepared to deal with an outsider trying to beat the system.

First time passwords are often an easy way to compromise an account. For example, when Steve joined his company, he was provided with a cell phone and a laptop. His user ID was his first initial and last name, and his password was "Newuser1." The initial password was the same for every user and would technically exceed the complexity requirements of PCI DSS. The password is alphanumeric and includes a mixture of uppercase and lowercase letters. But because every user gets the same password, compromising a new account might be a trivial operation with a little bit of social engineering. Requirement 8.5.3 mandates that all new accounts have a unique password that expires immediately after its first use. We'll cover configuration methods to do these for both Windows and UNIX in the "Windows and PCI Compliance" and "POSIX (UNIX/Linux-like Systems) Access Control" sections of this chapter.

Another source of compromise is old or stale authentication information from users no longer employed with your company. If you terminate a user, you must immediately revoke his or her access per Requirement 8.5.4. If a user does not authenticate with his or her password for a period of 90 days, the account must be removed or disabled per Requirement 8.5.5. Reviewing logs, as we cover in Chapter 9, "Logging Events and Monitoring the Cardholder Data Environment," is one of the ways to track successful access from terminated employees. The account login IDs should never be seen in access logs after their termination.

Requirement 8.5.6 mandates tight controls around accounts that vendors may use to support systems. Although vendor accounts vary in their level of authorization on systems, they should be disabled any time they are not being used and monitored while they are in use. These support accounts can come in more than one form. Sometimes the original equipment manufacturer supports it, such as IBM or Cisco, and other times you may have a third-party, such as SunGard or a division of a Big 4 to support it. Regardless, any common vendor accounts must be disabled when they are not in use. To monitor what happens during a session, you could have your vendor log into a Citrix portal to then access your machines and log the entire session. Command-based machines could make use of logging utilities built into common applications like `sudo`, or even using the history function of a UNIX shell and offloading the logs somewhere outside of the vendor's write access.

Finally, Requirement 8.5.7 mandates that you communicate all the password procedures in PCI DSS to the in-scope user base. An in-scope user is a user who has access to cardholder data as a normal part of his or her job. These users must be made aware of the password procedures, and your assessor will randomly sample users and ask them what they know about password procedures. Assessors may do this as a part of an interview for another area of PCI DSS, or they may specifically ask for a list of users and randomly call them for a phone interview.

TOOLS

Want to see how strong your passwords are? Mandylion Research Labs (www.mandylionlabs.com) created a fantastic brute force calculator that you can download (www.mandylionlabs.com/documents/BFTCalc.xls) and test to see how long it would theoretically take to break a password or key. Plugging in the elements of the password above (Newuser1), it would take the average computer just over 2½ hours to break that password. Let's say that you didn't know that the password contained one uppercase letter, six lowercase letters, and one number and assumed an eight-character random mix of uppercase and lowercase letters and numbers. If you made this assumption, the average computer would take a little more than 6300 h using a brute force attack to crack the password (an effective key strength of 2^{36}). Adding special characters in it would take over 117,000 h with an effective key strength of 2^{52}. This is where user education is important.

Educating Users

Although PCI's password requirements are not incredibly strict, they may be much stricter than what your company was using before becoming compliant. If your company is going from a very relaxed password policy to a stricter one, you will probably meet resistance from employees. Of all the changes you may have to make, this is one that affects an employee's day-to-day work. Some employees have a hard time seeing the benefits from using strict password policies – some may even grumble that this is just another way the IT department is making their lives more difficult.

Instead of forcing policy upon users and communicating it through e-mail or newsletters, meet with employees to personally explain the policy to them and answer any questions they may have. This is a great opportunity to educate them on what makes a good password and why they are important, and this could even be considered part of your security awareness training for Requirement 12.6.1. Management should be involved in this meeting, and it makes sense to tie it to some other form of All Hands event. As we learn from our mothers (thanks Mom!), it's best to lead by example. If employees observe management interested in and adhering to the policy, they will take it more seriously. You may want to get someone from management to briefly introduce that the company will be implementing a new password policy to become more secure.

One of the things you want to cover in this meeting is the password complexity requirements that will be enforced. Many times, users get frustrated when it's time for them to change their password because they don't understand why any of their new passwords are not being accepted. Give them examples of passwords that both conform and violate the policy, with information on why they do not comply.

You may also want to go over some tricks to help them choose good, secure passwords that will be easy to remember. For example, some security experts advocate writing out a sentence and using the first or second letter from each word. One of our colleagues suggests having users pick two items always present on their desk (such as a coffee cup and a monitor) and the password might be "c0ff33Cup&m0n!tor." Another trick is to take certain letters and interchange them for numbers that look like those letters (e.g., 3 for E, 7 for T, 1 for L) or take letters and interchange them for symbols the same way (e.g., # for H, $ for S). For example, the sentence "Bill grabbed a brewdog at the high school reunion gathering" could become the password "Bg4bathsrg," and the verse from one of the author's favorite songs "Show me, how you want it to be, tell me baby, cause I need-to-know" could become "Sm#yw1tbtmbc1ntk." The effective key strengths of those passwords are 2^{45} and 2^{72}, respectively. Users could also use a passphrase as long as it has uppercase and lowercase letters and numbers to comply with PCI requirements. A great reference is Mark Burnett's book, *Perfect Passwords: Selection, Protection, Authentication*, (ISBN 978-1-59749-041-2, Syngress). Much of the book is dedicated to helping users select passwords that are unique and easy to remember.

> **NOTE**
>
> Some of the most interesting research in recent years on how well users protect passwords has been done by the organizers of Infosecurity Europe. In 2002, they surveyed 150 workers on the way to work and found that two out of three were willing to give up their password when asked what their password was as part of a survey (www.managinginformation.com/news/content_show_full.php?id=469). In 2003, the survey participants were offered a cheap pen in exchange for their passwords; 90 percent of the 152 people surveyed gave up their passwords and some after a little coaxing by the person conducting the survey (www.theregister.co.uk/2003/04/18/office_workers_give_ away_passwords/). In 2004, they moved from pens to chocolate bars and found that 71 percent of those asked were willing to give up their passwords for the candy (www.informationweek.com/news/showArticle.jhtml?articleID=18902094). The organizers then decided to wait 3 years until 2007 to see if the situation had improved. In the 2007 survey, they also included some of the IT professionals attending the Infosecurity Europe conference. They found that 65 percent of the 300 people they surveyed were willing to give up their passwords in exchange for chocolate bars (www.theregister.co.uk/2007/04/17/chocolate_password_ survey/).

Users should be educated to never give out their passwords under any circumstances to anyone, including the IT staff. In the same 2007 survey from the Note above the users were asked if they knew any of their colleague's passwords and 29 percent responded that they did, and 39 percent said they would give their password to their IT staff if asked for it. Yikes! Looks like we have a lot of educating yet to do.

Use this opportunity to help them understand how often password changes will be required (at least every 90 days), and that they will not be allowed to reuse old passwords (at least the last four). You should also review company policies about disclosing passwords. Passwords should never be disclosed to anybody for any reason. Employees should understand the process that's in place to reset their passwords if they forget it. You should always ask users if they have any questions when rolling out a new policy.

Password Design for PCI DSS: Requirements 8.5.8 to 8.5.12

When PCI DSS was really gaining steam, one big complaint from companies forced to comply was that the password controls were too stringent or could not be supported on the hardware that ran their businesses. Nearly every currently supported system has the capability to comply with the PCI DSS password complexity requirements. If during your compliance efforts you find systems that are unable to comply, check to make sure that it is still supported by the vendor and is not just horribly out of date. To simplify the subrequirements contained within PCI DSS Requirement 8.5, see Table 5.1 that explains everything that your in-scope systems must enforce for password controls.

Table 5.1	PCI DSS Password Complexity Requirements
Req. No.	**Control**
8.5.8	No group or shared passwords. Each user should have his or her own user account and unique password not to be shared with others. Furthermore, requests for group or shared IDs should be denied
8.5.9	Expire passwords every 90 days. All users must be forced to create new passwords for their accounts at least quarterly
8.5.12	Password must be different from last four. When users change their passwords, they must not be able to use a password that has been used in the last four changes
8.5.10	Seven element minimum length. Users must be forced to create passwords of at least seven elements
8.5.11	Passwords must contain letters and numbers. Of the at least seven elements or positions in each password, at least one of them must be a number and at least one must be a letter

For these requirements, systems must enforce these controls. Having only a policy that describes the proper procedure for making passwords is not acceptable. All the above requirements can be met by modern UNIX and Windows operating systems. We'll show you how to accomplish this in the "Windows and PCI Compliance" and "POSIX (UNIX/Linux-like Systems) Access Control" sections of this chapter.

The Math of Password Complexity

We've thrown out some stats on how password complexity relates to the overall strength of the password. There are many measures to determine how strong a password is. One measure of password strength is the total possible combinations using your particular character set and length. Generally, the more possible combinations there are, the harder passwords are to crack. For example, using PCI requirements, you have 26 lowercase letters, 26 uppercase letters, and 10 numbers for a total of 62 total characters. PCI DSS requires that passwords are at least seven characters long, so for a seven-character password, there would be $62^7 = 3,521,614,606,208$ possibilities.

The number of possibilities increases exponentially with the length. If your company required eight-character passwords, that would be $62^8 = 218,340,105,584,896$ possibilities. On the other hand, if you left the length requirement at seven characters and instead required that users also use symbols or special characters in their passwords, it would add 32 more characters to the equation. Now you have $94^7 = 64,847,759,419,264$ – just over three times less than if we had required the password to be longer, but over 21 times better than one that only complies with PCI DSS.

Locking Users Out: Requirements 8.5.13 to 8.5.15

The first two requirements help to protect accounts against brute force attacks as well as the nefarious individual from abusing an abandoned, logged-in terminal. Requirement 8.5.13 mandates that systems automatically lock an account after six failed login attempts, and Requirement 8.5.14 mandates that systems maintain that locked status for at least 30 min for an automated system or until an administrator resets it for a manual system. To test this, an assessor may ask a user to perform six failed login attempts to make sure that the account locks, or they may just examine the system's settings to make sure it is set up properly.

Requirement 8.5.15 mandates that idle sessions time out after 15 min of inactivity. This requirement led to a myriad of interpretations, some of which actually broke a business function. For example, Matt manually runs some processes on a mainframe that takes just over 1 hour to complete. When he types in the command, the session essentially freezes while the task runs but becomes interactive again when the job completes. Some Qualified Security Assessors (QSAs) interpreted this to mean that after 15 min of starting the job, the session should time out (forcing the process to terminate abnormally). This requirement should not be applied to every possible way a session could be started but instead should be smartly applied to the environment as a whole. If all mainframe sessions must be initiated from a Windows-based workstation, then make sure the workstation meets the session timeout requirements since the mainframe session runs inside the Windows one. This may not work in every case, but take the concept and find the best way to implement it in your environment.

Databases and Requirement 8.5.16

Databases contain lots of information valuable to a hacker, yet the security around databases is sometimes the worst in the entire enterprise. Many compromises occur because of administrator-level accounts with blank passwords. Requirement 8.5.16 has two testing procedures. Procedure 8.5.16a requires assessors to verify that all users are authenticated prior to being granted access to the database, direct user interactions with the database are done through programmatic methods such as stored procedures, and that direct queries to the databases are restricted to administrators only. If you have power users that log into your database directly instead of going through an application, take any common actions they may perform and put them into stored procedures or functions, and then restrict their access to those elements. Better yet, code these actions into the application and force users to use that method instead.

Procedure 8.5.16b requires that assessors verify that application IDs and their passwords can only be used by the authorized applications and not by individual users or other processes. This can be challenging depending on your infrastructure. Older versions of database servers may not be able to sufficiently distinguish users from applications. Consider the following example.

Diana is a DataBase Administrator (DBA) and manages two main locations where enterprise data is stored. Her business critical information is stored in various locations on a mainframe. The security added to the mainframe allows batch processes to operate under noninteractive login credentials, thus preventing those credentials from being used for an interactive session with the data. Diana's Web farm for her e-commerce site pulls its data from a PostgreSQL database. In her pga_hba.conf, she set an Internet Protocol (IP)-based restriction on the application's ID by adding in the source IPs that are valid from her application servers. She has four different ones in her enterprise, so all four of the IPs are in her pga_hba.conf, and the application IDs can only be used from those machines which are considerably locked down.

TOOLS

Here is a sample pg_hba.conf with IP-based limitations. Assume that the database is called "CommWebsite" and the ID used for access is "CommUser." Your pg_hba.conf would look like this:

```
# TYPE DATABASE USER CIDR-ADDRESS METHOD
host CommSite CommUsr 10.4.30.0/29 password
```

Windows and PCI Compliance

If you work in an organization where Windows is widely deployed, you're probably using Active Directory to authenticate users. One of the great things about Active Directory is that it is easy to roll out many of the requirements for PCI to the enterprise. Using Group Policy Objects (GPOs), you can enable password-protected screen savers and set up password policies all from your domain controller. You may also have standalone Windows computers that aren't part of the domain (e.g., a Web server that's at a hosting company), so we'll show you how to configure these for PCI compliance as well.

Windows File Access Control

Windows access lists (ACLs), or Discretionary Access Control Lists (DACs), are used to configure and enforce access control. ACLs contain a list of Access Control Entities (ACEs), and each entity defines permissions. To set ACLs in Windows, you must have proper administrative privileges. Because Windows uses discretionary access control, the owner of the file and administrators can configure ACLs for an object. When using Windows access control mechanisms, you basically have three options: you can explicitly allow permission, explicitly deny permission, or implicitly deny permission.

When you implicitly deny permission, this means that you did not explicitly allow or deny access. By default, Windows denies all access to objects that do not have rights set on them. This is a great best practice to follow for all systems and is particularly good because it helps us comply with PCI Requirement 7.2.3 without doing anything. Because Windows implicitly denies access, explicitly denying access should only be used in special cases where you are denying permission to a subset of a group. One user you would normally never deny access to is the built-in "Everyone" group because this will deny access to all users including the administrator. The correct way to do this would be to add users and groups that should have access to the file and then simply remove the Everyone group from the allowed users. Because Windows follows an implicit deny for anyone not explicitly given permission, this will likely give you the desired result.

WARNING

System administrators are busy. Sometimes they will give all users administrative rights instead of properly reducing each user's (or role's) rights to the minimum necessary to do his or her job. This is bad for many reasons, including higher support costs when "Acts of CLOD" occur. With everyone acting as an administrator, Windows no longer follows the default deny policy required by PCI Requirement 7.2.3 because all users are allowed full access to all files.

When configuring access controls in Windows, there are several tricks that can save you time in initial configuration and later maintenance. Remember the roles you created as part of the Requirement 7, "How Much Access Should a User Have?" section earlier in this chapter? Here's where we use them! Once you have the role, you must create a group with those permissions and assign all the required users to that group. With users belonging to roles or groups, you can set access permissions for the whole group instead of each user individually. This also makes maintenance much easier because you can change permissions for the entire group and remove and add users whenever needed. It's not uncommon to have users who are assigned to more than one group. For example, one user may only need access to unprocessed cardholder information, whereas another user may need access to unprocessed and processed cardholder information. In this case, both users would be members of a group with access to cardholder information, but only the second user would also be a member of a group with access to processed cardholder data.

NOTE

The process of defining roles is not a weekend or after-hours gig. One author assisted a customer in creating a detailed set of roles for a top 10 financial institution (precrisis) in the United States. What started as an initial set of 900 defined roles escalated to over 3000. Although the exercise ultimately yielded a much more secure company with an easily managed set of permissions, the effort was much larger than anticipated.

Another great time saver, but a potential minefield, is to use inheritance as much as possible. When you set permissions on a file or folder, you can also specify how subfolders will inherit those permissions. This makes it much easier to configure access control on a few folders that are near the root folder, instead of needing to configure each subfolder individually. Just remember that if you set up inheritance, by default, subfolders have the same permissions. Security templates can assist with this if you find that you have common types of folders to which you grant access often. This keeps all security settings in the same location and makes them much easier to manage.

WARNING

To be able to effectively secure data in Windows, you should always use the New Technology File System (NTFS). FAT32 does not cut it because it does not have the capability to do access control.

Creating a New GPO

In a Windows Active Directory environment, the best way to roll out a password policy to all the computers is to use a GPO. On your Windows 2000 or 2003 server, click **Start | All Programs | Administrative Tools**. Inside the Administrative Tools dialog, click **Active Directory Users and Computers**. This will open up a dialog box that will show you your domain as well as several folders for configuring users and computers in your domain.

Right-click on your domain and click **Properties**, then click on the **Group Policy** tab. At this point, it is a good idea to create a new policy rather than modifying the default policy. This will make it much easier to revert later if problems occur. To do this, click the **New** button and then give the GPO a name such as **PCI Password Policy**. Next, you will click on your new policy and click the **UP** button. This will move your new GPO in front of the default one so that it will be evaluated before the default GPO. Next, left-click on the **PCI Password Policy** and click **No Override**.

Enforcing a PCI Compliant Password Policy in Windows Active Directory

Now that we have our new policy in place, we will configure the password policy on it. Double-click on the **PCI Password Policy** and the "Group Policy Object Editor" should appear. Expand **Windows Settings**, then expand **Security Settings**, and then expand **Account Policies**. Next, click on **Password Policy**. In Windows 2003, the default should look like Fig. 5.1.

- Enforce password history: The number of passwords that should be stored and not allowed to be reused. PCI requires at least four.

- Maximum password age: The longest time users can go before they must change their passwords. PCI requires that this happens at least every 90 days.

- Minimum password age: This is used to ensure that users don't change passwords back to the original ones, by changing them more times than is in the history and then back to their originals. This way they must keep their passwords for a certain amount of time.

- Minimum password length: This specifies how long the password must be. PCI requires at least seven characters.

- Password must meet complexity requirements: This must be enabled for PCI compliance, as it requires that a password is at least six characters long and contains characters from at least three of the following categories:
  - Uppercase letters
  - Lowercase letters
  - Numbers
  - Symbols
  - Unicode characters
- Store passwords using reversible encryption: This means that passwords will be stored in such a way that they can be retrieved if an application uses protocols that need the user's password. This is not much better than using plaintext passwords and should therefore be disabled.

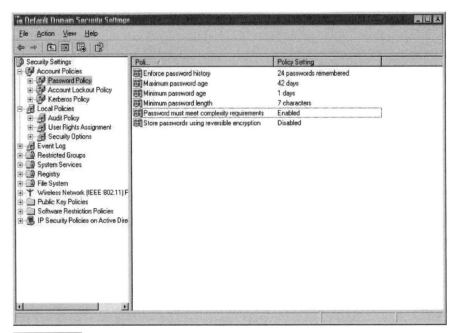

FIGURE 5.1 *Default Windows 2003 Password Policy*

NOTE

Remember that new password requirements will not be enforced until the next password change, so to be PCI compliant today, you would have to have all users change their passwords today.

Configuring Account Lockout in Active Directory

Although you're configuring the password policy settings, it's a good idea to also configure the Account Lockout Policy. To do this, expand Account Lockout Policy. Double-click on **Account lockout threshold**. In the Account lockout threshold Properties dialog box, change number of invalid login attempts to **6**. A dialog box will pop up and ask if it should also change the Account lockout duration and Reset account lockout counter after attributes as well. These should both be changed to 30 min to comply with PCI requirements, which is what the default is in this new dialog. Click **OK**. It should now look like Fig. 5.2.

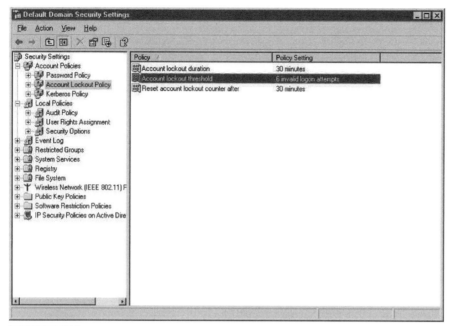

FIGURE 5.2 *PCI Compliant Windows 2003 Account Lockout Policy*

Setting Session Timeout and Password-Protected Screen Savers in Active Directory

Under User Configuration, go to **Administrative Templates | Control Panel | Display**. Double-click on **Activate screen saver**, click the radio next to **Enabled**, and then click **OK**. This will enable screen savers on all client machines. Now double-click on **Screen saver executable name** and click the radio next to **Enabled** and in the text box type **scrnsave.scr** (see Fig. 5.3).

This enables a blank screen saver on all computers in the domain. Now double-click on **Password protect screen saver**, click the radio next to **Enabled**, and then click **OK**. Last but not least, click on **Screen saver timeout** and then click on the radio next to **Enabled**. PCI requires that all sessions timeout after 15 min, which is equivalent to 900 s (see Fig. 5.4).

That's all there is to it. Now all the sessions on your Windows machines in your domain should time out after 15 min and require a login to get back in. In the end, your screen should look like Fig. 5.5.

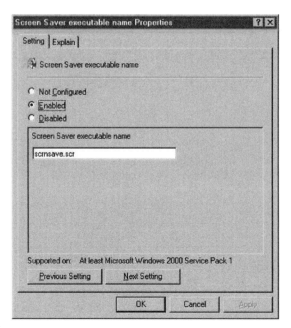

FIGURE 5.3 *Compliant Windows 2003 Screen Saver Properties*

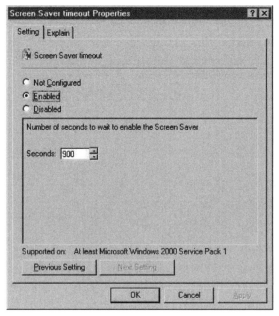

FIGURE 5.4 *PCI Compliant Windows 2003 Screen Saver Timeout Properties*

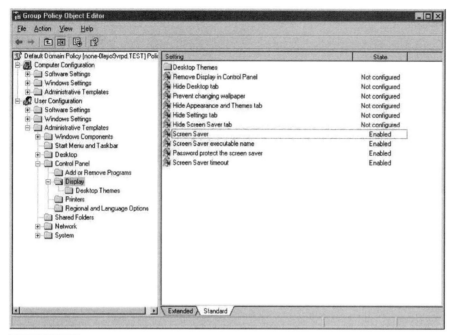

FIGURE 5.5   *Windows 2003 Display Properties*

Setting File Permissions Using GPOs

GPOs can also be used to set permissions for the file system. This makes permissions easy to maintain and keeps all of your security settings in one place.

In the GPO that we created in the last section, go to **Windows Settings | Security Settings**. Click on **File System**, and you will see a list of any files that have permission set on them in your GPO. To change the settings on a file currently listed, double-click on the **File** and a Properties dialog box will open. You can change inheritance settings in this dialog box to tell Windows how subfolders permissions should be affected (see Fig. 5.6).

Click on **Edit Security** and a dialog box will open that will allow you to view and modify what kinds of rights user and group accounts have. To add a user or group to the list of group or user names, click on the **Add button** and the Select Users, Computers, or Groups dialog box will appear. You can then type in the name of a **user** or **group**. The **Advanced** button gives you more options to help you find the correct group or user to add. After you click **OK**, the user or group appears in the previous dialog (see Fig. 5.7).

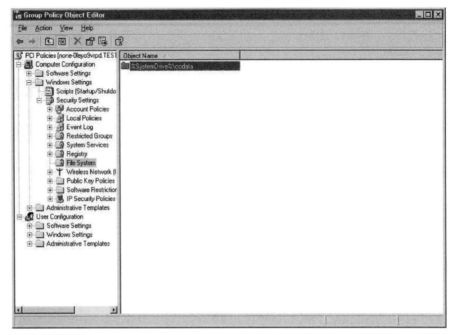

FIGURE 5.6 *Windows 2003 Access Control*

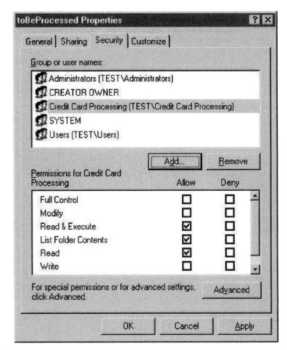

FIGURE 5.7 *Windows Access Control Settings*

By clicking on the **Advanced** button, you can view and change special permissions settings. You can also modify auditing settings and owner settings using the **Auditing and Owner** tabs.

Finding Inactive Accounts in Active Directory

One of the PCI requirements is to find all accounts that have been inactive for 90 days or more and remove or disable them. In Active Directory, there are several ways to find inactive accounts. If you are using Windows 2003, you can use the built-in dsquery tool. To find all users who have not logged in during the last 90 days, the syntax is as follows:

```
dsquery user -inactive 13
```

The tool expects the argument in weeks, so we supply 13 weeks equalling 91 days. For Windows 2000, there is a tool called `OldCmp` available at www.joeware.net. This tool works with both Windows 2000 and 2003 and has features to not only find inactive accounts but to automatically delete them as well. It also makes easy-to-read reports in Hypertext Markup Language (HTML). Windows 2000 does not have a method to return the last time a user logged into an account, and this was added to 2003. We can, however, tell when a user's password was last changed. PCI DSS requires that passwords are changed at least every 90 days, so if a password has not been changed in the last 180 days, then we know it has been inactive for at least 90 days. If you have configured your system to require that users change their passwords more often than 90 days, it would be that amount of time plus 90. `OldCmp` should be executed from the command prompt of the domain controller. The syntax to find inactive accounts using `OldCmp` is as follows:

```
oldcmp -report -users -b dc=mydomain,dc=com -age 180 -sh
```

If you would like to use OldCmp against a Windows 2003 to do the same thing, the syntax would be

```
oldcmp -report -users -b dc=mydomain,dc=com -llts -age 90 -sh
```

After the command runs, a browser window will automatically appear with a report in it of what `OldCmp` found. You can then review this list of accounts to verify that there's no good reason for the account to have been inactive (e.g., that person has been on the road for a long time and will return shortly). After you have reviewed, you can use the `-forreal` switch, which will tell `OldCmp` to delete the inactive accounts it reported previously.

Enforcing Password Requirements in Windows on Standalone Computers

To set password policies for a Windows computer (including 2000, XP, 2003, and Vista) that is not connected to the domain, you should use the Local Security Settings dialog box, which is set up basically the same way as a GPO, except that it will only affect the local computer.

- Windows XP: Click on **Start | Control Panel**. Inside the Control Panel, click on **Performance and Maintenance | Administrative Tools | Local Security Policy**.

- Windows 2000: Click on **Start | Programs | Administrative Tools**. Inside the Administrative Tools dialog box, click on **Local Security Policy**.

- Windows 2003: Click on **Start | All Programs | Administrative Tools**. Inside the Administrative Tools dialog box, click on **Local Security Policy**.

- Windows Vista: Click on **Start | Control Panel**. Inside the Control Panel dialog box, click on **System Maintenance | Administrative Tools**. In the Administrative Tools dialog box, click on **Local Security Policy**.

You should now have a dialog box open that looks something like Fig. 5.8. Now expand Account Polices, then click on **Password Policy** (for an explanation of what these settings mean, refer to the earlier section "Enforcing a PCI Compliant Password Policy in Windows Active Directory"). Enforce password history should be changed to at least four times to meet PCI requirements. The Maximum password age should be set to at most 90 to meet PCI requirements. The password length should be at least seven characters for PCI requirements, and passwords must meet complexity requirements and should be set to enabled. It's also a good idea to set the Minimum password age to at least 1. Otherwise, when a user is required to change their password, they could change it four times then back to their original password. When this setting is set to 1 or more, the user must keep the same password for at least that many days before they can change it again.

You should also configure the Account Lockout Policy to comply with PCI requirements. To do this, expand Account Lockout Policy. Double-click on **Account lockout threshold**. In the Account lockout threshold, Properties dialog box change number of invalid login attempts to **6**. A dialog box will pop up and ask if it should also change the Account lockout duration and Reset account lockout counter after attributes as well. These should both be changed to 30 min to comply with PCI requirements, which is what the default is in this new dialog. Click **OK**.

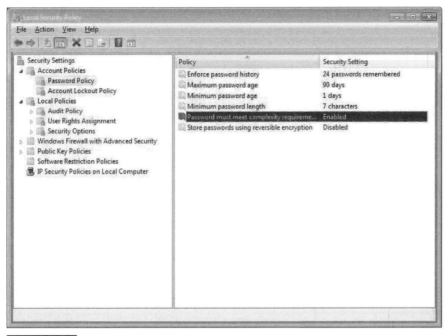

FIGURE 5.8 *Windows Vista Default Password Policy*

WARNING

All these settings are irrelevant if the users who connect to them have local administrator privileges! Do yourself a favor and remove all local administrator access from your users' accounts.

Enabling Password Protected Screen Savers on Standalone Windows Computers

Setting screen saver options is much easier to maintain and enforce using Active Directory. If you have computers that are not connected to a domain, these options can be set on each computer individually.

- Windows 2000, XP, and 2003 Server: Click on **Start | Control Panel**. In the Control Panel, double-click on **Display**. Inside the display dialog, click on the **Screen Saver** tab. The Wait option should be set to 15 min at the most. Also verify that **On Resume, password protect** is checked.

FIGURE 5.9 *Windows Vista Screen Saver Settings*

- Windows Vista: Click on **Start | Control Panel**. In the Control Panel, click on **Personalization** and then on **Screen Saver**. In the Screen Saver dialog box, set the Wait time to a maximum of 15 min. Also verify that **On Resume, display logon screen** is checked (see Fig. 5.9).

Setting File Permissions on Standalone Windows Computers

In Windows Explorer, navigate to the file or folder you would like to modify permissions on. Right-click on the **file** or **folder** and then click on **Properties**. In the Properties dialog, click on the **Security** tab. To add a user to the list of Group or user names, click on the **Add** button and the Select Users, Computers, or Groups dialog box will appear. You can then type in the name of a **user** or **group**. The **Advanced** button gives you more options to help you find the correct **group** or **user** to add. After you click **OK**, the user or group will appear in the previous dialog box (see Fig. 5.10).

By clicking on the **Advanced** button, you can view and change special permissions settings. You can also modify Auditing settings and owner settings.

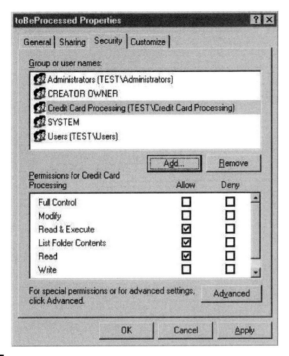

FIGURE 5.10 *Windows Access Control Settings Dialog*

POSIX (UNIX/Linux-like Systems) Access Control

UNIX-based systems such as Linux used POSIX-style access control lists. This means files have three permission modes: read (r), write (w), and execute (x). These modes can be assigned either using the letters just listed or they also have equivalent numbers. Read is 4, write is 2, and execute is 1. If file permissions are being set using letters, it will be a string of letters or dashes (e.g., a file with read-only permission would show r-- and a file with read, write, and execute would show rwx). When using numbers, they are added to denote permissions. Read permission would simply be a 4, and read and write permission would be 6 (4 plus 2). When using POSIX-style access controls, there are three groups or users you set permissions for. The first set is for that specific user who owns the file. The second set is for the group who owns the file. The third is for all other users who do not have any ownership over the file, similar to the Everybody group in Windows. So, a file that allows the owner to read and write, and everyone else only read access would look like this –rw-r--r-- or in numeric format it would be 644.

Linux has great command-line tools for changing file permissions and file ownership. Although exploring all that these commands can do is beyond the scope of this book, we will discuss some basics here. In Linux, to list file permissions, the `ls` command can be used. The syntax to list the file permission and the group and user who own the file is as follows:

```
ls -lg [filename]
```

To change file permissions in Linux, you usually use the `chmod` command. You can run the `chmod` command using numbers. The following example uses POSIX permission number format to set a file to allow the user who owns it to read, write, and execute the file, and everyone else to read and execute but not write to it, similar to a standard executable file.

```
chmod 755 filename
```

Or you could use letters and specify if you are going to add them or delete them from users (u), groups (g), others (o), or all (a). For example, to allow the user who owns the file to read from it and write to it, you would do the following:

```
chmod u=rw filename
```

To take away permissions use *a* – in front of the permissions parameter. To deny read, write, and execute permission to the group that owns the file and to all users other than the one that owns the file, you would do the following:

```
chmod go-rwx filename
```

To change the file ownership, use the `chown` command. To change the user and group that owns a file, do the following:

```
chown newuser:newgroup filename
```

In POSIX-style systems, there are three additional attributes that affect how files are executed are accessed. These are set user ID (SUID), the set group ID (SGID), and sticky. These settings work differently when they're applied to files or directories. The SUID bit can be configured to tell the file what user it should run under when the file is executed. Many times this is used to allow a nonroot user to run a file as the root user. This is used if a user needs to run a file that requires root access, and you don't want to give their account root access or the root password. SGID for a file works the same way as SUID, but it specifies what group the file should execute as. The sticky has no effect on individual files. The SUID bit has no effect on directories. If the SGID bit is set on a directory, any new files created in that directory will be owned by the group specified using the SGID instead of the group of the user who created the file. This is sometimes used in directories where many users will share files. When the sticky bit is set on a directory, only the user owner of the file or root can delete or rename a file (the group owner cannot). This is sometimes used in shared directories where you don't want users other than the owner or root to delete or rename a file.

In Linux, there are also several mandatory access control systems. Most of them are somewhat limited to protecting only a subset of files on the system (normally only critical system files). SE Linux is an example of this. SE Linux was developed by the National Security Agency (NSA) and has been incorporated into the 2.6 series Linux kernel. SE Linux uses targets to specify what files it will control and how it will control them. Other mandatory access control systems that are currently being used in Linux include Suse's AppArmor, Rule Set Based Access Control (RSBAC).

Linux Enforce Password Complexity Requirements

Most Linux distributions support password complexity enforcement using Pluggable Authentication Modules (PAM). This is normally set in /etc/ pam.d/system-auth. To comply with PCI requirements, a password must be seven characters long and contain uppercase, lowercase, and numeric characters. pam_cracklib has parameters to help you meet these requirements. The minlen parameter is used to specify the minimum length of a password. The dcredit parameter is used to requite digits, the ucredit is used to require uppercase letters, and the lcredit parameter is used to require lowercase letters. The retry parameter is used to specify how many attempts a user gets before the password program exits. Let's put all these together to show the entry in /etc/pam.d/system-auth:

```
    password  required  /lib/security/pam_cracklib.so  minlen=7
dcredit=1 ucredit=1 lcredit=1 retry=5
```

Depending on your implementation, you may see different names for the PAM configuration files where this information is placed (for example, in Debian, you would find this information in the /etc/pam.d/common-password configuration file).

Cisco and PCI Requirements

Cisco devices have some important settings that should be used for you to become PCI compliant. All passwords should be encrypted when stored or in transit. Most operating systems do this and do not really give you an easy way to store them unencrypted even if you want to. Cisco devices are an exception, however, so it's important to check this.

Cisco Enforce Session Timeout

To force Cisco devices to automatically timeout if a session is left inactive, use the exec-timeout configuration under the appropriate line configuration. The syntax for this command is exec-timeout [minutes] [seconds]. For PCI compliance, this should be set to as follows:

```
exec-timeout 15 0
```

Encrypt Cisco Passwords

The current best practice from Cisco is to always use "enable secret" and "username secret," instead of enable password. Enable password encrypts the password using a very weak encryption algorithm that has been broken for a long time. The secret command uses Message Digest 5 (MD5) to hash the password. Although MD5 has shown some weaknesses lately, this is far better than the alternative and the best Cisco is giving us right now. Alternatively, you can use directory-based authentication models such as RADIUS or TACACS+ to prevent these usernames and passwords from being stored directly on the device.

Setting Up SSH in a Cisco Environment

By default, Cisco routers allow Telnet access to the line vty 0 4 port for remote configuration. To disable this and set up an SSH server, you must first have an IOS version that supports IOS with the appropriate feature pack (typically the crypto pack). You need to set up either local authentication or as suggested above, tie the device to a directory. When managing any more than a few devices, pointing the authentication to a directory service makes administration much easier.

If you have already directed your device to a directory service, skip to the next configuration step. Otherwise, you need to enter this into your router after entering the "Terminal Configuration" mode by typing config t:

```
aaa new-model
```

The next command generates the keys required to perform SSH encryption:

```
cry key generate rsa
```

Then finally, to disable Telnet for remote access, type the following two commands:

```
line vty 0 4
transport input ssh
```

Then, save your configuration!

Requirement 9: Physical Security

There are three basic types of physical security. The first type is obstacles such as doors, walls, and other barriers, which can help stop or at least delay intruders. The second type is detection mechanisms such as alarms, lighting, guards, and television cameras that help detect attacks. The third type is response, which includes things you would put in place to stop an attack in progress or soon after. It's important to use all these types of physical security to protect sensitive information. For example, you may put sensitive data behind a locked door and have security cameras monitoring that door, recording everybody who goes in and out. You may also have a guard on duty who can quickly respond to stop anyone who's trying to circumvent the lock. Security measures in plain sight act as a deterrent to attackers, sometimes preventing the attack in the first place.

Requirement 9.1 mandates "facility entry controls" for in-scope areas including computer rooms, data centers, and other physical areas where in-scope systems may live. Acceptable controls include lock and key, badge access, or some other barrier that automatically locks and only unlocks for the people authorized to access these rooms (Hint: the President of your company should *not* have access). Requirement 9.1.1 mandates the use of video cameras or other access control mechanisms to monitor individual physical access to "sensitive areas." No doubt those areas include the ones mentioned in 9.1, but arguably they would include a large physical storage area of paper records that contain cardholder data. These large storage areas exist in many places in the United States, and the payment systems in some countries require exchanging a significant amount of paper data (such as Mexico). Those areas should be protected in the same way and should have cameras monitoring access. In addition to simply placing the camera there, you must protect the video data from modification and regularly review and correlate the data, as well as store it for a minimum of 3 months.

Before PCI DSS version 1.2, this requirement has been interpreted to mean a wide variety of controls. PCI version 1.2 does a good job clarifying exactly where these cameras should be stored. For example, placing cameras over each cash register is not required, but if you store cardholder data in a server room at a store, that would need to be monitored.

Requirements 9.1.2 and 9.1.3 aim to protect inherently vulnerable areas of your environment. Requirement 9.1.2 targets publicly accessible network jacks and mandates the access to such jacks be restricted. This one can be challenging as far as its intent. If you have conference rooms or common areas with network jacks that are outside the restricted areas of your company, you should disable them or segment them away from networks where cardholder data may be processed. This requirement would not apply to a conference room *behind* a secured area where visitors must be escorted. QSAs in the past have incorrectly read this requirement to mean that *all* conference room jacks must be disabled. This is incorrect, only those areas considered publicly accessible (i.e., with no physical access such as a badge reader protecting them). Another area to look out for with respect to 9.1.2 is retail store locations where network jacks may be placed throughout the store in plain view (or otherwise unrestricted) that might also sit on the point of sale (POS) network (or a network where cardholder data may be processed).

It is time for a real-life example. One of the authors was working with a customer who had a chain of cafes. When sitting down at one of the tables in the cafe, a network jack was discovered slightly obscured by a plant. This jack was actually hooked up to the same network as the POS systems, and an attacker could easily hide a device that could take advantage of this major design flaw.

Requirement 9.1.3, discussed in Chapter 7, "Using Wireless Networking," mandates protection for wireless access points, gateways, and hand-held devices.

Handling Visitors: Requirements 9.2 to 9.4

First, we begin with documentation! Requirement 9.2 talks about procedures to distinguish employees and visitors, and the testing procedure 9.2.a determines if the procedure covers granting badges, changing access, and revoking terminated or expired badges. The other testing procedure 9.2.b sees if you actually follow your own policies!

NOTE

During your assessment, *make sure* you make your assessor follow the procedures you set! There is nothing that says FAIL more than when a company being assessed forgets to give the assessor a visitor badge.

Requirement 9.3 deals with visitors exclusively. Requirement 9.3.1 is a test to make sure that the badge you give to the assessor does not open doors where sensitive information is stored. This is what the Council means by "unescorted access." You can expect your assessors to try and get their badge to open a data center door or other sensitive area. Obviously, if you issue plain paper badges to your assessors, this will be a fairly easy requirement to pass. Your assessor will also look at the badge you give them and compare it to your badge. Requirement 9.3.2 mandates that employee badges and visitor badges visually appear different and have distinguishing marks such that an employee of your company could easily identify someone as a visitor by the badge used to identify him. Finally, Requirement 9.3.3 mandates that visitor badges are surrendered upon leaving the facility. Your assessor will probably perform the required testing procedures without you even knowing, so be sure your company is following the policies and procedures you set out!

Requirement 9.4 is documentation-based but not in the way you might think. When visitors are allowed to visit the facility in general, data center or other sensitive areas, they must sign in. The three items that must be captured for every access are the person's name, the firm represented, and the name of the employee authorizing the access. You must also retain this log for at least 3 months (unless restricted by law), so expect to add dates and times to the above three items.

Handling Media: Requirements 9.5 to 9.10.2

Up to this point, the main focus with cardholder data has been online or live data. Data is not always online or live and exists in many different places. Requirement 9.5 deals with backup tapes and how they are stored off-site. These should be stored in a secure location, and if they are stored off-site, the security of the facility in question should be reviewed at least annually. Backups are not required to be stored off-site, however! Several companies make use of on-site tape vaults in their primary data centers to ensure that the data remains secure. If the media goes off-site, don't send it home with one of your employees to put in her house. Be sure it is a facility that is secure and that the contracts comply with Requirement 12.8.

Requirement 9.6 mandates physical protection of all kinds of media that contain cardholder data. The term "media" is intentionally broad here, and the examples they list include computers, removable electronic media (such as USB drives), communications hardware, telecommunication lines (arguably not required if all data over the wire is encrypted), and paper (receipts, sales reports, chargeback or dispute reports, faxes, mailrooms). Although this is a procedural requirement (your assessor must review your procedures to ensure that this is addressed), your assessor may validate that you follow your procedures and ask to see areas where this type of data may be stored.

When media is distributed outside your company's secure facility, you must protect the media in three distinct ways. First, Requirement 9.7 mandates a policy be put in place to strictly control the distribution of cardholder data. The fewer places you send in-scope data, the less likely you will have a breach because someone did not adequately protect the data. Requirement 9.7.1 states that all media must be classified in a manner such that it can be identified as confidential. This requirement could literally be interpreted to say that the media must have the term "CLASSIFIED" written on it, or more loosely interpreted to state that if you label tapes with a colored dot, the *red* ones are considered classified by your policies. Finally, Requirement 9.7.2 mandates that any media transported outside the facility is done so via a secure courier or in a manner by which it can be tracked. Something like your Iron Mountain driver or a Federal Express package would suffice.

When media is transported off-site, you need to enter it into a log so that you know where your media inventory is at any given point. Your assessor will review several months of logs, per Requirement 9.8, and make sure that both the tracking information are included as well as proper management authorization. Someone capable of providing proper management authorization could be your data center manager or another person with the delegated authority (and accountability) for authorizing the transport of media.

Requirement 9.9 mandates strict control over the media such that it is only accessible to the employees who need it and periodic inventory of the media (per a policy). The testing procedure for Requirement 9.9.1 requires your assessor to review the media inventory log to make sure that periodic inventories are performed.

NOTE

What is periodic? Good question! Version 1.2 of the PCI DSS removed many ambiguous terms like "periodic" and replaced them with concrete terms like "every quarter." Use this as a general rule of thumb. You must have an assessment performed annually, so do any periodic requirement at least annually so you have something recent to show your assessor.

Requirement 9.10 deals with the destruction of cardholder data. In cases where you need to dispose of any media containing cardholder data, it needs to be destroyed in a manner by which the data is not recoverable. This means that if you are done with a hard drive, you must either electronically destroy the data or physically destroy the media – a simple delete does not work. Requirement 9.10.1 describes some methods that could be used for hardcopy media and mandates that shred bins are available for employees to use (where applicable), and those bins are protected by some kind of locking device. Expect your assessor to walk through your areas and jiggle that lock a bit. Requirement 9.10.2 mandates that electronic media is destroyed appropriately. This type of media could be electronically destroyed with something like a bulk eraser (only for magnetic-based media) or physically destroyed with a giant shredder, incinerator, or just a bad day with a steam roller. Your assessor may want to review a sample of any electronically destroyed media to ensure that the data is not recoverable.

WHAT ELSE CAN YOU DO TO BE SECURE?

This chapter covers how to create PCI Compliant access controls for in-scope data. One of the most effective things you can do is reduce the storage of in-scope data to both make it easier to comply with these three major requirements and to improve your general security. Let's explore some areas where you might store in-scope data that could be reduced or eliminated.

Retail stores are notorious for storing data well beyond their useful lifespan for various purposes. When retailers started to embrace the concept of a computer to run their POS and process credit card transactions, it appears that the equipment first deployed was unreliable. Why else would you store 90 days of transaction logs on an in-store server? From an electronic perspective, remove all cardholder data older than 2 or 3 days from your POS controllers. POS terminals should never store this information once it has been passed to the controller (which could arguably be done on a daily batch basis). If you feel that you may need this data, collect the transaction logs or electronic journals in a central location. Bringing data from 50 stores is much easier to maintain in one place versus 50 individual places.

Next, look for paper data. If you are still printing the entire card number on the receipt that a customer signs, all of that paper must be protected in accordance with PCI. Get it centralized, then possibly imaged and destroyed. Even if you make a change to your process to mask that number when it is printed, be sure you don't have any legacy data in the stores. One of the authors remembers visiting a retail location that had 10 years of paper cardholder data in clearly labeled boxes next to the bathroom used by customers, even though corporate policy prohibited keeping data any longer than 1 year.

TOOLS

Did you know that you only need four elements to uniquely identify any transaction in your enterprise, and one of those is *not* the full card number? These elements are as follows:

- First six and last four (or just last four) digits of the card number
- Date and time of purchase
- Amount of purchase
- Authorization code

Customers who have used this method have never reported that two transactions matched these elements identically but had different card numbers.

Do your retail stores still contain knuckle-busters, those old manual credit card contraptions that used carbon paper and made a "kerCHUNK-kerCHUNK" sound as an imprint of a customer card is made? If so, you better believe there is probably someone who has used it recently and that some data is stored on hardcopy media (i.e., paper) in that store. Just like above, be sure that once you fix the policy or remove that equipment from the store that you have removed all the legacy data.

Here's another one that you may not have thought about. If you have certain business or high volume customers that phone or fax orders in, how do they pay for their orders? Do you keep a credit card on-file so that when they come in they can just sign and leave? Work on removing that data or changing how you deal with your high-profile customers.

If you run a call center, how are calls monitored? Do the phones rely on Voice Over IP (VoIP) technologies to operate? Do you record the calls? The Council has specific Frequently Asked Questions dealing with call centers on their Web site (www.pcisecuritystandards.org) that will address your particular situation.

Finally, look to your corporate headquarters. Do you really need a credit card more than a couple of months after the transaction was initially processed? Many companies tell you that they absolutely need it until you ask them why at least three times. Why is three the magic number? Who knows, but the truth usually sounds like "Well, we've always done it that way." Then, you ask them what they might do if the data was not available after 60 days. They will usually figure out a way to either handle the dispute with a truncated number or simply realize that the cost to secure this data far exceeds the potential losses associated with not having the data.

NOTE

Propaganda is powerful. Some industry pundits think that the card brands require merchants to store data. If you have heard this, read the next sentence very carefully. Card brands *do not* require that you store data! In most cases, your acquirer is taking a short cut, thus transferring risk to the merchant! In the authors' experience, companies can easily deal with dispute resolution without the full number when they press their acquirer. Acquirers will compete for your business, so if your current acquirer is not willing to help you, consider another one! You'd be amazed how quickly something like this is resolved. Furthermore, law enforcement typically provides you with the full card number they want you to pull transactions for, so you can still assist them by asking for specific dates and times. There are some exceptions to this rule, but virtually every one can be altered to off-load risk from the company trying to comply with PCI DSS.

TOOLS AND BEST PRACTICES

Aside from challenging the useful life of data and ensuring that you do not retain data longer than is absolutely required, here are a few other best practices you might consider.

Enforcement of a strong password policy helps to protect systems from potential compromise. Here are some simple password rules, above and beyond changing default passwords that will provide stronger security.

- Make user-level passwords expire every 60 days instead of 90 days.

- Accounts that have system-level privileges must have a unique password from all other accounts held by that user.

- Give administrators different accounts for administrative actions; do not tie the privileges to their primary domain accounts.

- Do not transmit passwords over the Internet by e-mail or any other form of communication without being encrypted.

- Make passwords be a minimum of eight characters in length, with a combination of uppercase and lowercase alpha and numeric characters and special characters as well (e.g., !%@$).

- Deploy a token-based, system-wide two-factor authentication solution such that any system access requires a token.

- Deploy a single sign-on solution that synchronizes passwords so that users do not have to remember multiple passwords, thus encouraging users to select more secure passwords.

- Do not share or write passwords down.

Many of these methods can help you bolster your overall security, but in many cases, they also make authentication easier on users. After all, if security professionals impose difficult requirements on users, they will come up with ever more creative ways to get around them!

Random Password for Users

PCI requires unique first time passwords. There are many possible ways to do this, and a quick Google search for password generators returns many options. These may work well for you; however, if you're ultra paranoid, then you may want to use one installed on your own computer.

Here is a short Ruby (www.ruby-lang.org) script to help you create good, first time passwords. Notice that certain letters and numbers will never be used in passwords that this program creates. For example, 1, l, and I are not included because they can often be mistaken for each other. Also 0 and O have been removed. To run this script, you must have Ruby installed (it runs on many operating systems including Windows and Linux) and have the Crypt::ISAAC module, which is a more secure random number generator than the one included with Ruby. This can be found at http://rubyforge.org/projects/crypt-isaac/.

```
#!/usr/bin/env ruby
require "crypt/ISAAC"
rng = Crypt::ISAAC.new
schars  =  "24356789abcdefghijkmnopqrstuvwxyzABCDEFGHJKLMN-
PQRSTUVWXYZ"
for i in 1..10
password  =  (1..10).collect  {  |i|  schars[rng.rand(schars.
length), 1]}
puts password.join
end
```

COMMON MISTAKES AND PITFALLS

This domain of PCI DSS starts with documentation, and poor documentation will set you up for failure when you try to meet the rest of it. Companies that struggle the most with this domain have two major issues they fight. The first is a poor analysis as part of Requirement 7, thus poor (if not non-existent) documentation to support this requirement. Because content in Requirements 8 and 9 often rely on Requirement 7 to be completed, companies that often miss parts of Requirements 8 and 9 have set themselves up for failure by missing Requirement 7. Do your homework, and make sure Requirement 7 is handled well!

The other big trip up is legacy systems. There aren't as many of them out there as there used to be, but with a new group of companies looking for the services of a QSA for the first time, there will be no doubt a ton of these out there. Legacy systems have many issues complying with PCI DSS, and this is one of the major ones.

Is there an avenue for a compensating control? There is always a possibility for a compensating control unless you are dealing with Requirement 3.2. For these systems, you will most likely need to use network segmentation and Virtual Private Networks (VPNs) or a "jump" server environment like a Citrix box or a Windows Terminal Server. Keep in mind, systems that are this legacy tend to be riddled with holes and struggle with just the basics of limiting network traffic to them. Most companies soon discover that this option will break their business, and they must ultimately upgrade.

For Requirement 9, the biggest mistakes people make are on camera coverage. PCI DSS version 1.2 does quite a bit to clarify where cameras are required, and what you must do with them. Don't over cover (i.e., put a camera on every cash lane), and don't under cover (i.e., no cameras in stores at all).

CASE STUDY

The following two case studies explore when bad things happen (or could happen) to people with good intentions. The PCI Requirements, when followed correctly, are designed to reduce the risk that companies carry by holding this data. The moral for both of these case studies is that you should store the absolute least amount possible, but protect what you store like a mama bear protects her cubs.

The Case of the Stolen Database

Alice's Activity Atrium is a startup that aims to revolutionize how families shop with young children in malls. Alice pitched the concept of an activity center inside her local mall, with a safe, indoor playground, physical security around the play area, and pagers to reach parents inside the mall if problems occur with their children. Her goal was not to take up a store front but to make use of existing atrium space in an aesthetic manner such that it could be part of a seasonal offering for malls. The general manager for the mall granted her proposal on a trial basis, allowing her to set her business up for the back-to-school rush. Provided that things went smoothly, she would win the contract for the coveted Christmas season shopping that often occurred during November and December.

Alice bought some daycare management software for her laptop based on Microsoft Access, and opened her business in late July with amazing success. Her quick rise in popularity required her to hire some additional help. Alice contracted Darlene to run the laptop during peak times so that Alice could help with keeping the kids busy and safe. The software on her laptop captured relevant information about each customer and captured a credit card for payment. Customers paid by the tenth of an hour for the service, so the card was preauthorized for a 6-h stay, much longer than any stay she envisioned, and then finally authorized and settled for the actual amount used. The laptop was placed at her location's entrance so that customers could check in and out quickly without having to step inside the facility, and repeat customers quickly were able to drop their kids off because the information was retrieved from storage.

One evening, one of the children under Alice's care fell at an awkward angle and sprained his ankle. During the commotion of moving the child to a safe place and calling the mall's medical personnel and the child's parents, Darlene left her post to help out. A passing thief seized a rare opportunity and stole Alice's new laptop.

Some readers may stop there and say, well, it's just a stolen laptop and that's not a big deal. Except, the laptop contained customer data on it, including credit card data. Although this is definitely a small scale breach, the concept could also occur at a well-established business (say at a day care or jewelry store) with thousands of customers. Alice made three key mistakes when she set up her business.

First, Although Alice took every precaution to prevent a child from "escaping" from her area, she didn't lock down the physical assets that ran her business. A laptop out in the open of a crowded mall won't last long before someone picks it up. Alice should have physically secured the laptop such that it was not openly available for a thief to steal it during a crisis.

Second, Alice's desire to make it easier for kids to be dropped off had good intentions, but fell short when she stored the cardholder data of all of her customers. Instead of storing all that data, Alice should have instructed Darlene to ask for the method of payment for every transaction. Although this request would force her customers to spend another 1 to 2 min per transaction, she would not put her customer data at risk, and this breach's reach would be much smaller.

Finally, the software Alice used to manage her business did not protect the information it stored. Because it was written in Microsoft Access, the data is easily retrieved. The thief not only had accesses to each of her customers' credit card numbers but also had their home addresses and medical insurance information too! Should the thief figure this out, he has more than enough data to begin the process of stealing an identity or fraudulently charging transactions.

The Case of the Loose Permissions

Melissa works in the marketing department for Ben's Body Boutique, a regional fitness and health center. Ben charged Melissa with merging data from a mass mailing campaign to purchase records from the last 6 months. Ben wanted to determine how effective the original marketing campaign was, and if there were certain geographic areas where the response was higher, so he could concentrate future outreach programs on those areas that yielded the largest amount of business.

Melissa made a request to IT to get access to the current customer database, and through her basic database skills, she learned as a business analyst in a former job, and she was able to perform direct queries against the data. IT gave Melissa a different username than her normal username, and she had to use a different password from her current Windows password because the complexity requirements did not match. She had a hard time remembering the password, so she temporarily wrote it down on a sticky-note and placed it inside her closed laptop.

Melissa began performing some basic queries based on the database layout provided by one of the DBAs. The data map seemed to be missing a few key elements that she needed to complete her analysis, so she tried calling the DBA. He was out sick, and nobody else was available to help her with her question. So relying on her previous experience, she ran a few commands to get a more complete layout of the schema. She noticed that most of the fields were ones she thought she would need, so to save time, she used a wildcard when listing the database columns she wanted to see, thus effectively dumping the entire contents of the table to the Excel spreadsheet she would use on her machine. Unfortunately, her wildcard selection pushed customer credit card data down to her machine without her immediate knowledge.

It was getting late in the day, and she decided to finish the analysis later that evening after she put her children to bed. Not realizing the data she had, she simply copied the customer data file and the direct mail list to a USB disk she kept in her purse, left her laptop at her desk, and headed home. After putting her kids to bed, she loaded the data on her home computer and started to perform her analysis.

Without going any farther into the story, let's stop for a minute and find the issues with this case, some of which happen every day in our companies. First, knowing Melissa's background, IT gave her a database account with unlimited select permissions on all the tables in the customer database. The IT department violated Requirement 8.5.16 by giving a user direct access into the database and not regulating her use to just the data she needed. Instead, they should have asked her for the requirements and performed the data dump themselves and further ensured that the data was not PCI related. Next, she wrote her password down because the authentication for the database was different from her main Windows account. This action should be prohibited by security and password policies. Finally, she took the data home and put it on a noncompany-owned or controlled PC. Although her home machine may have all of its patches and be up to date on antivirus, she may forget to delete the file and could open Ben's up for a breach further down the road if she sold the computer or fell victim to a Trojan horse or virus.

SUMMARY

Access controls are an extremely important part of protecting your data. It is important to understand your systems and the best ways to control access to your data. Once access controls are set, they must be constantly maintained to be effective. As we have talked about in this chapter, it's important to have many layers of security to be effective. Not only is it important to have strict access controls in place on computer systems, but it's also important to control physical access.

Spend time to fully define your access requirements for PCI so that you can comply with Requirement 7. Although this is the shortest of the three requirements we covered in this chapter, it may require the most amount of effort to effectively meet. Defining roles and access profiles takes time, but the work you put in will allow you to centrally manage a diverse set of permissions effectively and efficiently. Next, put those profiles into action and assign permissions to them on your systems. Put users into containers, and ensure that their access complies with the diverse requirements in Requirement 8.

Then, take a step back and focus on physical security, and don't forget stores and satellite locations! Don't defeat the corporate security at your headquarters by leaving wide open electronic access to your store or satellite locations. Finally, discover how much money you can save by destroying the data quickly after settlement. Remember, you don't have to protect what you don't store!

Protecting Cardholder Data

The Payment Card Industry Data Security Standard (PCI DSS) was created to decrease the risk of electronic card transactions by mandating security controls at merchants and service providers; it is, thus, obvious that protecting the data is one of the key goals of the standard. Most of the 12 requirements cover data protection at least indirectly. We can even say "it is all about the card data"; however, there are two requirements that particularly apply to protecting card data that is stored ("data at rest") or transmitted ("data in motion") in your environment. This chapter covers such narrow data security requirement, which is mostly related to avoiding the storage of data and encryption.

WHAT IS DATA PROTECTION AND WHY IS IT NEEDED?

Before we even start our discussion of data protection methods, we need to remind you that "the only good data is dead data." Humor aside, dropping, deleting, not storing, and otherwise not   the data is the best single trick to make your PCI DSS compliance easier and to make the transaction less risky, reduce your liability, chance of fines, and breach notification losses.

NOTE

Many times, the easiest way to protect data is not   you're keeping and verify that you really need to to store it at all! It's a good idea to review the data   keep it.

As mentioned above, PCI DSS requirement to protect cardholder data encompasses two elements:

- Protect stored cardholder data

- Encrypt transmission of cardholder data across open, public networks

The processes and activities necessary to meet these requirements and the specific subitems spelled out by the PCI DSS are simply the implementation of some of the fundamental components of a sound information security program, just as with other PCI DSS controls. In this particular case, the controls are about protecting "data at rest" and "data in motion."[1] Thus, it is possible to present PCI DSS data scope as a triad:

- Transmit

- Process

- Store

If you have already put into place the pieces of a solid information assurance program, or you are in the process of doing so, there won't be a great deal of extra work to do. Your current processes and technology may very well serve to quickly allow you to comply with these requirements without a great deal of additional effort or cost.

---

[1] Sometimes "data in use" is added to this; in the context of PCI DSS, "data in use" often translated to payment application security, covered by PA-DSS.

The Confidentiality, Integrity, Availability Triad

We define the Confidentiality, Integrity, Availability (CIA) triad in Chapter 5, "Strong Access Controls." Let's use them here to define our data protection efforts. These three tenets of information security are referred to as a triad because they are most commonly illustrated as three points of a triangle (See Fig. 6.1). All three principles must be considered as you manage your data. An undue degree of emphasis on one can lead to a deficiency in one of the others.

- **Confidentiality:** It strives to ensure that information is disclosed to only those who are authorized to view it. Most PCI DSS requirements apply to this leg of the CIA triad.

- **Integrity:** It strives to ensure that information is not modified in ways that it should not be. This can refer to modification by either people or processes. While not directly focusing here, many PCI controls help to assure data integrity.

- **Availability:** It strives to ensure that data is available to the authorized parties in a reliable and timely fashion. PCI DSS does not play in this particular sandbox. The requirement to keep the data available for your business is on you and your organization. No external guidance from PCI Council applies, even though many general security practices (such as Requirement 5 asking to deploy antivirus software) indirectly help in keeping the systems humming and data available.

In addition to the CIA triad, auditability component is often added to it. Specifically, in case of PCI DSS logging and monitoring requirements (covered in Chapter 9, "Logging Events and Monitoring the Cardholder Data Environment") are meant to provide auditing and monitoring for the infrastructure. This key tenet is about knowing who is doing what with the data at any given time and on being able to prove it via logging and monitoring.

Combining CIA with process-transmit-store, you arrive at the following complete structure for PCI DSS data protection (Table 6.1).

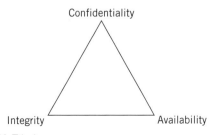

FIGURE 6.1   *The CIA Triad*

Table 6.1 PCI DSS Data Protection Mapped to CIA

	Transmit	Process	Store
Confidentiality	Don't transmit the data over less-secure networks, if possible. Encrypt data in transmission	Use secure applications (Payment Application Data Security Standard [PA-DSS], application security)	Don't store. If you have to, encrypt, mask, and truncate the data
Integrity	Don't transmit the data over less-secure networks, if possible. Encrypt data in transmission	Use secure applications (PA-DSS, application security)	Don't store. If you have to, encrypt the data. Other methods do not preserve data integrity
Availability	PCI does not apply. Your business does need card data availability to operate	PCI does not apply. Your business does need card data availability to operate	PCI does not apply. Your business does need card data availability to operate

Use this as a map for all relevant PCI DSS requirements covered in this chapter.

REQUIREMENTS ADDRESSED IN THIS CHAPTER

This chapter addresses the following PCI DSS requirements.

- Requirement 3: Protect stored cardholder data.
- Requirement 4: Encrypt transmission of cardholder data across open, public networks.
- Requirement 12: Include sections relevant to data protection.

Other chapters, such as Chapter 4, "Building and Maintaining a Secure Network," Chapter 5, "Strong Access Controls," Chapter 8, "Vulnerability Management," Chapter 9, "Logging Events and Monitoring the Cardholder Data Environment," cover additional requirements relevant to data protection as well:

- Requirement 7: Restrict access to cardholder data by business need-to-know (see Chapter 5 "Strong Access Controls").
  - Requirement 10: Logging access to data and monitoring the environment (see Chapter 9, "Logging Events and Monitoring the Cardholder Data Environment").

PCI REQUIREMENT 3: PROTECT STORED CARDHOLDER DATA

The most effective means of insuring that cardholder data is not exposed to unauthorized parties (confidentiality) is the proper destruction of that data.

There is no mistake here! Please keep this thought in mind. The best means of avoiding that data falling in the wrong hands is not having such data at all. In fact, this is not just the best way; this is the only way that 100% guarantees it. This fact also highlights that PCI has nothing to do with data availability for your business processes (whereas the last revision of the Visa Cardholder Information Security Program [CISP] standard required business continuity and disaster recovery procedures). It reminds that if you can avoid storing and moving the data around, you can be saved from a lot of trouble.

As a result, before you engage in any data protection project involving encryption, masking, sanitization, etc., consider doing a project that investigates removing the data from as many systems as possible. The author team is well aware of the fact that it is not possible for many organizations and many circumstances; thus, this chapter continues.

By the way, we are not talking about running the commands that are as follows:

```
DEL /Q /A credit_card_data.dat (Windows)
```

Or

```
/bin/rm -rf /opt/credit_card_data.data (Linux)
```

We are talking about assessing how your organization processes payment cards and whether any parts of that business process can be simplified and improved by not storing card data, storing it in smaller number of places, or not storing full primary account number (PAN, which is allowed as per PCI, but definitely not recommended). Storing some types of data is expressly prohibited by PCI DSS, and thus, no protection methods are required; such data simply must not exist in your environment.

Thus, only the second-most effective means of insuring that stored cardholder data is not exposed to unauthorized parties (confidentiality) is the encryption of that data. When implemented properly, the value of encryption is that even if an intruder is able to gain access to your network and your data, without access to the proper encryption keys, that data is still unreadable.

PCI standards dictate that stored cardholder data can be rendered unreadable, such as encrypted, masked, truncated, or tokenized. Encryption will protect your data from being used by the malicious hackers, and thus, the spirit of PCI DSS – to reduce the risk of transactions – will be preserved.

Only upon failing to protect the data with strong cryptography, PCI DSS allows you to implement compensating controls to mitigate the risk if you are unable to meet this requirement directly. See Chapter 12, "The Art of Compensating Control," for more details on selecting the compensating controls for encryption. Because encryption is such an effective and critical part of protecting data, we will discuss some of the details of encryption methods and the associated advantages and disadvantages.

Requirement 3 Walk-through

Let's walk through all the subrequirements of Requirement 3, "Protect stored cardholder data."

First, PCI DSS 3.1 highlights the mantra about not storing data: "Keep cardholder data storage to a minimum." It further specifies that an organization needs to "Limit storage amount and retention time to that which is required for business, legal, and/or regulatory purposes." This section of PCI DSS refers to the fact that sensitive-card data storage is not required by the card brands and the PCI Council. On the contrary, storage of some data is completely prohibited. A frequent argument of needing full PAN data for chargebacks is not entirely true as well, since many acquirers have other ways of handling it without mandating full-card data storage. Remember, keep cardholder data storage to a minimum, or better, don't store it at all.

There is a common misconception about the storage of PAN data proliferated by industry pundits. If your acquirer or processor is requiring that you store the PAN data, keep in mind that is *their* requirement, not the card brand's. Also, choosing another acquirer is definitively within your rights.

The next subrequirement flat-out bans the storage of some types of data (3.2): "Do not store sensitive authentication data after authorization." This is stated very clearly in PCI DSS, namely, *not* ever storing certain data after authorization. This requirement is also one of the key components of Phase 1 of PCI DSS Prioritized approach.

So, what data can *never* be persistently[2] stored if you are to have any hope of PCI DSS compliance for your organization? The answer is easy:

1. Full track data from the magnetic stripe, magnetic stripe image on the chip, or elsewhere

2. CAV2/CVC2/CVV2/CID code, a 3- or 4-digit value printed on the card

3. Personal identification number (PIN) or the encrypted PIN block

For example, here is a reference from PCI DSS documents (Fig. 6.2):

---

[2] Temporary memory storage is explicitly allowed by one of the PCI DSS clarification notes.

	Data element	Storage permitted
Cardholder data	Primary account number (PAN)	Yes
	Cardholder name[1]	Yes
	Service code[1]	Yes
	Expiration date[1]	Yes
Sensitive authentication data[2]	Full magnetic stripe data[3]	No
	CAV2/CVC2/CVV2/CID	No
	PIN/PIN block	No

FIGURE 6.2 *Banned Data*

It shows that such sensitive data must not be stored. Remember, if you are persistently storing any of the above (full track, CVV2, PIN), you are not PCI DSS compliant and cannot be PCI-validated.[3] For more information, see Visa Inc famous DropTheData site www.visa.com/dropthedata.[1]

NOTE

Track 1 contains the following data, as per ISO/IEC 7813:2006:

| SS | FC | PAN | FS | CC | Name | FS | Additional Data | CC | LRC

The field abbreviations are as follows:

SS: start sentinel

FC: format code

PAN: primary account number

FS: field separation

Name: primary account holder name

FS: field separation

Expiration date, offset, encrypted PIN, etc.

ES: end sentinel

CC: country code (3 characters minimum)

LRC: longitudinal redundancy check

Track 2 contains the following data, as per ISO/IEC 7813:2006:

SS | PAN | FS | ED | SC | Other Data | ES | LRC

---

[3] Not legitimately, at least! However, it is the authors' sincere belief that lying about it can only get your organization in trouble with your acquirer, card brands and, ultimately, with your customers and the public. Above all, in the US states where PCI DSS provisions are encoded as law, it will get you in trouble with authorities as well.

NOTE   (Continued)

The field abbreviations are as follows: SC: service code

  SS: start sentinel   Other data

  PAN: primary account number   ES: end sentinel

  FS: field separation   LRC: longitudinal redundancy check

  ED: expiration date

This requirement results in a simple action before even looking into encryption technologies at all:

- Find out if you have such data stored.

- If there happens to be an active business process that results in such data or that relies on having such data, adjust it.

- Destroy the data.

- Make sure that no accidental/undocumented storage is taking place.

As for a real-world example, remember that storage of prohibited data killed CardSystems back in 2005 or at least was a contributing factor in its demise.

TOOLS

Now you know that you cannot store sensitive authentication data, but what does it look like? The best thing you can do is search for valid PANs first and then manually verify what data is stored around it. Second, card verification values that appear on either the front or the back of the physical cards are hard to find programmatically. Track data is easier as it is a formally defined standard. For more information, point your browser to your favorite search engine and enter "ISO/IEC 7813" for the layout of track data. Also, a brief introduction on card track data as described in ISO/IEC 78xx family of standards is presented in the note.

The next subrequirement 3.3 covers the display of sensitive data – PAN. Given that an accidental disclosure of the number can lead to card fraud just as well as its theft, the DSS mandates that organizations "Mask PAN when displayed." Showing the first six (Bank Identification Number [BIN]) and last four (not sensitive) digits can be displayed if needed. It goes without saying that this guidance cannot be mandated for the employees that need to see a full account number for their business functions.

Requirement 3.4 mandates that you "render PAN, at minimum, unreadable anywhere it is stored." This is another reminder to you that not storing the data will make PCI DSS easier for your organization; clearly, if it is not stored anywhere, this requirement would not require any action on behalf of your organization.

This requirement, by the way, does not simply mandate encryption. It allows one of the following to be used:

1. One-way hashes based on strong cryptography

2. Truncation

3. Index tokens and pads

4. Strong cryptography with associated key-management processes and procedures (covered in Requirements 3.5 and 3.6)

TOOLS

PCI Knowledge Base Project (www.pciknowledgebase.com) is a very useful resource on what other organizations are doing for PCI compliance. You can search it by PCI DSS requirement, type of an organization, etc. Specifically, in this case, PCI KB members have highlighted the fact that focusing solely on removing the data reduces PCI DSS budget release power and thus reduces spending on useful security technologies. It means that adopting tokenization reduces encryption purchases that could have been useful for other types of sensitive data, and not only payment card data.

Please visit www.pciknowledgebase.com for "tokenization," and see how other organizations are handling the "protect the data versus destroy the data" debate.

All the above are equally acceptable. However, only encryption actually preserves the integrity of card data. Thus, it is the only acceptable method if you have to store the complete account number. Other methods are preferable if you do not have to store the number and should be tried first. Follow our main theme: if it is not stored, it cannot be stolen. We cover encryption in the next few sections in more depth.

Encryption Methods for Data at Rest

Disk encryption software can be broken down into two high-level categories:

- File- or folder-level encryption
- Full disk encryption
- Database encryption

Let's examine the advantages and disadvantages of each as you consider how and where they might fit into your program for protecting cardholder data.

File- or Folder-Level Encryption

File- or folder-level encryption (or file system level) is an encryption system where specific folders, files, or volumes are encrypted by a third-party software package or a feature of the file system itself.

Advantages:

- More granular control over what specific information needs to be encrypted can be accomplished. Card data files that you need to encrypt can be stored in a particular folder or volume, and data that does not need to be protected can be stored elsewhere. For example, some smaller organizations that do periodic billing actually use this method to encrypt all the numbers between the billing runs, thus satisfying PCI DSS requirements.

- Many file-level encryption products allow you to integrate access-level restrictions. This allows you to manage who has access to what. This helps satisfy data protection and access control.

- Some file-level encryption systems offer the capability to track who attempts to access a file and when. File-level encryption products allow you to add granular data logging, which helps satisfy Requirement 10 about logging access to card data.

- When there is a need to move the data, data can be encrypted on a file level and then moved off the storage location, one needs to make sure that the unencrypted copy is removed. This maintains the confidentiality of the data when it is moved to a backup tape. Backup tapes are known to have been used by attackers to compromise massive amounts of card data. Even accidental tape "loss" has caused companies embarrassment and triggered costly disclosure procedures.

- File encryption is less invasive to a database than column-level encryption. The schema of the database does not need to be modified and the access of data by authorized personnel (based on access control) is not hindered when querying and other management activities take place. This is an aspect of *availability*, one of the three tenets of the CIA triad; even though PCI DSS does not contain availability requirements, your business clearly has them.

- File-level encryption tends to consume less resource overhead, thus less impact on system performance. Modern operating systems can perform efficient file encryption on the fly.

Disadvantages:

- Performance issues can be caused for backup processes, especially with relational databases.

- Extra resources for key management are required since more keys need to be managed.

Windows Encrypted File System (EFS) with Microsoft operating systems is the primary example of such technology. Remember, if you deploy this type of encryption, you will need to ensure that the decrypting credentials are different from your standard Windows login credentials. Additional encryption products can be used as well. Here are some of the common free or open-source file encryption products, found in wide use:

- GNU Privacy Guard (GnuPG or GPG) from Free Software Foundation can be found at www.gnupg.org. It performs efficient file encryption using symmetric and public key cryptography and works on Windows and Unix operating systems.

- TrueCrypt is an other free open-source disk encryption software for Windows, Linux, and even MacOS. It can be found at www.truecrypt. org. It can perform file, folder, and full-disk encryption.

- AxCrypt (www.axantum.com/AxCrypt/) is another choice for Windows systems. It is also free and open-source.

Encrypting individual card data files is free and easy with the above tools. As with other domains, PCI DSS never mandates individual tools or vendors.

Full-Disk Encryption

Full-disk encryption (FDE) or "whole disk" encryption methods encrypt every file stored on the drive (or drives), including the operating system/file system. This is usually done on a sector-by-sector basis. A filter driver that is loaded into memory at boot encrypts every file as it is written to disk and decrypts any file that is moved off of the disk. This happens transparently to the end user or the application generating the files.

Advantages:

- Everything on the drive (or drives) is encrypted, including temporary files and swap space, increasing security of all your data, not just card data. If deployed on all in-scope systems, the card data would be guaranteed encrypted.

- Encryption of data is enforced on end user, alleviating decisions on what or what not to encrypt.

- Encryption/decryption is transparent. When information needs to be accessed, it can be saved off the system and is automatically decrypted. If a processing application is installed on the system, the use of encrypted data is also easy.[4]

- Since all data on the drive is encrypted, even if an alternative boot medium is used against an encrypted system, the data on the drive is unreadable and therefore useless to the thief. Thus, card data is protected even when the system is turned off.

Disadvantages:

- Some FDE programs can cause an increase in data access times. Slight delays in writing and reading data can occur, especially with very large files and high transaction volumes.

- System password management and key management processes have to be defined and put into place. If a user loses his password that grants access to the encrypted system, he has no access to his data at all. Key management procedures defined in Requirement 3.5 are more critical for full-disk encryption. By the way, as per 3.4.1, "Decryption keys must not be tied to user accounts!"

FDE is more suited to protecting data on workstations and mobile devices, whereas file-level encryption is more useful as a method on large-volume storage devices. The much publicized cases of database managers or analysts putting thousands of clients at risk because a laptop was stolen that had been used to download large volumes of sensitive data from a storage device only serve to demonstrate this fact.

Figure 6.3 illustrates the difference in architecture between file-level encryption and FDE.

BitLocker Drive Encryption, included with the newer Microsoft operation systems Windows Visa and Windows 7, is the primary example of such technology. Additional encryption products can be used as well. For example, TrueCrypt is a free, open-source disk encryption software for Windows, Linux, and even MacOS, which can perform full-disk encryption. It can be found at www.truecrypt.org. The latest PGP Whole Disk Encryption (www.pgp.com) is not free but is found in frequent use.

---

[4] However, in this case, the unencrypted card data may be stolen while in use. Such data theft has been reported to be used by attackers for some recent card processor breaches. Neither "data in motion" nor "data at rest" encryption techniques could have helped.

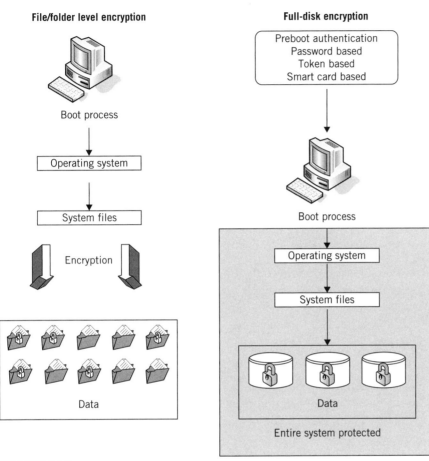

FIGURE 6.3   *File-based Encryption versus Full-disk Encryption*

TOOLS

Before you reach out for the encryption tools, remember and repeat the mantra: "Do I need to keep this data?"

Free notable encryption file and disk tools are as follows:

- The most popular and widely used tool GnuPG from Free Software Foundation can be found at www.gnupg.org. It performs efficient file encryption using symmetric and public key cryptography and works on Windows and Unix operating systems.

- TrueCrypt is another free open-source disk encryption software for Windows, Linux, and even MacOS. It can be found at www.truecrypt.org. It can perform file, folder, and full-disk encryption.

Database (Column-Level) Encryption

The most sensitive piece of cardholder data that is allowed to be stored is a PAN. Think of this as your crown jewel. This is the full card number that identifies both the issuer of the card and the cardholder account. PCI DSS 3.4 states "The MINIMUM account information that must be rendered unreadable is the PAN." If PANs are stored in a relational database and not in files, the column-level encryption becomes the only approach for rendering the key cardholder data unreadable.

Advantages:

- When a table is queried for data in a nonencrypted column, no performance impact is seen. Since no decryption activity is taking place, no delay in reading/writing and no performance hit by system because encryption software activity is seen.

- When a query for a record with data from an encrypted field is performed, the overhead is minimal. Since the decryption activity only has to take place on the individual field or fields that are encrypted, there is much lower overhead.

- It can be used in conjunction with other controls to protect data from administrators. Separation of duties between security and database administrators reduces the risk presented by allowing a database administrator (DBA) unlimited access to the data you need to secure for PCI compliance.

Disadvantages:

- Database encryption requires tight integration with the database or purchased separately from a database vendor.

- It is often highly invasive to the database design. To implement column-level encryption protection after the fact, you will likely have to change the following:
  - Data type of the field being encrypted.
  - References to and queries of the encrypted field(s) will have to be modified to limit access. Middleware and other applications that interact with the database will have to be comprehended and possibly reconfigured.

- Key management has to be well planned; if the encryption key is hard-coded into scripts, it defeats the security and violates Requirement 3.5. Keys themselves must be stored in an encrypted state and access controls placed around them.

- Merchants and service providers who perform batch processing will commonly end up storing sensitive data in flat files exported from a database. In this case, database encryption has to be combined with file or folder encryption.

As a result, column-level database encryption might be the answer for a piece of your overall plan for compliance to protecting cardholder data, but it is unlikely to be the entire plan.

At the time of writing, most major relational database vendors offer database encryption. In particular:

- Oracle database (www.oracle.com) offers multiple type of encrypted tables, including "transparent encryption" that can be integrated with applications. See [2] for more information.

- IBM DB2 database (www.ibm.com/db2) offers data field and column encryption as well. See [3] for more information.

- Microsoft MS SQL Server (www.microsoft.com/sqlserver) offers data encryption as well.

- Free open-source database MySQL (www.mysql.com), now owned by Oracle, offers nontransparent data encryption using the AES cryptographic algorithm.

As before, choose the solution that fits your overall IT strategy; you will likely not need to switch database vendors to fulfill your PCI obligations.

WARNING

Don't forget about portable storage devices that attach to laptops or desktops. There are some software-based solutions that can be configured to enforce encryption on any attached USB device, sometimes even based on the type of data being copied. While difficult to manage, this can also protect you from having your expensive encryption solution undone by a careless employee who stores sensitive data on an encrypted system, but then uses a nonprotected USB drive to transfer the card data, thus decrypting it as it is transferred to the device. Overall, minimize the use of portal devices to transport card data.

PCI and Key Management

Apart from making data unreadable, PCI DSS mandates certain key management practices if encryption is your chosen method of rendering data unusable. After all, the only thing that makes encryption a data protection mechanism is an encryption key. Let's continue to review PCI DSS Requirement 3.

Section 3.5 mandates that you "Protect cryptographic keys used for encryption of cardholder data against both disclosure and misuse." The document details 12 different items for the proper management of encryption keys. They include processes, procedures, and the custodian of these keys. The management of encryption keys is probably the most resource-intensive aspect of encryption and the most error prone one as well. Critical key management practices to keep in mind are as follows:

- "Restrict access to cryptographic keys" – only let those who need to see the key access it; this means that not everyone who needs to see card data needs to be in possession of an encryption key.

- "Store cryptographic keys securely in the fewest possible locations and forms" – while not in use, make sure that keys are protected from online and off line attacks. While encrypting the keys is not always realistic (since you will have a new set of keys to guard), such practice sometimes helps to reduce the number of keys you need to protect. A common way to address this is to use key storage software, a software vault, and then only guard one key for that software.

- "Decryption keys must not be tied to user accounts" (Requirement 3.4.1) – your system password must not be your key to decrypt all the data in case of full-disk encryption.

The next subrequirement (3.6) addresses the policy angle of the encryption; namely, "Fully document and implement all key-management processes and procedures for cryptographic keys used for encryption of cardholder data." PCI DSS explicitly states what practices must be documented:

- Generation of strong cryptographic keys

- Secure cryptographic key distribution

- Secure cryptographic key storage

- Periodic cryptographic key changes

- Retirement or replacement of old or suspected compromised cryptographic keys

- Split knowledge and establishment of dual control of cryptographic keys

- Prevention of unauthorized substitution of cryptographic keys

- Requirement for cryptographic key custodians to sign a form stating that they understand and accept their key custodian responsibilities

However, detailed coverage of cryptographic practices goes much out of scope of our book.

WHAT ELSE CAN YOU DO TO BE SECURE?

While encryption is one of the natural ways to protect stored data, it is not the only method to protect the data while stored. In some special cases, mainframe systems with strong access controls may be permitted to meet Requirement 3.4 without deploying encryption technologies. These circumstances are quite rare, and typically require no direct user access, encrypted connections into the mainframe, and storage limited to only a few small areas.

If you think you may fall into this category, contact a QSA and walk through the scenario to see whether they believe that it stands up to the definition of a compensating control.

PCI REQUIREMENT 4 WALK-THROUGH

As in the case of protecting stored data, the most reliable and efficient way to ensure that your transmitted data is not intercepted (confidentiality) or modified (integrity) is to not transmit it anywhere. At the very least, avoiding public and insecure networks will go a long way toward achieving compliance and risk reduction.

For data storage, the next most reliable and efficient way to ensure that your transmitted data is not intercepted (confidentiality) or modified (integrity) is to encrypt it during transmission.

PCI Requirement 4 spells out some specific details as it relates to these procedures for communication. Let's take a look at some of the specific PCI DSS subitems to illuminate some of the terminology and the implications.

Requirement 4.1 states: "Use strong cryptography and security protocols such as secure socket layer (SSL)/transport layer security (TLS) and Internet protocol security (IPSec) to safeguard sensitive cardholder data during transmission over open, public networks."

An open, public network is essentially any network that contains a gateway to the Internet at large. This describes the networks of pretty much every business today. Anytime your cardholder data is transmitted over the Internet or any network you are unsure is secure, that data has to be protected. PCI DSS documentation explains that the Internet, any wireless network, Global System for Mobile Communications (GSM), and General Packet Radio Service (GPRS) network are to be considered "open and public," while dedicated network relays are not.

Let's take a look at the specific protocols mentioned in DSS and used for securing card data when transmitted over these various types of networks, and the way they are applied.

Transport Layer Security and Secure Sockets Layer

Transport Layer Security (TLS) and the original Secure Sockets Layer (SSL) are cryptographic protocols that are used for transferring information over networks such as the Internet. They both encrypt the data transferred between communicating endpoints, such as a Web browser and a Web server. Use of SSL or TLS is mandated by PCI DSS Requirement 4.1. Describing the technical differences between TLS and SSL is beyond the scope of this chapter.

NOTE

A merchant asked one of the authors some time ago: if I have an SSL certificate on an e-commerce Web site, am I PCI DSS compliant?

After recovering from shock (after all, there about 220 more requirements in PCI DSS!), the author was able to explain that SSL obviously does *not* guarantee PCI compliance. However, transmitting card data without SSL or TLS will certainly guarantee the absence of such compliance.

All modern Web servers such as Apache (www.apache.org) and Microsoft IIS (www.iis.net) have long offered native SSL support. Configuration of SSL on each individual server is beyond the scope of the book. Google offers many pointers to enabling SSL on your Apache Web server.

Don't forget, per the Council, SSLv2 is no longer acceptable and cannot be deployed on systems that are involved in card processing and on external systems. You must at least use TLS 1.0 or SSLv3.

NOTE

A recent PCI DSS requirement clarification from the PCI Council now mandates that all approved scanning vendors (ASVs) detect the use of older cryptographic protocols and identify this as a failure to PCI validation via scanning, leading to loss of PCI compliance. We cover PCI ASV scanning in Chapter 8, "Vulnerability Management." Specifically, the PCI Council stated it is imperative that an ASV identifies the use of older versions of SSL (version 2.0 and older) to transmit cardholder data as a failure. Note that the PCI Council does not view this as a new requirement, but a clarification to an existing requirement in the ASV scanning guidelines. The PCI Council also clarified that the merchant can enable SSL 2.0 or even an older version for an initial handshake only to notify the user of the outdated browser that it needs to be updated, and then disallow access to the site until and unless the user updates his browser.

To resolve these failures for PCI validation, it is recommended that you discontinue the use of SSLv2 on all systems within the PCI scope. However, if you can't phase out the use of SSLv2, then you can discuss the issue with your ASV. By proving that the discovered SSLv2 connection does not transmit any cardholder data, you may receive an exception from this rule.

IPsec Virtual Private Networks

IPsec is technically not just a protocol, but a framework or set of security protocols for data protection with cryptography. IPsec is often used for site-to-site virtual private networks (VPNs). A VPN can be described as a network that uses public infrastructure (like the Internet) to create a connection between a remote host or network and an organization's main or home network. This is a much less expensive proposition than using dedicated leased lines to provide this kind of privacy. The way a VPN works is to set up a private "tunnel" using certain protocols, which causes the data to be encrypted at the sending end and decrypted at the receiving end. It can be configured in different ways, but typically involves the installation of connection software on the client, which establishes the secure tunnel to the home network, and network devices on the home network end to serve as the secure gateway.

Another option for VPN is SSL VPN. The main advantage of an SSL VPN solution is that it does not require any additional or specialized software package on the client end. A modern standard Web browser is all that is needed, which utilizes a small plug-in to the browser to configure it.

Wireless Transmission

In addition, Requirement 4.1.1 covers the transmission of card data via wireless networks. We cover wireless security in a dedicated chapter – Chapter 7, "Using Wireless Networking." For now, it would suffice to say that wireless networks are becoming much more common for transmission of card data within stores, hotels, and other environments. At the same time, several of commonly used wireless encryption protocols such as WEP have been shown to be broken and are in the process of being phased out.

Section 4.1.1 of the PCC DSS specifically states that the merchant must "ensure wireless networks transmitting cardholder data or connected to the cardholder data environment; use industry best practices to implement strong encryption for authentication and transmission." It also adds that "for current wireless implementations, it is prohibited to use WEP after June 30, 2010" since it is one of the protocols that was shown to be breached by the security researchers.

NOTE

Other protocols are mentioned in PCI DSS as well. GSM refers to the communication system that is used to support mobile phone networks. GPRS is a wireless communication service that provides connection to the Internet for data transfer for mobile phones and computers. Where this might affect a wireless network

> **NOTE   (Continued)**
>
> and transmission of card data would be the circumstances of using a GSM/GPRS modem card in a laptop for connection to the Internet. If the requirements for implementation of the VPN and wireless protocols have been observed, it will satisfy issues related to these cards as well. It appears that overall risks of using GSM and GPRS are lower than those for Wi-Fi networks because there are fewer publicly released attack tools for those networks.
>
> Finally, Bluetooth is another wireless protocol for short-range communication. Its use for card data transmission is extremely unlikely and this not covered in this book. Please let the authors know if your organization engages in such use of Bluetooth.

PCI Council has released "Information Supplement: PCI DSS Wireless Guideline" document in July 2009 to help merchants manage the security of their wireless requirements. The document can be found at www. pcisecuritystandards.org/pdfs/PCI_DSS_Wireless_Guidelines.pdf.

> **NOTE**
>
> The second-largest card data breach ever, at the time of this writing, at TJX, has in fact involved insufficient wireless security! In January of 2007, TJX Companies, which is the owner of several retail stores including TJ Maxx and Marshalls, reported a very large data breach of customer credit and debit-card numbers that occurred between 2005 and 2007. TJX reported the theft of at least 94 million credit-card numbers. Attackers were able to steal the data through an insecure wireless network at a Marshalls store in Minnesota. The Marshalls store's wireless network, which connected their credit-card processing hardware to the company's back-end systems, was not protected with Wi-Fi Protected Access (WPA) encryption, but rather was still using the unsafe and outmoded WEP standard. Despite the fact that the WPA standard was introduced in 2002 and TJX had their back-end systems protected, this vulnerability led to what is at this time the largest known breach of credit-card data in history, given TJX a very dubious distinction.
>
> As of March 2009, some of the perpetrators of this attack have been arrested!

Misc Card Transmission Rules

Finally, our Requirement 4 walk-through ends with what is simply an embodiment of common sense – Requirement 4.2: "Never send unencrypted PANs by end-user messaging technologies (for example, e-mail, instant messaging, chat)."

A true "no-brainer" requirement with nothing else to add is just to remember and follow. Never e-mail plain card numbers – and never deal with anybody who does. By the way, this applies to attachments as well, not just to plain text e-mail.

Some merchants have asked about fax data transmission. It is obviously allowed but received faxes, especially if electronic, are subject to all the data protection rules, including physical security that governs data protection and access control.

REQUIREMENT 12 WALK-THROUGH

Requirement 12, "Maintain a policy that addresses information security for employees and contractors", indirectly plays toward protecting card data from the "softer" side via policies and procedures. Given that Requirement 12 is covered in PCI DSS document with plenty of useful requirements, we are only providing a brief overview of all the requirements.

Requirement 12.1 starts us off, mandating we "Establish, publish, maintain, and disseminate a security policy." Details about the policy are specified in the document; the main idea is that the policy is present, contains all the needed components, and is actively being used. Needed components should at least include every policy required by PCI DSS (Requirement 12.1.1), includes a requirement for an annual risk assessment (Requirement 12.1.2), and mandates an annual review process based on the output of the risk assessment, or at least as a part of a normal review process to alter the policy based on changes to the business or the risk environment (Requirement 12.1.3). Remember, this policy may not need to be one massive document; it could be part of the policy framework in your governance structure.

Next, the requirement 12.2 "Develop daily operational security procedures that are consistent with requirements in this specification" covers the step down from the security policy; operational procedures that prove that your policy is not an empty piece of paper. Your daily operational procedures should at least include those items mandated by PCI DSS (such as log review, vulnerability discovery, and antivirus updates), but may also include other items relevant to your particular environment.

NOTE

Requirement 12.3 covers the need to "develop usage policies for critical employee-facing technologies." For more information on Requirement 12.3, see Chapter 7, "Using Wireless Networking."

The policy and procedures are further defined in the next few requirements. For example, Requirement 12.4 mandates you "ensure that the security policy and procedures clearly define information security responsibilities for all employees and contractors." The first step is to make sure that you actually delineate between the two distinct groups in your policy. Do you have an Acceptable Use Policy or an information security policy disclosure notice for visitors when they come on-site? That is one perfect way to make sure that visitors understand your policies and is a pretty easy way to show to an assessor that you are meeting this requirement.

Requirement 12.5, and its sub requirements, mandates assigning a particular team in your organization the responsibility for managing information security. You should have a formal chief security officer, or equivalent, named with board-delegated authority to carry out information security management (Requirement 12.5). The delegated authority and responsibility should include creating information security policies and procedures (Requirement 12.5.1); monitoring, analyzing, and reporting information security alerts and metrics, and sending relevant information back to the business (Requirement 12.5.2); creating and managing the incident response and escalation procedures, with proper escalation to management or authorities as needed (Requirement 12.5.3); responsibility for administering user authentication and authorization (Requirement 12.5.4); and monitoring and controlling all access to data (Requirement 12.5.5). Once companies start to get the hang of information security, this requirement is usually not a problem.

Part of complying with PCI DSS means that you will complete information security awareness training annually for your employees (Requirement 12.6). You can use multiple methods for accomplishing this, but at a minimum, you must perform some kind of awareness training annually, and make your employees acknowledge that they have read and understand your security policy and procedures.

Human resources get to have their very own requirement! Requirement 12.7 mandates employee background checks (within the constraints of local laws) be performed on all employees *prior* to hiring them. PCI DSS gives some examples of what type of checks could be performed, but keep in mind this may vary from country to country, depending on the laws or customs in place.

One of the most critical requirements is 12.8, which covers your work with service providers: "If cardholder data is shared with service providers, maintain and implement policies and procedures to manage service providers." This is one of the few requirements that is always present in your validation scope, even (especially!) if you outsource *all* operations with card data.

One way to determine your service providers is to ask one question. Could Rob's IT Shop affect the security of cardholder data? If the answer is yes, add them to the list of companies covered under Requirement 12.8. Once you have your list of companies, you must maintain the list you just created (Requirement 12.8.1), ensure you have written agreements whereby the service provider acknowledges they are responsible for cardholder data security (Requirement 12.8.2), any *new* service provider that is brought on board must go through a diligence process before engaging them (Requirement 12.8.3), and finally, make sure you have a program to monitor your service providers' compliance to PCI DSS (Requirement 12.8.4).

NOTE

Did you notice that PCI DSS version 1.2 removes the requirement that service providers must acknowledge in writing they are compliant with PCI DSS? Requirement 12.8 is mostly a protection requirement. If you are a merchant and a breach of your data is caused by one of your service providers, *you* are liable. This requirement helps make both of you as the merchant aware of this and also the service provider. If you are a service provider that uses a service provider (whew!), things may follow the same path.

Despite all protections, incidents will happen. In light of this, Requirement 12.9 requires that your organization "Implement an incident response plan. Be prepared to respond immediately to a system breach." Expect your assessor to thoroughly review your incident response plan while validating your compliance on-site. Requirement 12.9.1 lists all the things that your incident response plan must include, most of which would be found in any good incident response policy. The only exception is the last bullet, which mandates that you include the card brands in your incident response process. You must test the plan annually (Requirement 12.9.2). You don't have to hire someone to steal data to do this! A tabletop exercise should suffice. You must have 24×7 incident response capabilities, and you must monitor critical systems at all times (Requirement 12.9.3). Chapter 7, "Using Wireless Networking," reminds us that we must include wireless intrusions in our incident response plan as of PCI DSS 1.2 (also as Requirement 12.9.5). You must train your staff with incident response capabilities at least annually (Requirement 12.9.4). This could be a component of your tabletop exercise but should go beyond just the testing of your plan. Finally, you need procedures to update your plan based on things you learn and changes in the industry or threat landscape (Requirement 12.9.6).

The book Web site www.pcicompliancebook.info will contain sample policies and procedures, as well as links to resources that you can use to help jumpstart your Requirement 12 efforts.

APPENDIX A OF PCI DSS

The last set of requirements to discuss is a part of Appendix A. These require-ments only apply to shared hosting providers. If you use a shared hosting provider for any process in your company dealing with cardholder data, be sure that hosting provider complies with Appendix A. Either your shared hosting provider should have this filled out by a QSA during their normal PCI DSS assessment or you may have your assessor go to your shared host-ing provider to complete this portion of the assessment for you. If your QSA has to perform this, it most likely will add to the cost of your assessment from both a time and expenses basis.

For your hosting providers, here's what you need to do. Appendix A con-sists of eight testing procedures: one major, rollup requirement, and four subrequirements. The main focus of Appendix A is keeping every company's environment separate by way of access controls. Requirement A.1.1 man-dates that every merchant has their own ID, no shared IDs are permitted, and any Common Gateway Interface (CGI) scripts are run under the lower privilege merchant account, and not a shared account or as the same user that the Web server runs under.

Requirement A.1.2 further expands upon A.1.1 and has five unique test-ing procedures. Expect your assessor to verify: applications do not run under an elevated privilege account like *root* or *Administrator* (A.1.2.a), each com-pany's user ID has only permissions to its own files – none of which are group readable/writable – and suggest that these files exist in a *chroot* type jail (A.1.2.b), the company's user ID cannot overwrite system binaries (A.1.2.c), the company's user ID cannot read log files except those generated by its own applications (A.1.2.d), and that each hosting environment cannot take over the rest of the machines' disk space, bandwidth, memory, or CPU (A.1.2.e).

Requirement A.1.3 mandates that assessment trails or logs are enabled and consistent with Requirement 10. Finally, Requirement A.1.4 mandates that the hosting company's policies require timely forensic investigations in the event of a suspected compromise.

Your hosting provider should already have done these for you, but if they are not PCI DSS compliant and cannot supply this information for you, your QSA will need to validate it.

HOW TO BECOME COMPLIANT AND SECURE

Now that we've looked at the particulars of the PCI requirements for protecting cardholder data and discussed some of the technologies and methods available to achieve compliance, let's take a step back and briefly discuss your approach.

In many cases, organizations involved in handling PCI data existed and were involved with it before the PCI DSS came out. So, networks and architecture processes already existed. If you were designing your network and your plan from the ground up with PCI DSS in mind, you'd likely do it differently. For example, you would probably minimize the use, storage and transmission of card data on your network, and try to avoid storage altogether. Attempting to apply specific security standards after the fact is a different and difficult proposition.

By thinking logically through the requirement, their letter and spirit, your business processes, and your IT environment, you can avoid a haphazard approach that can lead to problems such as inefficiency, unnecessary cost, insufficient controls, as well as unidentified risks or controls that are more restrictive than necessary.

We'd like to propose a process to satisfy these requirements.

Step 1: Identify Business Processes with Card Data

The first step is to simply create a list of all business processes that involve the payment cards, electronic payments, card data, etc. Look at how those processes are implemented and what possible card data exposures there are. While doing it, start analyzing things such as follows:

- Is card data being stored? Where? Why?

- What is my card data flow?

- Can the process be improved by reducing card exposure?

- Is there any prohibited data – CVV2, PIN, etc. – storage?

Step 2: Focus on Shrinking the Scope

After creating the list of processes that involve cards and card data, even if you outsource, focus on improving by reducing card exposure. This step needs to happen before any talk about encryption, obfuscation, or anything begins. Also, at this stage, focus on eliminating the storage of prohibited data as this will block any chances at PCI DSS compliance.

Step 3: Identify Where the Data Is Stored

Databases might house cardholder data, but where else might it be found? Flat files that are results of batch processing, log files, backup tapes, and storage networks may all house sensitive information.

Ask the following questions:

- Where is the data located? Should it be?

- What format is it in (e.g., database, flat file)?

- What is the size of the data?

Answers to these questions will determine whether you have to make changes in your architecture to minimize the cost and work to protect the data.

Step 4: Determine What to Do About Data

For each found location, consider what happens with it to bring it into compliance and reduce risk.

- Data is removed, and exposure to PCI DSS is eliminated.

- Data is truncated or hashed, thus reducing the risk of theft or loss.

- Data is encrypted using one of the discussed methods.

Only resort to encryption after you have tried other methods.

Step 5: Determine Who Needs Access

Too often, data breaches take place simply because people and applications have access to data they do not need. You have to balance the need for access with the proper control on that access to keep doing business.

Answer these questions:

- Who currently has access to the remaining repositories of sensitive data?

- Do they need access to do their job?

- What applications, such as backup applications or Web sites, need access?

Plan changes based on what is found.

Step 6: Develop and Document Policies

Now that you have identified what data you have, where your data is located, how it is protected, and who and what needs to access it, you can define, document, and implement information-handling policies based on what, where, who, and how. This is where you establish such things as policies, standards, guidelines, and procedures. Such policies and procedures, as well as their implementation, are what a QSA would review to substantiate your claims of PCI DSS compliance.

COMMON MISTAKES AND PITFALLS

If you follow the media today, you might conclude that data encryption is everywhere. However, is this "good" encryption? Does it help you to protect the data from attackers while allowing for easy PCI compliance? A classic saying "Encryption is easy; key management is hard" illustrates one of the pitfalls that await those implementing encryption, and it is reflected in Requirement 3. While Requirement 3.4 simply states the need for encryption, the complexity of key management shows when you are reviewing Requirements 3.5 and 3.6 with their multiple subsection. Let's look at some of the common mistakes that often occur when organizations try to use encryption to protect data at rest and data in transit, as well as achieve PCI compliance.

Before we start with the first mistake, how about the one numbered 0, thinking that PCI DSS data protection requirements are about encryption. No, they are about not letting the hackers get the data. As you've learned, *data deletion* is more reliable than *data encryption* as a mean of denying your opponents access to data. So, don't encrypt what you can simply delete or not store.

The first mistake is not using encryption when it is both easy and mandatory. For example, why continue using those pesky plaintext protocols such as Telnet and FTP? One can argue that people should have abandoned the above protocols for a host of other reasons, not just PCI DSS, but as the fairly recent Solaris Telnet 0-day vulnerability fiasco indicates, enough people are still using them. If you insist on using them, make sure that card data never travels over them.

Similarly, while using HTTP for online purchases using a payment card is not common, one still sees such instances on lesser known e-commerce Web sites. Exposing card data information to known, actively used attacks, such as sniffing, is inexcusable in the age when anybody can configure SSL encryption. While risk of sniffing is typically overshadowed by the risks to stored card data, there is indeed no excuse to not encrypting the data in transit when it is easy and does not cost any extra.

The second mistake has been mentioned by most cryptographers out there: inventing your own cryptographic algorithm. Cryptography is a science just like physics and mathematics; in fact, we all know that it is based on the latter. This is an area where amateurs have no place. Use publicly vetted algorithms such as AES (www.nist.gov/public_affairs/releases/aesq&a.htm) or others with many secure implementations that can be used for free.

An interesting extension of this mistake has to do with failing to correctly implement a well-designed cryptographic algorithm. Indeed, algorithm design is hard, but quality implementation isn't an easy job either. As a result, people who chose to reimplement a "known good" crypto algorithm might be doing themselves a disservice, if a proven implementation exists (as a cryptographic library, for example).

Every reader will probably recognize the third mistake: "hard-coding" secrets, such as passwords and keys. As we know, security of a quality cryptographic algorithm does not depend on its secrecy, but on its key or password. If you inadvertently make such passwords available for attackers, the game is over. Embedding passwords in code (binaries), configuration files, Web pages, style sheets, or other "hidden" files is just providing your secret to attackers. And, no, your XORing the password with a string of characters does not count, it just replaces your credible "secured by AES" label by a purely humorous "protected by the power of XOR." You can only secure a password by encrypting it, and then your problem does not go away since you have to deal with a new password.

Hard-coded secrets led to many disasters in the recent history of information security. DVD and now HD-DVD encryption breaches are just the most famous of them. The extensions of such error, where passwords are "hidden" in files to enable scripting or automation, have helped attackers to extend their control over the compromised networks. One cannot argue that system administrators need to automate routine tasks, but "root" passwords in scripts and configuration files should be as archaic as double-digit years. Finally, the question of whether having passwords hardcoded in JavaScript code, visible on the website using 'view source' command is left as an exercise to the reader.

As we learned in this chapter, database data encryption is becoming more common and more database vendors natively support it – their claim is that it is easy to just protect your database by encrypting it. Great! The task is done and the data is secured by a well-implemented encryption algorithm. Now, where do we put the encryption keys? Ah, why not in the same database, just another table? Thus, the fourth mistake is manifested in the form of storing keys with data. The author is aware of a few organizations who sought to protect their credit-card databases by encrypting the tables with sensitive data and then storing the key in another table on the same database server.

Sometimes, one hears a claim that such "protection" works against fools and low-skill attackers – they would see a string of random binary data where a credit-card number should have been and then go away. However, a more correct way of putting it is that it works as a "checkbox encryption" against your own management – they can now claim that cryptography protects their organization's crown jewels, whereas in reality, it protects nothing and achieves no compliance benefits, either.

While we're at it, think about the following as well: while you might not be leaving the keys in an obvious place such as a database table, do you prevent key leakage into swap files, crash dumps, logs, and other areas that might be seen by attackers? This is much more insidious, and a detailed discussion goes beyond the scope of this book.

Finally, the fifth mistake turns encryption again into the very entity that is supposed to benefit from it (that is, your organization): not handling data recovery. Ask yourself if your crypto implementation passes the "bus test." If whoever knows the keys to data is hit by a bus, will you be able to get your data back? PCI DSS does not mandate that you create procedures to ensure the availability of decryption keys, but it does not mean that you can avoid it.

If you implemented cryptography correctly such that there is no way to bypass the security it provides, and at the same time, you didn't think about data recovery, your implementation will likely not pass the bus test. As a result, the data would be as good as gone in case of a key loss. Did we mention that cryptography is a science? Handling key revocation and data recovery is a critical piece of the security puzzle. For example, Windows EFS has support for such features. Thus, protecting data from theft is only half of the challenge – you need to protect the data from loss due to "good" crypto.

To conclude, data protection is a critical piece of information security, and encryption plays a major role in it. However, one should try to avoid the mentioned pitfalls and should consider data encryption to be that long-sought security "silver bullet." Finally, don't encrypt what you can destroy!

CASE STUDY

The case study below illustrates how removal of card data from the environment, as well as various security measures, help achieve compliance and security.

The Case of the Data Killers

Jozef's antique cartoon and paraphernalia store started selling stuff online to fans back in 1997. In that ancient age of e-commerce, when the terms *new economy*, *dot-coms*, and *e-commerce* were new and cool, most Web site owners who wished to sell something from their sites had to find shopping cart software and install it on their sites. Often, especially for free and open-source shopping cart tools, they had to get into the code and change a few things here and there to customize and adapt the tool for their sites.

This is exactly what Jozef and they did: they grabbed the Bob and Garry Epic Fail of a Shopping Cart, 4.1 software package from www.bobngarryepicfailcart.com and dropped it on their site. After the package was installed, they check whether the visitors of their site can click on the links and buttons, they went into the Perl code of the shopping cart to change variables as well as to configure the card processing capability.

While this scenario is unthinkable in the enlightened 2009, remember that this was 1997!

After all required configuration "magic" was done, they advertised to their customers and to a local community that they are the first to do e-commerce in the entire county.

For a few years, they were happily selling old cartoons and charging their customer cards, totally oblivious to the threats and the emergence of PCI DSS in later years. However, as they discovered later, someone was charging some of those cards as well. Unbeknownst to them, their shopping cart was deployed in debug mode and actually logged all the cards into a big text file, located in the same directory, and anybody browsing to www.jozefs/epicfail-cart/debug_card_log.txt will be able to download an ever-growing card log that contained the following:

```
date, time, name, PAN, exp, amount.
```

In other words, most of the details on the cardholders, with the exception of their address, which was not commonly needed for the transactions in the 1990s.

Unfortunately for them, this file location was well-known to more than a few malicious hackers, and the cards were always pilfered and used – in moderation, of course, to avoid the suspicions – for various purchases worldwide.

When Jozef came to grips that his data is being used for fraud as well as come to grips with the fact that PCI is a reality that he needs to adapt to, what was the first step he did?

Did he reach out for those encryption tools? Data masking? An advanced cart software?

No, he picked the right choice: he went with PayPay Checkout (see https://merchant.paypal.com for more information) for all payment processing. No more cards – far less risk!

SUMMARY

PCI DSS data protection requirements are among the most challenging parts of PCI; they also deal with esoteric technology subjects such as encryption algorithms. Many organizations are still not compliant, and risk fines and data breaches as a consequence.

Here is a deceptively simple answer to your encryption worries: don't do it! If only you eliminate data storage, you eliminate the need to protect data at rest, which takes care of a massive amount of complexity in Requirement 3.

Similarly, if you eliminate the movement of card data over insecure networks, Requirement 4 will become simpler. With the proper preparation and execution of your plan, you can protect the information you have been entrusted with.

REFERENCES

[1] Visa, Inc. DropTheData website. www.visa.com/dropthedata [accessed 12.07.2009]

[2] Transparent Data Encryption. www.oracle.com/technology/oramag/oracle/05-sep/o55security.html [accessed 30.07.2009]

[3] Encrypting Data Values in DB2 Universal Database. www.ibm.com/developerworks/data/library/techarticle/benfield/0108benfield.html [accessed 30.07.2009]

Using Wireless Networking

Wireless technologies continue to advance in both speed and proliferation. It seems like every spring season merchants start to get frisky and revisit the prospects of pushing wireless technologies down to their stores. Most big-box retailers already use wireless for inventory management and have dealt with the upgrading outdated technology to comply with Payment Card Industry Data Security Standard (PCI DSS). Smaller retailers have toyed with implementing the technology to cut costs on store buildout or even to add additional registers in parking lots or tent areas. To add to the capabilities of radio frequency (RF) communication, you could even build a point of sale (POS) network that functions over Bluetooth. We shudder to think about that kind of network, but it is possible. Wireless networks don't stop at Wi-Fi or Bluetooth, however.

Recent advancements in cellular data networks created opportunity for a new class of card processing terminals that can process cards without Wi-Fi or hard-wired Internet connections. As we saw the effects of convergence in our cellular telephones over the last 10 years, we are beginning to see the same effects in the payment terminal market. Not only are the terminals becoming smaller and more functional but also

some companies have gone completely paperless with their field technicians. One service company even deploys what can only be described as
minitablet PCs to its field technicians that prioritize their work lists,
give them directions on where to go, provide traffic updates to keep their
schedules efficient, keep track of spare part inventory and send that
information back to headquarters, and finally accepting a credit card for
payment.

These terminals don't need to be that sophisticated to be in-scope! Think
about the last time you went to an outdoor festival or arts and crafts fair.
If you ran out of cash, you had two options. You could either run over to
that ATM machine on the street that only seemed to need a long orange
extension cord to operate, or pay for your wares directly with the merchant
through a credit card terminal. Depending on how hot the sun was or how
many adult beverages you may have consumed, you probably didn't think
too much of it. Both of those options look and feel like the ones you see
indoors but with one major difference. They are not connected to any sort
of wired network!

The intent of PCI DSS with respect to wireless is to impose a subset of
the requirements on any communication between two devices that does not
occur over a wired network.

This chapter covers some of the basics in wireless payment processing as
well as the pitfalls for which you need to be aware. Although not foolproof,
the basic concepts here keep your assessors happy as well as placate the business development and security professionals at your company.

WHAT IS WIRELESS NETWORK SECURITY?

When one of the authors thinks about his first wireless network, he remembers that his access point (AP) was the only one within range of his laptop's
Wi-Fi card. You know, the big fat credit card-sized ones that plugged into that
fancy PCMCIA slot on your laptop? Or even better, that brick you carried
around that plugged into the USB port?

Technology has come a long way in the last 10 years.

Not long after his first foray into Wi-Fi, he noticed another wireless AP
suddenly appearing as an available network to join. He protected his Wi-Fi
network with a 64-bit Wired Equivalent Privacy (WEP) key (128 bits were
not available on the hardware at the time) just to see how it worked, but
he noticed that his new "target network" did not. Curious, he joined the
other network.

Although the signal strength was not fantastic, he was still able to browse the Internet at a slow pace, no doubt riding the same cable modem service that was coming into his own house. He decided to probe a little bit further, and sure enough, an open file share was available on one of the machines connected to the network!

Curiosity aside, the author's neighbor clearly believed that he was either the first person to install wireless in his area or that his signal did not extend beyond his four walls. The latter is the most common misconception carried by individuals, even though they can receive a cellular telephone, television, and radio signal inside the very same four walls that they expect will block Wi-Fi.

Now imagine that same individual several years later having a brilliant brainstorm that includes deploying Wi-Fi into his store location, so he can sit out among the patrons with his laptop but still get his company business done. You can probably see where this is going. He made the fatal mistake of assuming that nobody would want to tinker with his little store. Not long after putting up his cheap AP that he purchased from a local electronics shop, he received a phone call from his acquiring bank notifying him that he may have a problem.

Wireless networks, and specifically Wi-Fi networks, are frequently the target of both nuisance and sophisticated attacks. Wi-Fi networks in particular are attractive to attackers because the cost to acquire the equipment used in the attack is minimal. Cellular and satellite networks have an advantage over Wi-Fi networks in this regard as the equipment required to go after these networks is typically much more expensive and requires specific training or knowledge to carry out a successful attack. That does not mean that these networks should ignore things like good security and encryption, but often, these constraints are seen as security controls.

To clear the air, they are not.

Unfortunately, early implementations of Wi-Fi only offered WEP encryption. Although the underlying algorithm was solid (RC4), the implementation of the algorithm caused information to be leaked with each packet. When used in a certain way, this information leads to the compromise of the WEP key (see the "Common Mistakes and Pitfalls" section of this chapter). With the key in hand, attackers could decode every single packet over the air, dumping information in a manner not too unlike sniffing traffic via a network span port on a switch. Usernames, passwords, company secrets, and customer information were now all available until the key was changed. Because the keys could be compromised in 30 min or less, key changes did not stop the attacks.

Basic security functionality like disabling Service Set Identifier (SSID) broadcast and Media Access Control (MAC) address filtering adds to the illusion of security. These features are easily overcome by anyone with a solid understanding of wireless networking and the proper tools. Remember, wireless encryption only protects the payload, but it does not encapsulate the entire packet from a laptop to the AP. This means that both the SSID and MAC addresses can be seen by a casual observer regardless of the encryption technology deployed, and both of these values can be configured to perform a successful attack.

Worse yet, now that the attacker had examples of legitimate hosts (and their hardware addressing) as well as the key, he could join the network and poke around until a firewall stopped him. Store networks, and internal networks in general, tend to be devoid of firewalls. Thus, an attacker joining a remote store's Wi-Fi network generally gave him free rein of the corporate network and a launch pad for attacks on servers inside the "secured" area of the network. Many cardholder data compromises start like this.

WHERE IS WIRELESS NETWORK SECURITY IN PCI DSS?

For the most part, PCI DSS only sets the stage for a baseline of wireless security. PCI DSS's handling of wireless network security is a prime example of how PCI DSS compliance does not necessarily mean you are secure.

The new scoping section of PCI DSS 1.2 has a small section on wireless that is helpful to review. It's pretty complete as far as giving you a definition of what is in-scope for PCI DSS. When in doubt, assume it is in-scope.

WARNING

Manufacturers of cellular or satellite products tell you they are safer to use because of the difficulty in intercepting the traffic, just as the ones that manufacture and sell Frequency-Hopping Spread Spectrum (FHSS) radios will. Security by obscurity is a foolish way to protect yourself against the bad guys. Eventually, someone will figure out a cheap way to intercept fancier communications like this and the game will be over. The technology probably lends itself to a lower risk of compromise today, but that doesn't mean it will be that way forever. Be sure you are using industry standard stream-ciphers over these networks. And remember that *any* wireless technology in use must comply with these requirements!

Companies wishing to comply with PCI DSS must minimally address several requirements, even if wireless is not deployed in the target environment. Those are 1.1.2, 1.2.3, 2.1.1, 4.1, 4.1.1, 9.1.3, 10.5.4, 11.1, 12.3, and 12.9.3. Let's explore how companies can meet those requirements.

NOTE

If you think that you have no legitimate wireless in your production environment, at a minimum you still must address the actions mandated by Requirements 11.1 and 12.9.3. "Rogue" APs in your cardholder environment can be lurking without your knowledge.

Requirements 1 and 12: Documentation

The first step, as is with most parts of PCI, is to document! 1.1.2 was referenced in Chapter 4, "Building and Maintaining a Secure Network," but it has applicability here specifically for wireless networks. Any wireless networks that are permissible in your environment should be documented in the network diagram you present to assessors. As an example, let's say that the only wireless permitted in your environment is a vendor wireless network that only has limited Internet access. Your network should already have a firewall between the unsecured wireless network and the corporate network. That action alone helps you meet most of PCI DSS. Even though it is not connected to any card processing networks, nor does it process cards itself, placing it on the diagram helps to illustrate that you have your ducks in a row.

Requirement 1.2.3 mandates that firewalls be installed between any in-scope networks and the wireless network. This is pretty self explanatory, but the part that can trip companies up is defining what is acceptable as a firewall. Because PCI DSS uses the word "perimeter" to describe the kind of firewalls you should use, many Qualified Security Assessors (QSAs) interpret that to mean a stateful inspection firewall like what you see in Requirement 1.3.6. Some QSAs might consider stateless packet filtering firewalls as a way to meet this requirement. With the flexibility that Reflexive Access Lists (RACLs) afford you as a stateful inspection access list, consider deploying those instead of new hardware. Watch your resource management, as any time you add filtering like this to your switches or routers, you will be adding both overhead and memory usage. Routers and switches at or near capacity should be upgraded before considering this type of deployment. The main point here is to put some kind of enforcement point between the wireless network and the wired network – preferably a stand-alone firewall – with the wireless network being on the untrusted side of the device.

Zooming to Requirement 12, we have more documentation-related items to address. Requirement 12.3 now includes wireless technologies. Remember, this is a policy document. If you set a company policy, your internal assessment group should conduct periodic reviews to ensure that the policies are being followed. Your QSA is not required to dig that deep, but a corporate policy that has not followed leads to a breach could prevent you from receiving safe harbor protection under the various card brand operating rules or applicable state or federal laws. The policies for Requirement 12.3 should address all the following before deploying wireless in your environment:

- Explicit management approval for the use of wireless

- An authentication scheme to identify users

- A list of all such devices and personnel with permission to use them

- Labeling of devices with owner, contact information, and purpose (use this for the infrastructure side, like an AP)

- Acceptable uses

- Acceptable network locations for wireless

- List of company-approved products

- Automatic disconnect of sessions after a specific period of inactivity (think more virtual private network (VPN) access, less standard Wi-Fi)

- Activation of remote-access technologies for vendors only when needed by vendors, with immediate deactivation after use

Most companies that deploy this type of technology can address the wireless components as part of their broader policy covering Requirement 12.3.

Next in Requirement 12 is 12.9.3, now expanded to include an incident response plan specifically for unauthorized wireless APs. If you follow PCI DSS to the letter, the possibility of activating this clause in your incident response plan may seem remote. It is. We'll get into that more later in the "Testing for Unauthorized Wireless: Requirement 11.1" section of this chapter.

Actual Security of Wireless Devices: Requirements 2, 4, and 9

By now, you are probably wondering when we will get to those fancy encryption requirements! It goes without saying, but building a secure environment where you operate any technology starts with documentation. Part of your wireless usage and deployment standards should include select elements from Requirements 2 and 4.

Wireless encryption technologies have come a long way in the last several years. Just 10 years ago, the only options for wireless encryption were using WEP or tunneling encryption inside your wireless connection such as a VPN or Secure Socket Layer (SSL) connection. Now, there are a multitude of options for both encryption and authentication. As of PCI DSS 1.2, WEP is no longer permitted as an acceptable protection technology. By the time you read this, no new installations using WEP may be deployed, and all existing ones must be upgraded by June 30, 2010.

Security professionals are quick to point out that WEP is simply encrypting packet payloads, and with additional protection like tunneled encryption and endpoint firewall technologies, it could still be a secure way to deploy wireless. Unfortunately for PCI DSS compliance, WEP is not allowed.

Requirement 2.1.1 lists five items that QSAs must check for to validate compliance. Your wireless installation should (at a minimum)

- Have unique encryption keys (i.e., not default) that are changed anytime anyone with knowledge of the keys leaves the company or changes positions (for shared keys only);

- Change default Simple Network Management Protocol (SNMP) community strings;

- Change default passwords/passphrases used for administration on APs;

- Support strong encryption for authentication and transmission over wireless networks – for example, Wi-Fi Protected Access (WPA) or WPA2 (WPA2/802.11i); and

- Change other security-related wireless vendor defaults.

This dovetails nicely into Requirement 4.1.1 that simply reiterates that industry best practices should be used for encryption and authentication of wireless devices. This requirement overlaps with Requirement 2.1.1 somewhat but still should be viewed separately.

NOTE

WEP may no longer be used for new in-scope networks. Existing networks must be converted by June 30, 2010 per PCI DSS version 1.2, Requirement 4.1.1. Deploy WPA (WPA and WPA2/802.11i) on these networks instead.

Many of the attacks against wireless networks start by gathering lots of traffic, either by performing injection attacks or by selectively targeting users and having them download large attachments or stream media. The more traffic you have, the more cryptanalysis you can perform, and the more likely the attack against the key will be successful. On top of that, shared keys are just that – *shared*. Everything about security screams "Don't do that!"

WPA2 or 802.11i provides networks with a significant boost in security by authenticating individual users through certificates or usernames and passwords. Additionally, devices that use WPA2 or 802.11i benefit from mutual authentication, meaning that the device itself can authenticate the AP it uses making evil-twin type attacks much more difficult to perform.

What constitutes an industry best practice for wireless security? For Wi-Fi installations, WPA or WPA2 should be deployed. WPA is increasingly coming under attack due to its reliance on WEP to function. WPA was designed as an interim fix to WEP until the 802.11i standard was finalized (also known as WPA2) and has recently demonstrated vulnerability to dictionary and "chop-chop" like attacks due to its reliance on WEP. Details of these attacks can readily be found via your favorite search engine. New installations using Wi-Fi should absolutely use WPA2 with some form of unique authentication, sometimes called WPA2 "Enterprise." Don't use shared keys (sometimes called WPA2 "Personal"). They are a pain to deal with and, for large installations, virtually impossible to maintain according to PCI DSS.

For other wireless technologies such as satellite, cellular, or microwave, encrypt transmissions with Triple-DES (3DES) or the Advanced Encryption Standard (AES) stream ciphers (or an industry-accepted algorithm of equivalent or better strength). Don't rely on the cost of communication interception equipment to secure these increasingly popular forms of communication. Such reliance is both risky and could lead to a false sense of security, further putting your company at risk.

Requirement 9.1.3 mandates physical protection for wireless devices. APs should be kept under lock and key, behind badged access doors, or in some cases, it should be protected with a cage. The intent of this requirement is to prevent an unauthorized user from tampering with the device. Don't rely on a 12-foot ceiling to protect the APs deployed on or above it. Ladders are readily available here in the 21st century. For that reason, don't rely on other physical hiding techniques, such as making your AP look like a smoke detector, to secure your hardware.

Logging and Wireless Networks: Requirement 10.5.4

Wireless gets a quick mention in the dreaded logging requirement for PCI DSS. Be sure to include wireless logs from your AP in your centralized logging solution. Different vendors have different ways of communicating logging data but most can dump data via syslog(). Piggybacking on the same infrastructure that collects logs from routers and switches should be trivial to accomplish.

Testing for Unauthorized Wireless: Requirement 11.1

When it comes to wireless, there is no requirement more debated than 11.1. Security and compliance may not be farther apart anywhere else in the standard than they are right here. On one side, merchants are equipping district managers with basic wireless tools and making sure they hit each of their stores at least once a quarter. These merchants rarely are able to be compliant with the standard all year long as invariably stores are missed and equipment fails. Managers don't understand why they have to do it, and every merchant has at least one maverick out there that would opt to buzz the tower instead of respecting the controller's wishes.

NOTE

The intent of Requirement 11.1 is to discover unauthorized wireless devices. Unauthorized devices can show up in your environment even with a "No Wireless" policy. As the "Property of IT" example in the "Why Do We Need Wireless Network Security?" section of this chapter illustrates, breaches can easily come from the wireless device you don't know is there.

On the other end of the spectrum, you have wireless defense vendors who tell their prospects that they cannot comply with PCI DSS unless they buy and deploy their wireless intrusion detection system (IDS) or intrusion prevention system (IPS) solution. One author knows he has ruined a few sales people's quarters by giving merchants alternatives to deploying wireless IPS. Early deployments were often costly, and retailers of any substantial size face mounting costs in deploying the technology in each store. A $2000 cash outlay for one location is easy to swallow, but that same outlay for a thousand locations suddenly becomes significant.

Then, in extremely rare cases, merchants have sophisticated enough network equipment to positively identify every device plugged into their network with automatic quarantine capabilities when devices that should not be active are plugged in. The number of ways you can attack this particular requirement are numerous, and the effective security of these solutions varies greatly.

The authors would like all those wireless IDS and IPS vendors to cover their ears for the duration of this paragraph. Just skip the rest of this paragraph, and go to the next one. Neither author wants to see this show up in a marketing slick, seriously. For the rest of you, the wireless vendors really do have your best interests in mind when they are pushing their products as a method to meet this requirement. One vendor in particular has a great analogy about scanning each store once per quarter (as the requirement states). It's equivalent of turning your firewall on for 1 day each quarter, then assuming nobody would want to come in and attack you until you turn it on for that 1 day next quarter. This analogy is fitting because it helps put things into context. It's also a great illustration on the difference between compliance and security.

Compliance with Requirement 11.1 means that at a minimum, you must scan each location with a wireless analyzer each quarter to identify all wireless devices. Should an unauthorized one show up in the scan, it should be traced down and efforts made to ensure that it is not affecting the security of the cardholder network. Alternatively, you can use a Wireless IDS or IPS to identify these devices in real-time, and in some cases, take action against them to prevent them from functioning on the network. Requirement 11.1.b mandates that if you do choose to use a Wireless IDS or IPS, it can generate alerts when unauthorized devices are detected, and should that event occur, 11.1.c ties into Requirement 12.9.3 discussed above (the incident response plan).

If you are using a wireless POS system for your stores, do yourself a favor and deploy an AP that has IDS and IPS functionality out of the box. Then, enable them and ensure that they can meet Requirement 11.1.b. If your plans include wireless POS, you should do everything you can to defend those devices. Make no mistake; if you deploy it, the attackers will come.

Quarterly Sweeps or Wireless IDS/IPS: How to Choose

As with most parts of complying with PCI DSS, there is no clear solution or silver bullet. Let's explore where one might be better than the other.

Automated solutions are slick. They provide scalability (usually) and do much of the thinking for us. If you have wireless technology in your locations, using a Wireless IDS or IPS solution is probably going to be the best way to handle security and compliance with PCI DSS. If you have a proven rapid response time in the field, a Wireless IDS may work well for you. The difference is similar to network IDS and IPS technologies we discussed in Chapter 4, "Building and Maintaining a Secure Network." Wireless IDS will only tell you about the problem, and then, you must take action. All 24/7 shops with appropriate response staff are required to make IDS an effective technology.

Wireless IPS solutions typically come on the same hardware and carry incrementally insignificant costs over the Wireless IDS solutions. If you don't have a proven response time or don't want to staff up accordingly, go with the IPS solution instead. Let it alert, but also let it take action. You will spend more time up front configuring it to not interrupt normal business activities, but overall IPS will carry a lower cost to your organization (when properly tuned and maintained).

So with all this fancy, whiz-bang technology, why would we go the manual route? For a couple of reasons, but the number one reason typically being cost. Companies considering this option would have limited network capabilities in their locations, such as a store front. If all of the network connectivity comes in through a Digital Subscriber Line (DSL) line on a modem with four ports on it, and all four ports are in use by equipment required to run the business, regular (shift change is a good time to do this) visual inspection of this equipment may be sufficient enough to protect the enterprise and only rely on the quarterly sweep to identify any devices. It's not foolproof (as any number of security pundits could no doubt come up with a list of ways to defeat this control), but based on the risk, it could definitely be both an acceptable compliance and security control.

This is where training is key. Good security includes all the principals of technology, process, and people. The impact that skimmers have on credit card fraud committed against fixed devices (such as unattended fuel pumps or cash machines) could be dramatically reduced by visual inspection at a shift change and other random times during the day. This is another argument for keeping your networking simple. A shift manager or even an individual contributor taking a few minutes each day to visually inspect all equipment and network jacks can be an effective control against unauthorized wireless devices.

WHY DO WE NEED WIRELESS NETWORK SECURITY?

Corporate networks are protected by many layers of security, one of which being physical security. Think about how difficult it is to get into the data center at your company. It probably includes going through multiple layers of physical security controls such as parking access gates, fences, and security guards. Employees can easily get access to the facility, but getting access to the data center is usually limited to a select group of individuals.

Wireless networking cannot rely on physical security to completely secure it. Yes, it is possible to use directional antennas to contain the signal inside your four walls or even use specially designed mesh surfaces inside your walls to create something like a Faraday cage for Wi-Fi signals, but that is not foolproof nor 100 percent secure. Worse, those techniques generally don't work for other wireless technologies, and it won't protect your network against a hot-shot user who puts a generic AP in his office, so he can work on his laptop from the conference room.

Because we lack physical security controls, we must rely almost entirely on technical controls to protect our wireless networks. Defense technologies have come a long way since the first corporate AP was deployed, but companies still need to install and configure these technologies properly in order for them to be effective.

PCI DSS only requires a minimum baseline for wireless security. In the authors' opinion, companies relying on wireless technology for their business should go beyond PCI DSS and choose the appropriate defensive solution to protect their networks.

TOOLS AND BEST PRACTICES

Wireless technologies have permeated virtually every part of our technologically advanced society from the use of cellular technology to enter credit cards and process payments to the casual Wi-Fi device lurking at a sleepy cafe. There are numerous tools you can use to both detect networks and defend against potential hackers.

Beginning with detecting, there are both commercial and open source solutions. Commercial solutions are readily discovered through your favorite search engine, and many of the major AP manufacturers also have similar capabilities built into their devices. The solution that fits best for you may just come down to your specific requirements and budget.

As far as open source tools, three in particular lead the pack by far. NetStumbler (www.netstumbler.com) for Windows was one of the first tools with a graphical interface that was easy for any casual wireless junkie to use. It did have limitations (and in some cases still does) but is a decent tool for beginners.

NOTE

Although wireless scanning software has come a long way over the years, especially free ones like NetStumbler, users performing serious scanning activities should always use a combination of tools, not relying on any one single tool for all their results.

On the UNIX side, two tools top our list. Kismet (www.kismetwireless.net/) uses a curses interface, so users run it from a terminal window, but it visually displays its information (as well as creates detailed logs with GPS data if enabled) in a format that is easy to navigate and understand. The other tool to consider is aircrack-ng (www.aircrack-ng.org). It has a great traffic dumping utility but is reserved for more advanced users. This tool has excellent encryption cracking capabilities and was a staple in one author's toolkit during wireless assessments for customers.

From the hardware side, consider getting a high-power Wi-Fi card. For 802.11b and 802.11g targets, high-power cards with external antenna capabilities are readily available through various electronics outlets. You should also consider a good antenna. An omnidirectional antenna is probably the most useful for PCI DSS scanning, though you may have more fun with a "Pringles Can" or another yagi Wi-Fi antenna. 802.11a networks differ slightly in both their frequency and channel designations. Only certain channels are allowed to have a detachable antenna per the FCC requirements. Outside the United States, check with your regulatory body for specific rules and standards.

> **WARNING**
>
> Keep in mind that illegally modifying equipment can land you in a heap of trouble with the various authorities that govern RF communications. Do yourself a favor and ensure that you do not break the rules!

There are plenty of tutorials for wireless scanning and penetration testing available through your favorite search engine or book store. If you are not a professional, your best bet is to leave this particular task to individuals who are. Whether you contract with a security consulting company or choose a wireless hardware vendor, be sure to select the most appropriate technology for your business and risk appetite. As with most things, you get what you pay for!

> **TOOLS**
>
> Here are several examples of good tutorials on wireless scanning and penetration testing:
>
> - Essential Wireless Hacking Tools: www.ethicalhacker.net/content/view/16/24/
> - Wireless Scanning by Andy, IT-Guy: http://andyitguy.blogspot.com/2008/04/wireless-scanning.html
> - Wi-Foo, The Secrets of Wireless Hacking: www.wi-foo.com/
>
> Use these tools and methods at your own risk.

COMMON MISTAKES AND PITFALLS

Wireless networks should be treated the same as a wired network when it comes to security, with some added hiccups. Remember, wireless stretches the boundaries of your network past your brick and mortar walls to areas where you may not have a physical security presence. Per the requirements, one of the most basic prevention measures you can deploy is changing the default settings.

- Change the default passwords. Be sure you work with your manufacturer to find them all. Some APs come with several default accounts with varying levels of security permissions.

- Change any shared key at least quarterly, and after any individual with knowledge of the key changes departments or leaves the company.

- Change the default SSID. The SSID differentiates one network from another. When coming up with an SSID for your AP, don't use the organization's name, address, or any identifying characteristics that would either draw attention to it or assist an attacker in singling out your company's wireless. Disabling SSID broadcasting characteristics is a good idea as well, but remember that most modern wardriving tools can still extract an SSID from packets over the air even if your AP leaves that field blank while broadcasting its beacon frames. Thus, you should not rely on "SSID Hiding" as a method of security.

■ Enable enterprise strength WPA2 or 802.11i for encryption. Preshared keys are not preferable because you have to change them frequently and have to touch every device to do so. If this is not an issue for your company, then be sure your preshared keys are as random as possible and use the entire key length allowed.

> **NOTE**
>
> Enterprise type authentication or authentication that uses a unique username and password or certificate per device is much preferred over a preshared key. Most network setups can handle this type of authentication with minimal cost of hardware or software.

Why Is WEP So Bad?

WEP has been proven to be a very weak encryption technique to secure a wireless connection. The article, "Breaking 104-bit WEP in less than 60 seconds" (http://eprint.iacr.org/2007/120.pdf), discusses how easy it is to break WEP. In a nutshell, there is a 3-byte vector called an initialization vector (IV). The IV is prepended onto packets based on a preshared key that all clients who need to authenticate must know. For most WEP hacks, you will probably only need tools like Kismet and the aircrack-ng suite. These tools can be downloaded freely from the Internet.

CASE STUDY

Wireless compromises give security professionals plenty to write about when it comes to what not to do with respect to wireless. Let's walk through a couple of examples.

The Case of the Untethered Laptop

Ashley's Archery Adventures aims to revolutionize hunting through archery. Ashley started her business last year and has seen steady growth as adults and kids alike take on the challenge of archery. Ashley's business is built on a small 50-acre plot of land just outside of several large suburbs. Luckily, she was close enough to those suburbs to get high-speed Internet access for her office and POS devices.

Ashley spends much of her time out in the field (literally) and has set up several small covered areas where her customers can enjoy water and packed lunches in between archery stations. Because Ashley found herself away from her desk quite often, she put a small Wi-Fi antenna on a modest 100-foot tower by the main office so that she could use her laptop. She took the appropriate precautions to secure her network and used a long preshared key that she changed every quarter.

One day while at the main office, she noticed some strange pop-up windows appearing on her computer and suffered intermittent network blackouts. She installed antivirus and set her automatic patch update to run weekly, so she thought that maybe it was one of her software programs automatically updating itself. If that was not the case, she thought maybe the weather caused her wireless network to go on the fritz. She made a mental note of it and went on with her day. That evening, she noticed that the problem seemed to go away and things were back to normal. Two months later, she learned that she had been compromised.

Ashley was a victim of a common attack against laptops with Wi-Fi cards called the Evil Twin. Ashley frequently visited her local coffee shop on the weekends and used their Wi-Fi connection from her laptop. When the owner of the coffee shop added free Wi-Fi for his customers, he dropped a basic wireless router with default settings on a separate broadband connection for his customers. He didn't want to mess with security settings for his customers and get involved with fixing esoteric problems with each patron's laptop. Default settings seemed to avoid those problems. He also didn't want one of his users to potentially use so much of the Wi-Fi network that his store network was at, or beyond, capacity. This solution worked well for him and his customers.

When Ashley's laptop was acting funny 2 weeks prior, an attacker was cycling through commonly used default SSIDs and got her laptop to associate with his attack machine. Because he provided a stronger signal than the one Ashley was using at the time, her laptop automatically associated with his machine, and he was able to launch an endpoint attack against it. Ashley's laptop had not yet downloaded and installed a patch that fixed a remote vulnerability in the operating system, allowing the attacker to exploit the vulnerability and gain control of her machine. From there, he installed a rootkit and was able to gain access to other machines on the network, including her POS devices. He was also able to grab the Wi-Fi key and casually observe and participate in the network at will.

One of the dangers of wireless networking is the devices that use it. One author has enjoyed watching overly confident security professionals boast about the security of their Wi-Fi networks, only to have a savvy consultant attack a laptop directly (instead of trying to break the network encryption) to gain access. Sometimes computers try to out think their users and do things they "believe" are in the best interest of their users. One of those things is to choose the strongest wireless signal to get the best possible Internet connection.

You can combat this by never "remembering" the networks that you connect to, requiring users to specifically choose each network in which they want to participate.

The Case of the Expansion Plan

After learning her lesson, Ashley quickly cleaned up her breach and was able to refocus on her business. She kept her wireless network intact, but she added additional protection with a host-based firewall for her laptop and then removed all stored profiles except for her office Wi-Fi. Her device is the only authorized device on the network at this time, but part of her improvement plan for this year is to put small POS terminals in some of the covered areas. She plans to offer more products for sale like cold beverages and food or snack items. Each covered area would have a PC to keep track of inventory or allow employees to send quick notes via instant messages or e-mail.

Ashley has budgeted a small amount of money to purchase both the hardware for the expansion plan and to build a small back-office network to maintain these devices. She wanted to provide network services to the devices to back them up daily and put important files on a network file server for all machines to use. Being as these machines would be somewhat exposed to the elements, she knew that equipment failure was a much bigger possibility than if those devices were kept in a climate-controlled office environment.

She purchases and deploys a Microsoft Windows 2003 Server and sets up her new employees in Active Directory with usernames and passwords. Each machine must log into the domain, and her "Rent-an-IT-Guy" sets up some basic network shares and permissions for each user. After he finished setting everything up, he left a small easy-to-follow guide for Ashley should she need to make minor changes.

Now Ashley must decide how she wants these machines to connect to the wireless network. It's impractical to go change Wi-Fi keys on these devices by hand every quarter, so she wants to find an automated solution or replace shared keys all together. What should she do?

Ashley has two choices. The first is to have her "Rent-an-IT-Guy" write a script that will change the Wi-Fi keys automatically on each PC in the field. This gives Ashley the advantage of keeping her existing setup that she is familiar with, but allowing the machines to easily change their keys while avoiding the headache of visiting each terminal and typing in the complex key by hand.

Ashley's second choice is to upgrade her Wi-Fi router to one that will support an enterprise authentication scheme with 802.11i or WPA2. From there, she can add an agent into each field computer's installation that requires users to authenticate with the network first with their existing username and password. This username and password could be part of their Active Directory credentials and would only require setting up a RADIUS server on the domain controller to enable this functionality.

Before security purists jump down the authors' throats, yes, we do realize that a single username and password that accesses all resources may add additional risk of compromise. That said, in this instance, the risk is relatively low provided that each user receives training on how to create good passwords or pass phrases, and they are changed regularly. Alternatively, Ashley could deploy an inexpensive token-based solution to provide a second factor of authentication that would effectively remove this weakness.

The Case of the Double Secret Wireless Network

James's Junker Jubilee, a car rental facility that rents run down automobiles for a fraction of the cost of a traditional rental company, recently went through a PCI assessment. Upon arriving at their corporate headquarters, the assessors were placed into a conference room for the duration of the assessment. When it came time to ask about wireless technologies, Sally, a risk manager, proudly stated that wireless technologies were prohibited at James's and that employees found using these technologies were reprimanded with penalties up to termination.

The lead assessor casually looked over in the corner of the conference room where the audio/visual (A/V) equipment was stored and pointed out a blue device with two antennas on it. It oddly enough had a label on it that proclaimed "Property of IT, DO NOT REMOVE." When the lead assessor examined it closer, it was an AP from a well-known supplier and was plugged into the Ethernet port in the wall. The assessor had an older model in his house, so he was sure he was looking at an AP and not something related to the A/V features of the conference room. Sally looked at the device and said, "Well, that showed up last month and we just assumed it belonged to IT and didn't touch it. The CIO has a lot of political power at James's, and most employees have learned not to cross him."

It turns out, a hacker posing as a flower deliveryman gained access to the facility around Valentine's Day that year and placed the curiously labeled device in the conference room. He had been poking around the network ever since and had stolen both customer data and intellectual property. Because he had used several techniques to hide the device, the basic wireless sweeps that the company was performing did not pick up that device. To the wireless analyzer, it appeared to be coming from the community laptop at the front desk that was used to enter and print visitor badges.

Had James's used a Wireless IDS or IPS to bolster his security instead of relying on his quarterly wireless analysis as part of Requirement 11.1, chances are he would have had a much better chance of catching the hacker in the act and shutting down the connection before the breach of data could occur.

SUMMARY

Wireless networking can be both safe and effective in extending your network's functionality for special events or as a normal course of business. From mobile users who have all-in-one devices that manage their inventory, schedules, and payments, to that cash machine at an outdoor arts festival, to a trendy bar with an outdoor patio and deck area in the spring and fall, wireless payments are here to stay.

As we have learned by reading this chapter, there are several things that companies must be aware of when they venture into potentially uncharted waters of mobile or wireless payments. This goes without saying, but be sure you understand both the technology you are implementing and have a trusted third-party review it for compliance and security (the latter probably being much more important in the grand scheme of things). Too many companies have ventured down this road with big ideas only to deploy an insecure technology and end up with a massive compromise bill.

Finally, pay close attention to the security features of your particular infrastructure components. Use all the capacity available (that makes the most sense for your network and setup), in your keys, and use the best encryption available.

Vulnerability Management

Before we discuss Payment Card Industry (PCI) requirements related to vulnerability management in deep, and find out what technical and nontechnical safeguards are prescribed there and how to address them, we need to address one underlying and confusing issue of defining some of the terms that the PCI Data Security Standard (DSS) documentation relies upon.

These are as follows:

- Vulnerability assessment

- Penetration testing

- Testing of controls, limitations, and restrictions

- Preventing vulnerabilities via secure coding practices

Defining vulnerability assessment is a little tricky, since the term has evolved over the years. The authors prefer to define it as a process of finding and assessing vulnerabilities on a set of systems or a network, which is a very broad definition. By the way, the term *vulnerability* is typically used to mean a software flaw or a weakness that makes the software susceptible to an attack or abuse. In the realm of information security, vulnerability assessment is usually understood to be a vulnerability scan of the network with a scanner, implemented as installable software, dedicated hardware appliance, or a scanning software-as-a-service (SaaS). Sometimes using the term *network vulnerability assessment* adds more clarity to this. Terms *network vulnerability scanning* or *network vulnerability testing* are usually understood to mean the same. In addition, the separate term *application vulnerability assessment* is typically understood to mean an assessment of application-level vulnerabilities in a particular application; most frequently, a Web-based application deployed publicly on the Internet or internally on the intranet. A separate tool, called application vulnerability scanner (as opposed to the network vulnerability scanner mentioned above), is used to perform application security assessment. By the way, concepts such as port scan, protocol scan, and network service identification belong to the domain of network vulnerability scanning, whereas concepts such as site crawl, Hypertext Transfer Protocol (HTTP) requests, cross-site scripting, and ActiveX belong to the domain of Web application scanning. We will cover both types in this chapter as they are mandated by the PCI DSS, albeit in different requirements (6 and 11).

Penetration testing is usually understood to mean an attempt to break into the network by a dedicated team, which can use the network and application scanning tools mentioned above, and also other nontechnical means such as dumpster diving (i.e., looking for confidential information in the trash), social engineering (i.e., attempting to subvert authorized information technology [IT] users to give out their access credential and other confidential information). Sometimes, penetration testers might rely on other techniques and methods, such as custom-written attack tools.

Testing of controls, mentioned in Requirement 11.1, does not have a simple definition. Sometimes referred to as a "site assessment," such testing implies either an in-depth assessment of security practices and controls by a team of outside experts or a self-assessment by a company's own staff. Such control assessment will likely not include attempts to break into the network.

Preventing vulnerabilities, covered in Requirement 6, addresses the vulnerability management by assuring that newly created software does not contain the known flaws and problems. Requirements 5, 6, and 11 also mandate various protection technologies, such as antivirus, Web firewalls, intrusion detection and prevention, and others.

The core of PCI Requirement 11 covered in this chapter covers all the above and more. The requirement covers all the above types of testing and some of the practices that help mitigate the impact of problems, such as the use of intrusion prevention tools. Such practices fall into broad domains of vulnerability management and threat management. Although there are common definitions of vulnerability management (covered below), threat management is typically defined ad hoc as "dealing with threats to information assets."

PCI DSS REQUIREMENTS COVERED

Vulnerability management controls are present in PCI DSS Requirements 5, 6, and 11.

- PCI Requirement 5 "Use and regularly update anti-virus software or programs" covers antimalware measures; these are tangentially related to what is commonly seen as vulnerability management, but it helps deal with the impact of vulnerabilities.

- PCI Requirement 6 "Develop and maintain secure systems and applications" covers a broad range of application security subjects, application vulnerability scanning, secure software development, etc.

- PCI Requirement 11 "Regularly test security systems and processes" covers a broad range of security testing, including network vulnerability scanning by approved scanning vendors (ASVs), internal scanning, and other requirements. We will focus on Requirements 11.2 and 11.3 in this chapter.

VULNERABILITY MANAGEMENT IN PCI

Before we start our discussion of the role of vulnerability management for PCI compliance, we need to briefly discuss what is commonly covered under vulnerability management in the domain of information security. It appears that some industry pundits have proclaimed that vulnerability management is simple: just patch all those pesky software problems and you are done. Others struggle with it because the scope of platforms and applications to patch and other weaknesses to rectify is out of control in most large organizations with compliance networks and large numbers of different products. The problems move from intractable to downright scary when you consider all the Web applications being developed in the world of Web 2.0, including all the in-house development projects, outsourced development efforts, partner development, etc. Such applications may never get that much needed patch from the vendor because you are simultaneously a user and a vendor; a code change by your own engineers might be the only way to solve the issue.

Thus, vulnerability management is not the same as just keeping your systems patched; it expands into software security and application security, secure development practices, and other adjacent domains. If you are busy every first Tuesday when Microsoft releases its batch of patches, but not doing anything to eliminate a broad range of application vulnerabilities during the other 29 days in a month, you are not managing your vulnerabilities efficiently, if at all. Vulnerability management was a mix of technical and nontechnical process even in the time when patching was most of what organizations needed to do to stay secure; nowadays, it is even more of a process that touches an even bigger part of your organization: not only network group, system group, desktop group, but also your development and development partners, and possibly even individual businesses deploying their own, possible "in the cloud" applications (it is not unheard of that such applications will handle or contain payment card data).

Clearly, vulnerability management is not only about technology and "patching the holes." As everybody in the security industry knows, technology for discovering vulnerabilities is getting better everyday; for instance, Qualys vulnerability scanning today offers 99.997 percent accuracy [1]. Moreover, the missing of vulnerability scanning is broadening; the same technology is also used to detect configuration errors and nonvulnerability security issues. For instance, a fully patched system is still highly vulnerable if it has a blank administrator or root password, even though no patch is missing. The other benefit derived from vulnerability management is the detection of "rogue" hosts, which are sometimes deployed by business units and are sitting outside of control of your IT department, and thus, might not be deployed in adherence with PCI DSS requirements. One of the basic tenants of adhering to the PCI standard is to limit the scope of PCI by strictly segmenting and controlling the cardholder data environment (CDE). Proper implementation of internal and external vulnerability scanning can assist in maintaining a pristine CDE.

As a result, it would be useful to define vulnerability management as managing the lifecycle of processes and technologies needed to discover and then reduce (or, ideally, remove) the vulnerabilities in software required for the business to operate, and thus, bring the risk to business information to the acceptable threshold.

Network vulnerability scanners can detect vulnerabilities from the network side with high accuracy and from the host side with even better accuracy. Host-side detection is typically accomplished via internal scans by using credentials to log into the systems (the so-called "authenticated" or "trusted" scanning), so configuration files, registry entries, file versions, etc. can be read; thus, increasing the accuracy of results. Such scanning is performed only from inside the network, not from the Internet.

NOTE

Sometimes vulnerability scanning tools would be capable of running trusted or authenticated scanning where the scanner tools will actually log into the system, just like the regular user would, and then perform the search for vulnerabilities. If you successfully run a trusted or authenticated scan from the Internet and discover configuration issues and vulnerabilities, you have a serious issue because no one should be able to directly log into hosts or network devices directly from the Internet side, whether to network device or servers. Believe it or not, this has happened in real production environments, subject to PCI DSS! Also, PCI ASV scanning procedures prohibit authentication scanning when performing ASV scan validation. Authenticated or trusted scans are extremely useful for PCI DSS compliance and security, but they should always be performed from inside the network perimeter.

However, many organizations that implemented periodic vulnerability scanning have discovered that the volumes of data far exceed their expectations and abilities. A quick scan-then-fix approach turns into an endless wheel of pain; such wheel of pain is obviously more dramatic for PCI DSS external scanning because you have no choice in fixing vulnerability, which leads to validation failure (we will review the exact criteria for failure below). Many free and low-cost commercial-vulnerability scanners suffer from this more than their more advanced brethren; thus, exacerbating the problem for price-sensitive organizations such as smaller merchants. Using vulnerability scanners efficiently presents other challenges, including having network visibility of the critical systems, perceived or real impact on the network bandwidth, as well as system stability. Overall, it is more clear that vulnerability management involves more process than technology and should be based on the overall risk and not simply on the volume of incoming scanner data.

Stages of Vulnerability Management Process

Let's outline some critical stages of the vulnerability management process. Even though Gartner analysts have defined [2] that the vulnerability management process includes the steps below; vulnerability management starts from software creation when vulnerabilities are actually introduced. Thus, investing in secure coding practices (prescribed in Requirement 6) helps make the vulnerability management life cycle much less painful; it is the only choice for the application created within your organization. The following steps are commonly viewed as composing the vulnerability management process [2]:

1. Policy definition is the first step and includes defining the desired state for device configurations, user identity, and resource access.

2. Baseline your environment to identify vulnerabilities and policy compliance.

3. Prioritize mitigation activities based on external threat information, internal security posture, and asset classification.

4. Shield the environment, prior to eliminating the vulnerability, by using desktop and network security tools.

5. Mitigate the vulnerability and eliminate the root causes.

6. Maintain and continually monitor the environment for deviations from policy and to identify new vulnerabilities [2].

Policy Definition

Indeed, the vulnerability management process starts from the policy definition that covers organization's assets, such as systems and applications and their users, as well as partners, customers, and whoever touches the resources. Such documents and the accompanying detailed security procedures define the scope of the vulnerability management effort and postulate a "known good" state of those IT resources. Policy creation should involve business and technology teams, as well as senior management who would be responsible for the overall compliance. PCI DSS requirements directly affect such policy documents and mandate its creation (see Requirement 12 that states that one needs to "maintain a policy that addresses information security"). For example, marking the assets that are in scope for PCI compliance is also part of this step.

Data Acquisition

The data acquisition process comes next. A network vulnerability scanner or an agent-based host scanner is a common choice. Both excellent freeware and commercial solutions are available. In addition, emerging standards for vulnerability information collection, such as OVAL (http://oval.mitre.org), established standards for vulnerability naming, such as CVE (http://cve.mitre.org) and vulnerability scoring, such as Common Vulnerability

Scoring System ([CVSS], www.first.org/cvss) can help provide a consistent way to encode vulnerabilities, weaknesses, and organization-specific policy violations across the popular computing platforms. Moreover, an effort by US National Institute of Standards and technology called Security Content Automation Protocol (SCAP) is underway to combine the above standards into a joint standard bundle to enable more automation of vulnerability management. See http://scap.nist.org for more details on SCAP.

Scanning for compliance purposes is somewhat different from scanning for remediation. Namely, PCI DSS reports that Qualified Security Assessor (QSA) will ask to validate your compliance should show the list of systems that were scanned for all PCI-relevant vulnerability, as well as an indication that no systems has any of the PCI-relevant vulnerabilities. Scanning tools also provide support for Requirements 1 and 2 secure-system configurations and many other requirements described below. This shows that while "scanning for remediation" only requires a list of vulnerable systems with their vulnerabilities, "scanning for compliance" also calls for having a list of systems found not to be vulnerable.

Prioritization

The next phase, prioritization, is a key phase in the entire process. It is highly likely that even with a well-defined specific scan policy (which is derived from PCI requirements, of course) and a quality vulnerability scanner, the amount of data on various vulnerabilities from a large organization will be enormous. Even looking at the in-scope systems might lead to such data deluge; it is not uncommon for an organization with a flat network to have thousands of systems in scope for PCI DSS. No organization will likely "fix" all the problems, especially if their remediation is not mandated by explicit rules; some kind of prioritization will occur. Various estimates indicate that even applying a periodic batch of Windows patches ("black" Tuesday) often takes longer than a period between patch releases (longer than 1 month). Accordingly, there is a chance that the organization will not finish the previous patching round before the next one rushes in. To intelligently prioritize vulnerabilities for remediation, you need to take into account various factors about your own IT environment as well as the outside world. Ideally, such prioritization should not only be based on PCI DSS but also on organization's view and approach to information risk. Also, even when working within PCI DSS scope, it makes sense to fix vulnerability with higher risk to card data first, even if this is not mandated by PCI DSS standards. A recent document from PCI Council "Prioritized Approach for PCI DSS 1.2" [3] mandates that a passing ASV scan is obtained in Phase 2 out of

6 phases of PCI DSS implementation, next only to removing the storage of prohibited data.

Those include the following:

- Specific regulatory requirement: fix all medium- and high-severity vulnerabilities as indicated by the scanning vendor; fix all vulnerabilities that can lead to Structured Query Language (SQL) injection, cross-site scripting attacks, etc.

- Vulnerability severity for the environment: fix all other vulnerabilities on publicly exposed and then on other in-scope systems.

- Related threat information and threat relevance: fix all vulnerabilities on the frequently attacked systems.

- Business value and role information about the target system: address vulnerabilities on high-value critical servers.

To formalize such prioritization, one can use the CVSS (www.first.org/CVSS), which takes into account various vulnerability properties such as priority, exploitability, and impact, as well as multiple, local site-specific properties. The CVSS scheme offers a way to provide a uniform way of scoring vulnerabilities on a scale from 0 to 10. PCI DSS mandates the use of CVSS by ASVs; moreover, PCI validation scanning prescribes that all vulnerability with the score equal to or higher than 4.0 must be fixed to pass the scan. National Vulnerability Database (NVD) located at http://nvd.nist.org provides CVSS scores for many publicly disclosed vulnerabilities (see Fig. 8.1 below).

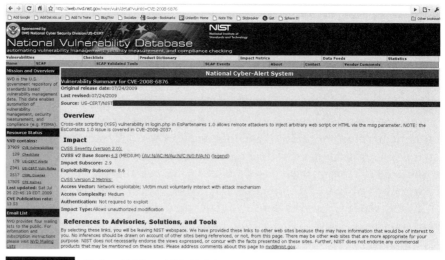

FIGURE 8.1 *National Vulnerability Database*

Mitigation

The next phase of mitigation is important in many environments where immediate patching or reconfiguration is impossible, such as a critical server running unusual or custom-built applications. Despite the above, in some cases, when a worm is out or a novel attack is being seen in similar environments, protecting such a system becomes unavoidable. In this case, one immediately needs to do something to mitigate the vulnerability temporarily. This step might be performed by a host or network intrusion prevention system (IPS); sometimes even a firewall blocking a network port will do. The important question here is choosing the best mitigation strategy, which will also not create additional risk by blocking legitimate business transactions. In case of Web application vulnerability, a separate dedicated device, a Web application firewall, needs to be deployed in addition to the traditional network security safeguards such as firewalls, filtering routers, IPSs, etc.

In this context, using antivirus and intrusion prevention technologies might be seen as part of vulnerability mitigation because these technologies help protect companies from the vulnerability exploitation (either by malware or human attackers).

Ideally, all vulnerabilities that impact card data needs to be fixed, such as patched or remediated in some other way in the order prescribed by the above prioritization procedure, and taking into account the steps we took to temporarily mitigate the vulnerability above. In a large environment, it is not simply the question of "let's go patch the server." Often, a complicated workflow with multiple approval points and regression testing on different systems is required.

To make sure that vulnerability management becomes an ongoing process, an organization should monitor the vulnerability management process on an ongoing basis. This involves looking at the implemented technical and process controls aimed at decreasing risk. Such monitoring goes beyond vulnerability management into other security management areas. It is also important to be able to report to senior management about the progress.

It should be added that vulnerability management is not a panacea even after all the "known" vulnerabilities are remediated. "Zero-day" attacks, which use vulnerabilities with no resolution publicly available, will still be able to cause damage. Such cases need to be addressed by using the principle of "defense in-depth" during the security infrastructure design.

Now, we will walk through all the requirements in PCI DSS guidance that are related to vulnerability management. We should again note that vulnerability management guidance is spread across Requirements 5, 6, and 11.

REQUIREMENT 5 WALK-THROUGH

While antivirus solutions have little to do with finding and fixing vulnerabilities, in PCI DSS, they are covered under the broad umbrella definition of vulnerability management. One might be able to argue that antivirus solutions help when vulnerability is present and is being exploited by malicious software such as a computer virus, worm, Trojan horse, or spyware. Thus, antivirus tools help mitigate the consequences of exploited vulnerabilities in some scenarios.

Requirement 5.1 mandates the organization to "use and regularly update antivirus software or programs." Indeed, many antivirus vendors moved to daily (and some to hourly) updates of their virus definitions. Needless to say, virus protection software is next to useless without an up-to-date malware definition set.

PCI creators wisely chose to avoid the trap of saying "antivirus must be on all systems," but instead chose to state that one needs to "Deploy antivirus software on all systems commonly affected by malicious software (particularly personal computers and servers)." This ends up causing a ton of confusion, and in many cases, companies fight deploying antivirus, even when the operating system manufacturer recommends it (for example, Apple's OS X). A good rule of thumb is to deploy it on all Microsoft Windows machines and any desktop machine with users regularly accessing untrusted networks (like the Internet) that have an antimalware solution.

Subsection 5.1.1 states that one needs to "Ensure that all antivirus programs are capable of detecting, removing, and protecting against all known types of malicious software." They spell out all the detection, protection, and removal of various types of malicious software, knowing full well that such protection is highly desirable, but not really achievable, given the current state of malware research. In fact, recent evidence points that guaranteeing that an antivirus product will protect you from all the malware, is becoming less certain everyday as more backdoors, Trojans, rootkits, and other forms of malware enter the scene, where virus and worms once reigned supreme.

Finally, Section 5.2 drives the point home: "ensure that all antivirus mechanisms are current, actively running, and capable of generating audit logs." This combines three different requirements, which are sometimes overlooked by organizations that deployed antivirus products. First, they need to be current – updated as frequently as their vendor is able to push updates. Daily, not weekly or monthly, is a standard now. Second, if you deploy a virus-protection tool and then the virus or even an "innocent" system reconfiguration killed or disabled the security tool, no protection is present. Thus, the running status of security tools needs to be monitored. Third, as mentioned in Chapter 9, "Logging Events and Monitoring the Cardholder Data Environment," audit logs are critical for PCI compliance. This section reminds PCI implementers that antivirus tools also need to generate logs, and such logs need to be reviewed in accordance with Requirement 10. Expect your Assessor to ask for logs from your antimalware solution to substantiate this requirement.

What to Do to Be Secure and Compliant?

Requirement 5 offers simple and obvious action items:

1. Deploy antivirus software on in-scope systems, wherever such software is available and wherever the system can suffer from malware. Free antivirus products can be downloaded from several vendors such as AVG (go to http://free.avg.com to get the software) or Avast (go to www.avast.com to get it). It is reported that the next version of Windows will include its own antimalware defenses. This will help with Requirement 5.1.

2. Configure the obtained antimalware software to update at least *daily*. Please forget the security advice from the 1990s when weekly updates were seen as sufficient. Daily is the minimum acceptable update frequency. This will deal with Requirement 5.1.1.

3. Verify that your antivirus software can generate audit logs. This will take care of Requirement 5.2. Please refer to Chapter 9, "Logging Events and Monitoring the Cardholder Data Environment," to learn how to deal with all the logs, including antivirus logs.

> **NOTE**
>
> For example, Symantec AntiVirus will log all detections by default; there is no need to "enable logging." To preserve, please make sure that the setting shown in Fig. 8.2 allows your centralized log collection system to get the logs before they are deleted.

REQUIREMENT 6 WALK-THROUGH

Another requirement of PCI covered under the vulnerability management umbrella is Requirement 6, which covers the need to "develop and maintain secure systems and applications." Thus, it touches vulnerability management from another side: making sure that those pesky flaws and holes never

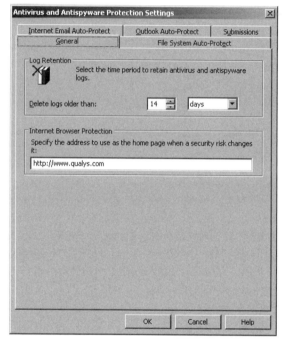

FIGURE 8.2 *Antivirus Log Setting*

appear in software in the first place. At the same time, this requirement covers the need to plan and execute a patch-management program to assure that, once discovered, the flaws are corrected via software vendor patches or other means. In addition, it deals with a requirement to scan applications, especially Web applications, for vulnerabilities.

Thus, one finds three types of requirements in Requirement 6: those that help you patch the holes in commercial applications, those that help you prevent holes in the in-house developed applications, and those that deal with verifying the security of Web application (Requirement 6.6). It states to "Ensure that all system components and softwares have the latest vendor-supplied security patches installed" [4]. Then, it covers the prescribed way of dealing with vulnerabilities in custom, homegrown applications, lies in careful application of secure coding techniques, and incorporating them into a standard software-development lifecycle. Specifically, the document says "for in-house developed applications, numerous vulnerabilities can be avoided by using standard system-development processes and secure coding techniques." Finally, it addresses the need to test the security of publicly exposed Web applications by mandating that "for public-facing Web applications, address new threats, and vulnerabilities on an ongoing basis."

Apart from requiring that organizations "ensure that all system components and software have the latest vendor-supplied security patches installed," Requirement 6.1 attempts to settle the debates in security industry, which is between a need for prompt patching in case of an imminent threat and a need for careful patch testing. They take the simplistic approach of saying that one must "install relevant security patches within one month of release." Such an approach, while obviously "PCI-compliant," might sometimes be problematic: one month is way too long in case of a worm outbreak (all vulnerable systems will be firmly in the hands of the attackers), and on the other hand, too short in case of complicated mission-critical systems and overworked IT staff. Therefore, after PCI DSS was released, a later clarification was added, which explicitly mentions a risk-based approach. Specifically, "An organization may consider applying a risk-based approach to prioritize their patch installations"; this can allow an organization to get an extension to the above one-month deadline "to ensure high-priority systems and devices are addressed within one month, and less-critical devices and systems are addressed within 3 months."

Further, Requirement 6.2 prescribes "establishing a process to identify newly discovered security vulnerabilities." Note that this doesn't mean "scanning for vulnerabilities" in your environment, but looking for newly discovered vulnerabilities via vulnerability alert services, some of which are free such as the one from Secunia (see www.secunia.com), whereas others such as VeriSign's iDefense Threat Intelligence Service can be highly customized to only send alerts applicable to your environment, and also fixes vulnerabilities that are not public, are not free, but may surely be worth the money paid for them. One can also monitor the public mailing lists for vulnerability information (BugTraq is a primary example: www.securityfocus.com/archive/1), which usually requires a significant time commitment.

NOTE

If you decide to use public mailing lists, you need to have a list of all operating systems and commercial software that is in-scope. You may want to set up a specific mailbox that multiple team members have access to, so new vulnerabilities are not "missed" when someone is out of the office. Checking these lists as part of your normal Security Operation Center (SOC) analyst duties can help ensure this activity regularly takes place. In fact, this is even explicitly mandated in PCI DSS, Requirement 12.2: "Develop daily operational security procedures that are consistent with requirements in this specification." Even if your organization is small and does not have a SOC, checking the lists and services frequently will help satisfy this requirement.

Other aspects of your vulnerability management program apply to securing the software developed in-house. Section 6.3 states that one needs to "develop software applications based on industry best practices and incorporate information security throughout the software-development life cycle." The unfortunate truth, however, is that there is no single authoritative source for such security "best practices" and, at the same time, current software "industry best practices" rarely include "information security throughout the software-development life cycle." Here are some recent examples of projects that aim at standardizing security programming best practices, which are freely available for download and contain detailed technical guidance:

- BSIMM "The Building Security In Maturity Model"; see www.bsi-mm.com/

- OWASP "Secure Coding Principles"; see www.owasp.org/index.php/Secure_Coding_Principles

- SANS and MITRE "CWE/SANS TOP 25 Most Dangerous Programming Errors"; see www.sans.org/top25errors/ or http://cwe.mitre.org/top25/

- SAFECode "Fundamental Practices for Secure Software Development"; see www.safecode.org/

Detailed coverage of secure programming topic goes far beyond the scope of this book.

In detail, Section 6.3 goes over software development and maintenance practices. Requirement 6.3 mandates that for PCI compliance, an organization must "develop software applications in accordance with PCI DSS (for example, secure authentication and logging) and based on industry best practices, and incorporate information security throughout the software development lifecycle." This guidance is obviously quite unclear and should be clarified in future versions of PCI DSS standard; as of today, the burden of making the judgment call is on the QSAs, who are not always experts in secure application development lifecycle.

Let's review some of the subrequirements of 6.3, which are clear, specific, and leave the overall theme of "following industry best practices" to your particular QSA.

So, specifically, 6.3.1 covers the known risky areas in its "Testing of all security patches, and system and software configuration changes before deployment" guidance, namely, input validation (6.3.1.1), error handling (6.3.1.2), stored of encryption keys (6.3.1.3), and others.

The next one simply presents security common sense (Requirement 6.3.2): "Separate development/test and production environments." This is very important because some recent attacks penetrated the publicly available development and testing or staging sites.

A key requirement 6.3.4, which states "production data (live primary account numbers [PANs]) are not used for testing or development," is one that is the most critical and also the most commonly violated with the most disastrous consequences. Many companies found its data stolen because their developers moved the data from the more secure production environment to a much less-protected test environment, as well as on mobile devices (laptops), remote offices, and so on.

On the contrary, contaminating the production environment with test code, utilities, and accounts is also critical (and was known to lead to just as disastrous compromises of production data) and is covered in Sections 6.3.5 and 6.3.6, which regulate the use of "test data and accounts" and prerelease "custom application accounts" "custom code." Similarly, recent attackers have focused on looking for left over admin login, test code, hard-coded password, etc.

The next requirement is absolutely a key to application security (6.3.7): "Review of custom code prior to release to production or customers to identify any potential coding vulnerability." Please also pay attention to the clarification to this requirement: "This requirement for code reviews applies to all custom codes (both internal and public-facing), as part of the system development life cycle required by PCI DSS Requirement 6.3. This mandates application security code review for in-scope and public applications.

Further, Section 6.4 covers a critical area of IT governance: change control. Change control can be considered a vulnerability management measure because unpredicted, unauthorized changes often lead to opening vulnerabilities in both custom and off-the-shelf software and systems. It states that one must "follow change control procedures for all system and software configuration changes," and even helps the organization define what the proper procedures must include:

- 6.4.1: Documentation of impact

- 6.4.2: Management sign-off by appropriate parties

- 6.4.3: Testing of operational functionality

- 6.4.4: Back-out procedures

The simple way to remember is: if you change something somewhere in your IT environment, document it. Whether it is a bound notebook (small company) or a change control system (large company) is secondary, leaving a record is primary.

To put this into context, most other IT governance frameworks, such as COBIT (www.isaca.org/cobit) or ITIL (www.itil.co.uk/), cover change control as one of the most significant areas that directly affect system security. Indeed, having documentation and sign-off for changes and an ability to "undo" things will help achieve both security and operation goals by reducing the risk, and striving toward operational excellence. Please refer to Chapter 14, "PCI and Other Laws, Mandates, and Frameworks," to learn how to combine multiple compliance efforts.

Another critical area of PCI DSS covers Web application security; it is contained in Sections 6.5 and 6.6 that go together when implementing compliance controls.

Web-Application Security and Web Vulnerabilities

Section 6.5 covers Web applications, because it is the type of application that will more likely be developed in-house and, at the same time, more likely to exposed to the hostile Internet (a killer combo – likely less-skilled programmers with larger number of malicious attackers!). Fewer organizations choose to write their own Windows or Unix software from scratch compared to those creating or customizing Web application frameworks.

Requirement 6.5 points toward the Open Web Application Security Project (OWASP) as the main source of secure Web application programming guidance. The OWASP "Secure Coding Principles" document mentioned above covers the issues leading to critical Web application vulnerabilities. Such vulnerabilities are covered in another OWASP document called Top Ten Web Application Security Issues (www.owasp.org/index.php/OWASP_Top_Ten_Project). In addition, it also calls to "review custom-application code to identify coding vulnerabilities." Although a detailed review of secure coding goes much beyond the scope of this book, there are many other books devoted to the subject. Also, detailed coverage of secure Web application programming, Web application security, and methods for discovering Web site vulnerabilities goes well beyond the scope of this book. See *Hacking Exposed Web Applications*, Second Edition, and *HackNotes*™ *Web Security Portable Reference* for more details. OWASP has also launched a project to provide additional guidance on satisfying Web application security requirements for PCI (see "OWASP PCI" online).

PCI DSS goes into great level of details here, covering common types of coding-related weaknesses in Web applications. Those are as follows:

- 6.5.1: Cross-site scripting (XSS)

- 6.5.2: Injection flaws, particularly SQL injection; also consider LDAP and Xpath injection flaws and other injection flaws

- 6.5.3: Malicious file execution

- 6.5.4: Insecure direct object references

- 6.5.5: Cross-site request forgery (CSRF)

- 6.5.6: Information leakage and improper error handling

- 6.5.7: Broken authentication and session management

- 6.5.8: Insecure cryptographic storage

- 6.5.9: Insecure communications

- 6.5.10: Failure to restrict URL access

In addition to secure coding to prevent vulnerabilities, organizations might need to take care of the existing deployed applications by looking into Web application firewalls and Web application scanning (WAS). An interesting part of Requirement 6.6 is that PCI DSS recommends either a vulnerability scan followed by a remediation ("Reviewing public-facing Web applications via manual or automated application vulnerability security assessment tools") or a Web application firewall ("Installing a Web application firewall in front of public-facing Web applications"), completely ignoring the principal of layered defense or defense-in-depth. In reality, deploying both is highly recommended for effective protection of Web applications.

WAS

Before progressing with the discussion of WAS, we need to remind our readers that cross-site scripting and SQL injection Web site vulnerabilities account for a massive percentage of card data loss. These same types of Web vulnerabilities are also very frequently discovered during PCI DSS scans. For example, Qualys vulnerability research indicates that cross-site scripting is one of the most commonly discovered vulnerabilities seen during PCI scanning; it was also specifically called out by name in one PCI Council document [4] as a vulnerability that leads to PCI validation failure.

You need to ensure that whichever solution you use covers the current OWASP Top Ten list. This list may change over time and you need to ensure your Web application security scanner (WAS) you are using keeps up with the changes. Some WAS products will need to add or modify detections to continue to meet this requirement. If you are using a more full-featured WAS, you may need to modify the scan options from time-to-time as the Top Ten list changes.

There are many commercial and even some free WAS solutions available. Common examples of free or open-source tools are as follows:

- Nessus, free vulnerability scanner, now has some detection of Web application security issues, see www.nessus.org.

- WebScarab, direct from OWASP Project (see www.owasp.org/index.php/Category:OWASP_WebScarab_Project) is also a must for your assessment efforts. The new one, WebScrab NG, is being created as well (see www.owasp.org/index.php/OWASP_WebScarab_NG_Project).

- w3af, is a Web Application Attack and Audit Framework (see http://w3af.sourceforge.net/), which can be used as well.

- Wikto, even if a bit dates, is still useful (see www.sensepost.com/research/wikto/).

- Ratproxy is not a scanner, but a passive discovery and assessment tool (see http://code.google.com/p/ratproxy/).

- Another classic passive assessment tool is Paros proxy (http://sourceforge.net/projects/paros).

- The whole CD of Web testing tools Samurai Web Testing Framework from InGuardians can be found at http://samurai.inguardians.com/

Commercial tools' vendors include Qualys, IBM, HP, and others. Apart from procuring the above tools and starting to use them on your public Web applications, it is worthwhile to learn a few things about their effective use. We will present those below and highlight their use for card data security.

First, if you are familiar with ASV network scanning (covered below in the section on Requirement 11), you need to know that Web application security scanning is often more intrusive than network-level vulnerability scanning that is performed by an ASV for external scan validation. For example, testing for SQL injection or cross-site scripting often requires actual attempts to perform an injection of SQL code into a database or a script into a Web site. Doing so may cause some databases/applications to hang or to have spurious entries to appear in your Web application.

Just as with network scanning, application scanners may need to perform authentication to get access to more of your application. Many flaws that allow a regular user to become an application administrator can only be discovered via a trusted scan. If the main page on your Web application has a login form, you will need to perform a trusted scan, i.e., one that logs in. In addition to finding flaws where a user can become an admin, you also need to ensure that customers cannot intentionally, or inadvertently, traverse within the Web application to see other customers' data. This happened many times in Web applications. See Fig. 8.3, which shows an example of such vulnerability.

Also, depending on how your Web site handles authentication, you may need to log in manually first with the account you will use for scanning, grab the cookie by using a tool like Paros or WebScarab, and then load it into the scanner. Depending on time-outs it takes, you may need to perform this activity just before the scan. In this case, do not plan on being able to schedule scans and have them run automatically.

In addition, WAS requires a more detailed knowledge of software vulnerabilities and attack methodologies to allow for the correct interpretation of results than network-based or "traditional" vulnerability scanning does. Remember to always do research in a laboratory environment, not connected to your corporate environment!

WARNING

It is perfectly reasonable to use an advanced Web application security scanner to scan applications deployed in production environment, but only *after* you tried it more than a few times in the laboratory.

When Web farms and Web portals are in the mix, scoping can become somewhat cloudy. Sometimes, you may have a Web portal that will send all

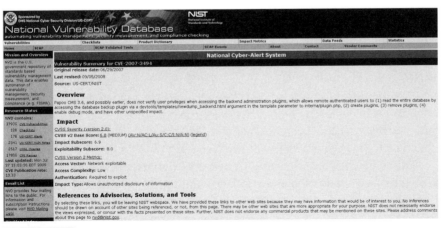

FIGURE 8.3   *User Privilege Violation Vulnerability in NVD*

transactions involving the transmission or processing of credit-card data to different systems. It is likely that the entire cluster will be in-scope for PCI in this case.

Finally, WAS (mandated in Requirement 6.6) is not a substitute for a Web application penetration test (mandated in Requirement 11.3). Modern web application scanners can do a lot of poking and probing, but they cannot completely perform tasks performed by a human who is attacking a Web application. For example, fully automated discovery of cross-site requirement forgery flaws is not possible using automated scanners today.

WARNING

Network vulnerability scanning (mandated in Requirement 11.2) and Web application security testing (mandated in Requirement 6.6) have nothing to do with each other. Please don't confuse them! Network vulnerability scanning is mostly about looking for security issues in operating systems and off-the-shelf applications, such as Microsoft Office or Apache Web server, while Web application security testing typically looks for security issues in custom and customized Web applications. Simply scanning your Web site with a network vulnerability scanner does not satisfy Requirement 6.6 at all.

PLEASE REMEMBER

Scanning your Web site with a network vulnerability scanner is *not* web application security assessment!

Let's go through a complete example of performing a PCI DSS Web application scan using Qualys as an example.

PCI Web Application Scan

Let's go through a complete scan from its initiation to report analysis.

First, we need to define the Web application we are planning to scan; see Fig. 8.4.

The definition shown in Fig. 8.4 includes the server where the Web application is deployed, such as www.example.com or 10.10.10.10, as well as a starting Web address (URL), such as /blog or /payapp or even simply "/." Then, defining the scan that will run; see Fig. 8.5.

This step includes choosing from a few options such as the desire to probe the Web application as an outside would (with no authentication) or to log in first as a user, and then look for security issues (with authentication). Additional common options that might be presented to you by a Web application scanner are the HTTP methods to try (GET, POST, etc.) and specific vulnerabilities to test for.

FIGURE 8.4   *Defining a New Web Application to Scan*

FIGURE 8.5   *Defining a New Web Application Scan*

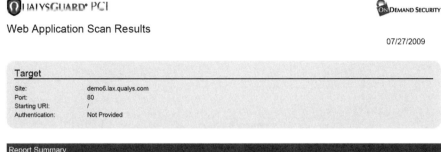

FIGURE 8.6   *Observing the Results of the Scan*

Next (Fig. 8.6), we observe the results when the scan completes.

The Fig. 8.6 presents some general information about the Web application security scan we just ran; the vulnerability results follow below (Fig. 8.7).

Specifically, the above view shows the so-called blind SQL injection, which is a specialized type of SQL injection. For more information, refer to the corresponding OWASP Top 10 entry: www.owasp.org/index.php/Blind_SQL_Injection. Such an issue will enable an attacker to modify the syntax of a SQL query to retrieve, corrupt, or delete data. The typical causes of this vulnerability are lack of input validation and insecure construction of the SQL query. In other words, this vulnerability may enable the attacker to either retrieve or corrupt your database!

How do you fix it? The scanner tells you what you need to do. See Fig. 8.8 for what to do.

SQL injection vulnerabilities can be addressed in three areas: input validation, query creation, and database security. All input received from the Web client should be validated for correct content. If a value's type or content range is known beforehand, then stricter filters should be applied. For example, an e-mail address should be in a specific format and only contain characters that make it a valid address; or numeric fields like a USA zip code should be limited to five digit values [5].

Again, just a reminder, whether network or application, the act of scanning is not sufficient as it is because it will only tell you about the issues but

Blind SQL Injection   port 80/tcp

QID:	150012	CVSS Base:	-
Category:	Web Application	CVSS Temporal:	-
CVE ID:	-		
Vendor Reference:	-		
Bugtraq ID:	-		
Last Update:	06/10/2009		

THREAT:
Blind SQL injection is a specialized type of SQL injection.

It enables an attacker to modify the syntax of a SQL query in order to retrieve, corrupt or delete data. This is accomplished by manipulating query criteria in a manner that affects the query's logic. The typical causes of this vulnerability are lack of input validation and insecure construction of the SQL query.

Queries created by concatenating strings with SQL syntax and user-supplied data are prone to this vulnerability. If any part of the string concatenation can be modified, then the meaning of the query can be changed.

Examples:

These two lines demonstrate an insecure query that is created by appending the user-supplied data (userid):

dim strQuery as String
strQuery = "SELECT name,email FROM users WHERE userid=" + Request.QueryString("userid")

If no checks are performed against the userid parameter, then the query may be arbitrarily modified as shown in these two examples of a completed query:

Web Application Scan Results   page 2

FIGURE 8.7   *Web Application Security Scan Results: Vulnerability Description*

IMPACT:
The scope of a SQL injection exploit varies greatly. If any SQL statement can be injected into the query, then the attacker has the equivalent access of a database administrator. This access could lead to theft of data, malicious corruption of data, or deletion of data.

SOLUTION:
SQL injection vulnerabilities can be addressed in three areas: input validation, query creation, and database security.

All input received from the Web client should be validated for correct content. If a value's type or content range is known beforehand, then stricter filters should be applied. For example, an email address should be in a specific format and only contain characters that make it a valid address; or numeric fields like a USA zip code should be limited to five digit values.

Prepared statements (sometimes referred to as parameterized statements) provide strong protection from SQL injection. Prepared statements are precompiled SQL queries whose parameters can be modified when the query is executed. Prepared statements enforce the logic of the query and will fail if the query cannot be compiled correctly. Programming languages that support prepared statements provide specific functions for creating queries. These functions are more secure than string concatenation for assigning user-supplied data to a query.

Stored procedures are precompiled queries that reside in the database. Like prepared statements, they also enforce separation of query data and logic. SQL statements that call stored procedures should not be created via string concatenation, otherwise their security benefits are negated.

SQL injection exploits can be mitigated by the use of Access Control Lists or role-based access within the database. For example, a read-only account would prevent an attacker from modifying data, but would not prevent the user from viewing unauthorized data. Table and row-based access controls potentially minimize the scope of a compromise, but they do not prevent exploits.

Example of a secure query created with a prepared statement:

PreparedStatement ps = "SELECT name,email FROM users WHERE userid=?";
ps.setInt(1, userid);

FIGURE 8.8   *Web Application Security Scan Results: How to Fix It?*

will not make you occure, you need to either fix the issue in code or deploy a Web application firewall to block possible exploitation of the issues.

That is what we are going to discuss next.

WARNING

While talking about network or application scanning, you rarely if ever scan to "just know what is out there." The work does not end when the scan completes; it only begins. The risk reduction from vulnerability scanning comes when you actually remediate the vulnerability or at least mitigate the possible loss. Even if scanning for PCI DSS compliance, your goal is ultimately risk reduction, which only comes when the scan results come back clean.

Web Application Firewalls

Let's briefly address the Web application firewalls. Before the discussion of this technology, remember that a network firewall deployed in front of a Web site does not a Web firewall make. Web application firewalls got their unfortunate name (that of a firewall) from the hands of marketers. These fine folks didn't consider the fact that a network firewall serves to block or allow network traffic based on network protocol and port as well as source and destination, whereas a Web application firewall has to analyze the application behavior before blocking or allowing the interaction of a browser with the Web application framework.

A Web application firewall, like a network intrusion detection system (IDS) or IPS, needs to be tuned to be effective. To tune it, run reports that give total counts per violation type. Use these reports to tune the web application firewall (WAF). Often, a few messages that you determine to be acceptable traffic for your environment and applications will clean up 80 percent of the clutter in the alert window. This sounds like an obvious statement, but you would be amazed how many people try to tune WAF technologies in blocking mode while causing the application availability issues in your environment.

If you have a development or quality assurance (QA) environment, placing a WAF (the same type you use in production) in front of one or more of these environments (even in just read/passive mode) can assist you, to some extent, in discovering flaws in Web applications. This then allows for a more planned code fix. Sometimes, you may need to deploy to production with blocking rules until the code can be remediated. In addition, place a WAF in a manner that will block all the direction from where the application attacks might come from (yes, including the dreaded insider attacks).

Finally, unlike the early versions, Web application firewalls are now actually usable and need to be used to protect the Web site from exploitation of the vulnerabilities you discover while scanning.

What to Do to Be Secure and Compliant?

Requirement 6 asks for more than a few simple things; you might need to invest time to learn about application security before you can bring your organization into compliance.

- Read up on software security (pointers to OWASP, SANS, NIST, MITRE, BSIMM are given above).

- In particular, read up on Web application security.

- If you develop software internally or use other custom code, start building your software security program. Such a program must focus on both secure programming to secure the code written within your organization and on code review to secure custom code written by other people for you. No, it is not easy, and likely will take some time.

- Invest in a Web application security scanner; both free open-source and quality commercial offerings that cover most of OWASP Top 10 (as mandated by PCI DSS) are available.

- Also, possibly invest in Web application firewall to block the attacks against the issues discovered while scanning.

REQUIREMENT 11 WALK-THROUGH

Let's walk through the entire Requirement 11 to see what is being asked. First, the requirement name itself asks users to "Regularly test security systems and processes," which indicates that the focus of this requirement goes beyond just buffer overflows and format string vulnerabilities from the technical realm, but also includes process weaknesses and vulnerabilities. A simple example of a process weakness is using default passwords or easily guessable passwords (such as the infamous "password" password). The above process weaknesses can be checked from the technical side, for example during the network scan by a scanner that can do authenticated policy and configuration audits, such as password strength checks. However, another policy weakness, requiring overly complicated passwords and frequent changes, which in almost all cases lead to users writing the password on the infamous yellow sticky notes, cannot be "scanned for" and will only be revealed during an annual penetration test. Thus, technical controls can be automated, whereas most policy and awareness controls cannot be.

The requirement text goes into a brief description of vulnerabilities in a somewhat illogical manner: "Vulnerabilities are being discovered continually by hackers and researchers, and being introduced by new software." Admittedly, vulnerabilities are being introduced first and then discovered by researchers (which are sometimes called "white hats") and attackers ("black hats").

The requirement then calls for frequent testing of software for vulnerabilities: "Systems, processes, and custom software should be tested frequently to ensure security is maintained over time and with any changes in software." An interesting thing to notice in this section is that they explicitly call for testing of systems (such as operating systems software or embedded operating systems), processes (such as the password-management process examples referenced above), and custom software, but don't mention the commercial off-the-shelf (COTS) software applications. The reason for this is that it is included as part of the definition of "a system" because it is not only the operating system code, but vendor application code contains vulnerabilities. Today, most of the currently exploited vulnerabilities are found in applications and even in desktop applications such as MS Office, and, at the same time, there is a relative decreased weakness in core Windows system services.

The detailed requirement starts from Requirement 11.1, which mandates the organization to "test security controls, limitations, network connections, and restrictions annually to assure the ability to adequately identify and to stop any unauthorized access attempts." This requirement is the one that calls for an in-depth annual security assessment. Note that this assessment of controls is not the same as either a vulnerability scan or a penetration test. Obviously, if your organization is already doing more rigorous security testing, there is no need to relax it down to PCI DSS standard once per year. Also notice the list of controls, limitations, network connections, and restrictions, which again covers technical and nontechnical issues. The term *controls* is broad enough to cover technical safeguards and policy measures.

In addition, wireless network testing states: "use a wireless analyzer at least quarterly to identify all wireless devices in use." Indeed, the retail environment of 2007 makes heavy use of wireless networks in a few common cases where POS wireless network traffic was compromised by the attackers. Please refer to Chapter 7, "Using Wireless Networking," for wireless guidance.

Further, Section 11.2 requires one to "run internal and external network vulnerability scans at least quarterly and after any significant change in the network (such as new system component installations, changes in network topology, firewall rule modifications, product upgrades)." Even though many grumble that "after any changes" is not stated clearly enough (after all, one would not scan the entire enterprise network after changing a single rule on a router somewhere deep in the test environment), this requirement does catch both needs to assess the vulnerability posture, periodically and after a change, to make sure that new vulnerabilities and weaknesses are not introduced.

This requirement has an interesting twist, however. Quarterly external vulnerability scans must be performed by a scan vendor qualified by the payment card industry. Thus, just using any scanner won't do; one needs to pick it from the list of ASVs, which we mentioned in Chapter 3, "Why Is PCI Here?" Specifically, the site says: "The PCI Security Standards Council has assumed responsibility for the Approved Scanning Vendor (ASV) program previously operated separately by MasterCard Worldwide." At the same time, the requirements for scans performed after changes are more relaxed: "Scans conducted after network changes may be performed by the company's internal staff." This is not surprising given that such changes occur much more frequently in most networks.

The next section covers the specifics of ASV scanning and the section after covers the internal scanning.

External Vulnerability Scanning with ASV

We will look into the operational issues of using an ASV, cover some tips about picking one, and then discuss what to expect from an ASV.

What Is an ASV?

As we mentioned in Chapter 3, "Why Is PCI Here?," PCI DSS validation also includes network vulnerability scanning by an ASV. To become an ASV, companies must undergo a process similar to QSA qualification. The difference is that in the case of QSAs, the individual assessors attend classroom training on an annual basis, whereas ASVs submit a scan conducted against a test network perimeter. An organization can choose to become both QSA and ASV, which allows the merchants and service providers to select a single vendor for PCI compliance validation.

So, to remind, ASVs are security companies that help you satisfy one of the two third-party validation requirements in PCI. ASVs go through a rigorous laboratory test process to confirm that their scanning technology is sufficient for PCI validation.

ASV existence and operation is governed by PCI DSS Requirement 11.2, which states: "Quarterly external vulnerability scans must be performed by an Approved Scanning Vendor (ASV) qualified by Payment Card Industry Security Standards Council (PCI SSC)."

In addition, the particulars of becoming an ASV as well as the specifics of scanning that ASV must perform and other details of ASV operation are governed by two other documents:

1. Technical and Operational Requirements for Approved Scanning Vendors (ASVs) [6]

2. Validation Requirements for Approved Scanning Vendors (ASV) [7]

Also, it is worthwhile to mention that validation via an external ASV scan only applies to those merchants that are required to validate requirement 11. In particular, those who don't have to validate Requirement 11 are those that outsource payment processing, those who don't process any data on their premises and those with dial-up (non-Internet) terminals. This is important, so it bears repeating; if you have no system to scan because you don't process in-house, you don't have to scan. Of course, it goes without saying that deploying a vulnerability management system to reduce your information risk is appropriate even if PCI DSS didn't exist at all.

Considerations when Picking an ASV

First, your acquiring bank might have picked an ASV for you. In this case, you might or might not have to use its choice. Note, however, that such prepicked ASV might be neither the best nor the cheapest.

While looking at the whole list of ASVs and then picking the one that "sounds nice" is one way to pick, it is likely not the one that will ensure trouble-free PCI validation and increased card data security as well as reduced risk of data theft. At the time of this writing, the ASV list boasted more than 90 different companies, from small 1 to 2 persons consulting outlets to IBMs and VeriSigns of the world, located on all the continents (save Antarctica). How do you pick?

First, one strategy, that needs to be unearthed and explained right away, is as simple as it is harmful for your card data security and PCI DSS compliance status. Namely, organizations that blindly assume that "all ASVs are the same" based on the fact that all are certified by the PCI Council to satisfy PCI DSS scan validation requirements would sometimes just pick on price. This same assumption sometimes applies to QSAs, and as many security industry insiders have pointed out (including both authors), they all are not created equal!

As a result, passing the scan validation requirement and submitting the report that indicates "Pass" will definitely confirm your PCI validation (as long as your ASV remains in good standing with the Council). Sadly, it will not do nearly enough for your cardholder data security. Even if certified, ASVs coverage of vulnerabilities varies greatly; all of them do the mandatory minimum, but more than a few cut corners and stay at that minimum (which, by the way, they are perfectly allowed doing), while others help you uncover other holes and flaws that allow malicious hackers to get to that juicy card data.

Thus, your strategy might follow these steps.

First, realize that all ASVs are not created equal; at the very least, prices for their services will be different, which should give you a hint that the value they provide will also be different.

Second, realize that all ASVs roughly fall into two groups: those that do the minimum necessary according to the above guidance documents (focus on compliance) and those that intelligently interpret the standard and help you with your data security and not just with PCI DSS compliance (focus on security). Typically, the way to tell the two groups apart is to look at the price. In addition, nearly 60 percent of all currently registered ASVs use the scanning technology from Qualys (www.qualys.com), while many of the rest use Nessus (www.nessus.org) to perform PCI validation.

In addition, the pricing models for ASV services vary; they roughly fall into two groups: in one model, you can scan your systems many times (unlimited scanning) while the other focuses on providing you the mandatory quarterly scan (i.e., four a year). In the latter case, if your initial scan shows the vulnerabilities and need to fix and rescan to arrive at a passing scan, you will be paying extra. Overall, it is extremely unlikely that you can get away with only scanning your network from the outside four times a year.

Third, even though an ASV does not have to be used for internal scanning, it is more logical to pick the same scanning provider for external (must be done by an ASV) and internal (must be done by somebody skilled in using vulnerability management tools). Using the same technology provider will allow you to have the same familiar report format and the same presentation of vulnerability findings. Similarly, and perhaps more importantly, even though PCI DSS–ASV scanning does not allow for authenticated or trusted scanning, picking an ASV that can run authenticated scans on your internal network is useful since such scanning can be used to automate the checking for the presence of other DSS controls, such as password length, account security settings, use of encryption, availability of antimalware defenses, etc. For example, an authenticated scan of a Windows server can help.

Table 8.1 shows a sample list of PCI DSS controls that may possibly be performed using automated scanning tools that perform authenticated or trusted scanning.

Fourth, look for how ASV workflow matches your experience and expectation. Are there many manual tasks required to perform a vulnerability

Table 8.1 Automatic Validation of PCI DSS Controls

Requirement	PCI DSS 1.2 Requirement	Technical Validation of PCI Requirements
1.4	Install personal firewall software on any mobile and/or employee-owned computers with direct connectivity to the Internet (for example, laptops used by employees), which are used to access the organization's network.	Automated tools are able to check for the presence of personal firewalls deployed on servers, desktops, and laptops remotely.
2.1	Always change vendor-supplied defaults before installing a system on the network – for example, include passwords, simple network management protocol (SNMP) community strings, and elimination of unnecessary accounts.	Automated tools can be used to verify that vendor defaults are not used by checking for default and system accounts on servers, desktops, and network devices.
2.1.1	For wireless environments connected to the CDE or transmitting cardholder data, change wireless vendor defaults, including but not limited to default wireless encryption keys, passwords, and SNMP community strings. Ensure wireless device security settings are enabled for strong encryption technology for authentication and transmission.	Automated tools can be used to verify that default settings and default passwords are not used across wireless devices connected to the wired network.
2.2	Develop configuration standards for all system components. Assure that these standards address all known security vulnerabilities and are consistent with industry-accepted system hardening standards.	Automated tools can validate the compliance of deployed systems to configuration standards, mandated by the PCI DSS.
2.2.2	Disable all unnecessary and insecure services and protocols (services and protocols not directly needed to perform the device's specified function).	Automated tools can help discover systems on the network as well as detect the network-exposed services that are running on systems, and thus significantly reduce the effort needed to bring the environment in compliance.
2.2.4	Remove all unnecessary functionality, such as scripts, drivers, features, subsystems, file systems, and unnecessary Web servers.	Automated tools can help discover some of the insecure and unnecessary functionality exposed to the network, and thus significantly reduce the effort needed to bring the environment in compliance.
2.3	Encrypt all nonconsole administrative access. Use technologies such as Secure Shell (SSH), virtual private network (VPN), or Secure Sockets Layer/Transport Layer Security (SSL/TLS) for Web-based management and other nonconsole administrative access.	Automated tools can help validate that encrypted protocols are in use across the systems and that unencrypted communication is not enabled on servers and workstations (SSH, not Telnet; SSL, not unencrypted HTTP, etc).
3.4	Render PAN, at minimum, unreadable anywhere it is stored (including on portable digital media, backup media, in logs).	Automated tools can confirm that encryption is in use across the PCI in-scope systems by checking system configuration settings relevant to encryption.
3.5	Protect cryptographic keys used for encryption of cardholder data against both disclosure and misuse.	Automated tools can be used to validate security settings relevant to protection of system encryption keys.

Table 8.1	Automatic Validation of PCI DSS Controls *Continued*	
Requirement	**PCI DSS 1.2 Requirement**	**Technical Validation of PCI Requirements**
4.1	Use strong cryptography and security protocols such as SSL/TLS or Internet Protocol Security (IPsec) to safeguard sensitive cardholder data during transmission over open, public networks.	Automated tools can be used to validate the use of strong cryptographic protocols by checking relevant system configuration settings and detect instances of insecure cipher use across the in-scope systems.
4.1.1	Ensure wireless networks transmitting cardholder data or connected to the CDE, use industry best practices (for example, IEEE 802.11i) to implement strong encryption for authentication and transmission.	Automated tools can attempt to detect wireless access points from the network side and to validate the use of proper encryption across those access points.
5.1	Deploy antivirus software on all systems commonly affected by malicious software (particularly, personal computers and servers).	Automated tools can validate whether antivirus software is installed on in-scope systems.
5.2	Ensure that all antivirus mechanisms are new, actively running, and capable of generating audit logs.	Automated tools can be used to check for running status of antivirus tools.
6.1	Ensure that all system components and software have the latest vendor-supplied security patches installed. Install critical security patches within one month of release.	Automated tools can be used to detect missing OS, application patches, and security updates.
6.2	Establish a process to identify newly discovered security vulnerabilities (for example, subscribe to alert services freely available on the Internet).	Automated tools are constantly updated with new vulnerability information and can be used in tracking newly discovered vulnerabilities.
6.6	For public-facing Web applications, address new threats and vulnerabilities on an ongoing basis and ensure these applications are protected against known attacks by either of the following methods: reviewing public-facing Web applications via manual or automated application vulnerability security assessment tools or methods, at least annually and after any changes.	Automated tools can be used to assess Web application security in support of PCI Requirement 6.6.
7.1	Limit access to system components and cardholder data to only those individuals whose job requires such access.	Automated tools can analyze database user right and permissions, looking for broad and insecure permissions.
8.1	Assign all users a unique ID before allowing them to access system components or cardholder data.	In partial support of this requirement, automated tools are used to look for active default, generic accounts (root, system, etc.), which indicate that account sharing takes place.

Continued

Table 8.1 Automatic Validation of PCI DSS Controls *Continued*

Requirement	PCI DSS 1.2 Requirement	Technical Validation of PCI Requirements
8.2	In addition to assigning a unique ID, use at least one of the following methods to authenticate all users: Password or passphrase.	Automated tools can be used to look for user accounts with improper authentication settings, such as accounts with no passwords or with blank passwords.
8.4	Render all passwords unreadable during transmission and storage on all system components using strong cryptography.	Automated tools can be used to detect system configuration settings, permitting unencrypted and inadequately encrypted passwords across systems.
8.5	Ensure proper user authentication and password management for nonconsumer users and administrators on all system components.	Automated tools can be used to validate an extensive set of user account security settings and password security parameters across systems in support of this PCI requirement.
11.1	Test for the presence of wireless access points by using a wireless analyzer at least quarterly or deploying a wireless IDS/IPS to identify all wireless devices in use.	Automated tools can attempt to detect wireless access points from the network side, thus to help the detection of rogue access points.
11.2	Run internal and external network vulnerability scans at least quarterly and after any significant change in the network (such as new system component installations, changes in network topology, firewall rule modifications, and product upgrades).	Automated tools can be used to scan for vulnerabilities both from inside and from outside the network.

scan and create a report or is everything automated? Fully automated ASV services where launching a scan and presenting a compliance report to your acquirer can be done from the same interface are available. Still, if you need help with fixing the issues before you can rescan and validate your compliance, hiring an ASV that offers help with remediation is advisable. It goes without saying that picking an ASV that requires you to purchase any hardware or software is not advisable; all external scan requirements can be satisfied by scanning from the Internet.

Finally, even though this strategy focuses on picking an ASV, you and your organization have a role to play as well, namely, in fixing the vulnerabilities that the scan discovered to arrive at a compliant status – clean scan with no failures. We discuss the criteria that ASVs use for pass/fail below.

How ASV Scanning Works

ASVs use standard vulnerability scanning technology to detect vulnerabilities that are deemed by the PCI Council to be relevant for PCI DSS compliance. This information will help you understand what exactly you are dealing with when you retain the scanning services of an ASV. It will also help you learn how to pass or fail the PCI scan criteria and how to prepare your environment for an ASV scan.

Specifically, the ASV procedures mandate that ASV covers the following in its scan (the list below is heavily abridged, please refer to "Technical and Operational Requirements for Approved Scanning Vendors (ASVs)" [4] for more details):

- Identify issues in "operating systems, Web servers, Web application servers, common Web scripts, database servers, mail servers, firewalls, routers, wireless access points, common (such as DNS, FTP, SNMP, etc.) services, custom Web applications."

- "ASV must use the CVSS base score for the severity level" (please see the main site for CVSS at www.first.org/cvss for more information).

After the above resources are scanned, the following criteria are used to pass/fail the PCI validation (also [4]):

- "Generally, to be considered compliant, a component must not contain any vulnerability that has been assigned a CVSS base score equal to or higher than 4.0." Any curious reader can look up a CVSS score for many publicly disclosed vulnerabilities by going to NVD at http://nvd.nist.gov.

- "If a CVSS base score is not available for a given vulnerability identified in the component, then the compliance criteria to be used by the ASV depend on the identified vulnerability leading to a data compromise." This criterion makes sure that ASV security personnel can use their own internal scoring methodology when CVSS scores cannot be produced.

There are additional exceptions to the above rules. Some vulnerability types are included in pass/fail criteria, no matter what their scores are, while others are excluded. Here are the inclusions:

- "A component must be considered noncompliant if the installed SSL version is limited to Version 2.0, or older."

- "The presence of application vulnerabilities on a component that may lead to SQL injection attacks and cross-site scripting flaws must result in a noncompliant status" [4].

The exclusions are as follows:

- "Vulnerabilities or misconfigurations that may lead to DoS should not be taken into consideration" [4].

The above criteria highlight the fact that PCI DSS external scanning is not everything you need to do for security. After all, PCI DSS focuses on card data loss, not on the availability of your key IT resources for your organization and not on their resistance to malicious hackers.

Each ASV will interpret the requirements a little differently; Table 8.2 shows an example from Qualys.

However, quality ASV identifies many different types of vulnerabilities in addition to PCI DSS. For example, Qualys uses the following scan policy to run its PCI DSS scanning, as shown in Fig. 8.9.

As you can see, it scans for all possible vulnerabilities, not just for PCI relevant ones, which allows you to reduce the risk of data exposure, not just achieve PCI DSS compliance validation.

Table 8.2 QualysGuard PCI Pass/Fail Status Criteria
Vulnerabilities with a NIST CVSS v2.0 base score of either 4.0 or higher will cause PCI compliance to fail on the scanned IPs.
Vulnerabilities that do not have a NIST CVSS score, or have a NIST CVSS score of 0, will be rated using the QualysGuard severity ranking. A severity of three or above will cause PCI compliance to fail on the corresponding IP.
An IP will be considered noncompliant if the SSL version installed on it is limited to 2.0 or older.
Vulnerabilities that may lead to SQL injection attacks and cross-site scripting will result in a noncompliant status on the corresponding IP.
Vulnerabilities or misconfigurations that may lead to denial of service are not taken into consideration for PCI compliance.
The PCI Technical Report will include a list of all vulnerabilities discovered; however, the PCI vulnerabilities that drive the pass/fail criteria will be indicated as such.

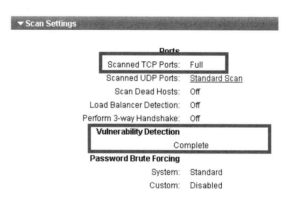

FIGURE 8.9 *PCI DSS ASV Scan Options*

When the scan completes, the report is generated, which can then be used to substantiate your PCI validation via vulnerability scanning.

PCI DSS Scan Validation Walk-through

Let's analyze a complete report and learn how to go from its current status (PCI FAILED) to successful PCI validation (PCI PASSED). Your PCI scan validation endeavor starts from a view presented by your ASV, which is similar to this (Fig. 8.10).

The scan report shown in Fig. 8.10 indicates that several of your scanned systems have failed the scan for various reasons. Let's walk through one of the systems, which failed the scan. For example, vulnerability such as the following will be grounds for a failed scan validation (Fig. 8.11).

This particular vulnerability has a CVSS score of 4.3 (which is more than 4.0 needed for PCI criteria to fail); thus, the PCI validation for this machine and, consequently, for the entire scanned environment fails. As a side note, in addition to being severe, this particular vulnerability can enable data theft via phishing because it enabled the attacker to run the cache poisoning attack.

How do we get out of this conundrum and back to security and PCI DSS scan passing? We need to fix the issue. Specifically, upgrade your Domain Name System (DNS) server software (such as BIND in this case) to a version that does not have these issues, such as the one newer than 9.2.8. To do that, see the BIND Web site at www.isc.org/products/BIND/ for patches and updates or contact your OS vendor for the same.

As a result of those efforts, you will be looking at a very different picture (Fig. 8.12).

PCI Status

The following table highlights the overall compliance status and each individual system's compliance status.

Overall PCI Status	FAILED

Live IP Addresses Scanned	Security Risk Rating	PCI Status
24	2.0	PASSED ✔
64	5.0	FAILED ✗
64	5.0	FAILED ✗
64	3.0	FAILED ✗
65	3.0	FAILED ✗
66	4.0	FAILED ✗

FIGURE 8.10 *PCI DSS Scan Failure*

FIGURE 8.11 PCI DSS Scan Failure Vulnerability

PCI Status

The following table highlights the overall compliance status and each individual system's compliance status.

FIGURE 8.12 PCI DSS Scan Pass

To summarize, ASV quality scanning will detect all possible external vulnerabilities and highlight those that are reasons for PCI DSS validation failure. The same process needs to be repeated for quarterly scans – usually toward the end of the quarter but not during the last day because remediation activities needs to happen before a final rescan takes place. In fact, let's talk about operationalizing the ASV scanning.

Operationalizing ASV Scanning

To recap PCI DSS Requirement 11.2 calls for quarterly scanning. In addition, every scan may lead to remediation activities, and those aren't limited to patching. Moreover, validation procedures mention that a QSA will ask for four passing reports during an assessment.

The above calls for an operation process for dealing with this requirement. Let's build this process together now.

First, it is a very good idea to scan monthly or even weekly if possible. Why would you be doing it to satisfy a quarterly scanning requirement? Well, consider the following scenario: on the last day of March, you perform an external vulnerability scan and you discover a critical vulnerability. The discovered vulnerability is present on 20 percent of your systems, which totals to 200 systems. Now, you have exactly 1 day to fix the vulnerability on all systems and perform a passing vulnerability scan, which will be retained for your records. Is this realistic? The scenario can happen and, in fact, has happened in many companies that postpone their quarterly vulnerability scan until the very last day and did not perform any ongoing vulnerability scanning. Considering the fact that many acquiring institutions are becoming more stringent with PCI validation requirements, and will not grant you an exception. Beyond the first day over the next month, the scenario will certainly incur unnecessary pain and suffering on your company and your IT staff. What is the way to avoid it? Performing external scans every month or even every week. It is also a good idea to perform an external scan after you apply a patch to external systems.

NOTE

Most companies run their external scans monthly, even though those are called "quarterly scans." That way, issues can be resolved in time to have a clean quarterly report since there are no surprises. There are known cases where organizations have been burned by waiting until the last month of a quarter to run an external scan. This can cause a serious amount of last-minute, emergency, code and system configuration changes, and an overall sense of panic, which is not conducive to good security management.

After you run the scan, carefully review the results of the reports. Are those passing or failing reports? If the report indicates that you do not pass the PCI validation requirement, please note which systems and vulnerabilities do not pass the criteria. Next, distribute the report to those in your IT organization who is responsible for the systems that fail the test. Offer them some guidance on how to fix the vulnerabilities and bring those systems back to PCI compliance. These intermediate reports will absolutely not be shared with your acquiring institutions.

When you receive the indication that those vulnerabilities have been successfully fixed, please rescan to obtain a clean report. Repeat the process every month or week.

Finally, scan a final round before the end of the quarter and preserve the reports for the assessor. Thus, your shields will be up at all times. If you are only checking them four times a year, you're suffering from two problems. First, you are most likely not PCI compliant throughout most of the year. Second, you burden yourself with a massive emergency effort right at the end of the quarter when other people at your organization expect IT systems to operate at its peak. Don't be the one telling finance that they cannot run that quarterly report!

What Do You Expect from an ASV?

Discussing the expectations while dealing with an ASV and working toward PCI DSS scan validation is a valuable exercise. The critical considerations are described below.

First, ASV can scan you and present the data (report) to you. It is your job to then bring the environment in compliance. After that, ASV can again be used to validate your compliant status and produce a clean report. Remember, ASV scanning does not make you compliant, you do, by making sure that no PCI-fail vulnerabilities are present in your network.

Second, you don't have to hire expensive consultants just to run an ASV scan for you every quarter. Some ASVs will automatically perform the scan with the correct settings and parameters, without you learning the esoteric nature of a particular vulnerability scanner. In fact, you can sometimes even pay for it online and get the scan right away – yes, you guessed right – using a credit card.[1]

Third, you should expect that a quality ASV will discover more vulnerabilities than is required for PCI DSS compliance. You'd need to make your own judgment call on whether to fix them. One common case where you might want to address the issue is vulnerabilities that allow hackers to crash your systems (denial of service [DoS] vulnerabilities). Such flaws are out of scope for PCI because they cannot directly cause the theft of card data; however, by not fixing them, you are allowing the attackers to disrupt your online business operation.

---

[1] How do you think the companies that provide PCI DSS and security services process their card payments? They outsource it, of course, no data – no risk. We will likely repeat this advice many more times in this book.

Finally, let us offer some common tips on ASV scanning.

First comes the question: what system must you scan for PCI DSS compliance? The answer to this splits into two parts, for external and internal scanning.

Specifically, for external systems or those visible from the Internet, the guidance from the PCI Council is clear: "all Internet-facing Internet Protocol (IP) addresses and/or ranges, including all network components and devices that are involved in e-commerce transactions or retail transactions that use IP to transmit data over the Internet" (source: "Technical and Operational Requirements for Approved Scanning Vendors (ASVs)" [4] by PCI Council). The obvious answer can be "none" if your business has no connection to the Internet.

For internal systems, the answer covers all systems that are considered in-scope for PCI, which is either those involved with card processing or directly connected to them. The answer can also be "none" if you have no systems inside your perimeter, which are in-scope for PCI DSS.

Second, the question about pass/fail criteria for internal scans often arises as well. While the external ASV scans have clear criteria discussed above, internal scans from within your network have no set pass/fail criteria. The decision is thus based on your idea of risk; there is nothing wrong in using the same criteria as above, of course, if you think that it matches your view of risks to card data in your environment.

Another common question is how to pass the PCI DSS scan validation? Just as above, the answer is very clear for external scans: you satisfy the above criteria. If you don't, you need to fix the vulnerabilities that are causing you to fail and the rescan. Then, you pass and get a "passing report," that you can submit to your acquiring bank.

For internal scans, the pass/fail criteria are not expressly written in the PCI Council documentation. Expect your assessor to ask for clean internal and external scans as part of Requirement 11.2. Typically, QSAs will define "clean" internal scans as those not having high-severity vulnerability across the in-scope systems. For a very common scale of vulnerability ranking from 1 to 5 (with 5 being the most severe), vulnerability of severities 3 to 5 are usually not acceptable. If CVSS scoring is used, 4.0 becomes the cutoff point; vulnerabilities with severities above 4.0 are not accepted unless compensating controls are present and are accepted by the QSA. It was reported that in some situations, a QSA would accept a workable plan that aims to remove these vulnerabilities from the internal environment.

Also, people often ask whether they become "PCI compliant" if they get a passing scan for their external systems. The answer is certainly a "no." You only satisfied one of the PCI DSS requirements; namely, PCI DSS validation via an external ASV scan. This is not the end. Likely, this is the beginning.

INTERNAL VULNERABILITY SCANNING

As we mentioned in the section, "Vulnerability Management in PCI," internal vulnerability scanning must be performed every quarter and after every material system change, and no high-severity vulnerability must be present in the final scan preserved for presentation to your QSA. Internal scanning is governed by the PCI Council document called Security Scanning Procedures [8].

First, using the same template your ASV uses for external scanning is a really good idea, but you can use more reliable trusted or authenticated scanning, which will reveal key application security issues on your in-scope systems that regular, unauthenticated scanning may sometimes miss.

Remediation may take the form of hardening, patching, architecture changes, technology/tool implementations, or a combination thereof. Remediation efforts after internal scanning are prioritized based on risk and can be managed better than external ASV scans. Something to keep in mind for PCI environments is that the remediation of critical vulnerabilities on all in-scope systems is mandatory. This makes all critical and high-severity vulnerabilities found on in-scope PCI systems a high priority. Follow the same process we covered in the "operationalizing ASV scanning" section and work toward removing the high-severity vulnerabilities from the environment before presenting the clean report to the QSA.

Reports that show the finding and remediation of vulnerabilities for in-scope systems over time become artifacts that are needed to satisfy assessment requirements. You should consider that having a place to keep archives of all internal and external scan reports (summary, detailed, and remediation) for a 12-month period is a good idea. Your ASV may offer to keep them for you and also as an added service. However, it is ultimately your responsibility.

This is a continuous process. As with other PCI compliance efforts, it is important to realize that PCI compliance is an effort that takes place 24/7, 365 days a year.

For Internal scanning, you can create different reports for technicians who will fix issues found and summary reports for management. However, overdoing it is bad as well: handing a 10,000-page report to a technician will typically not result in remediation taking place. We are not even talking about a possibility of showing such a report to senior management. Working with the team responsible for remediation to ensure the reports give them actionable data, without overwhelming them, is very much worth the time spent.

Servers that are in-scope are usually scanned off-hours. Be sure your scan windows do not occur during maintenance windows or the target hosts may be off-line for maintenance. If you have workstations in-scope, scans may need to be run during business hours. For systems that must be scanned during business hours, you may need to make the scans run at a lower intensity.

Until you have thoroughly defined processes (documentation again – many efforts in PCI DSS require both "doing" and "recording") for all scanning, remediation, and reporting functions tied to your PCI needs, you do not truly "own" the tool you are using.

Finally, issues will undoubtedly occur as you begin your scanning efforts. Here, having a well-defined root cause analysis helps a lot. The sidebar covers how to handle such issues.

TOOLS

Here is a sample PCI DSS scan issue tracking process in four steps:

Step 1: Gather inputs from the issue.

Gather Host/Application information: application name, version, patch level, port usage information, etc.

- Was the application disrupted, a system service, or the entire operating system?

- What had to be done to recover from the outage? Service restart or host reboot?

Step 2: Verify that the issue was caused by the scan.

Check system logs and try to match the time of the incident to the time of the scan.

Step 3: Place a support call with the application vendor or development team.

Verify that all patches have been applied to the application for "denial of service" and "buffer overflow" problems.

Step 4: If the issue is not resolved by the application vendor, engage support from your scanning vendor.

*Thanks to Derek Milroy for providing the sample process.

Let's also address the issues of a system change. PCI DSS Requirement 11.2 gives the following example of system changes:

- New system component installations, which covers new systems, new system components, and new applications.

- Changes in network topology, such as new network paths between the in-scope systems and the outside world, especially the Internet.

- Firewall rule modifications, especially additional rules allowing traffic to or from the cardholder environment.

- Product upgrades, examples are changes to payment applications, servers, network devices, etc.

It is your responsibility to perform a scan after these events have taken place.

Finally, remember that internal scanning is as mandatory for in-scope systems as the ASV scanning is mandatory for external systems.

Penetration Testing

Requirement 11.3 covers penetration-testing requirements. It says: "Perform penetration testing at least once a year and after any significant infrastructure or application upgrade or modification (such as an operating system upgrade, a subnetwork added to the environment, or a Web server added to the environment)." The logic here is again similar: periodic (annual) and after major changes. It appears that in this case, the changes that trigger a penetration test should be of a much larger scale because penetration test services aren't exactly cheap.

By the way, multiple books have been written on the art and science of the penetration test. There is no chance to cover it in our book. However, it makes sense to remind people that a penetration test will always involve a skilled, human attacker, not an automated tool.

Every penetration test begins with one concept – communication. A penetration test should be viewed by a security team as a hostile act – provided they are not asleep at the wheel. After all, the point is to break through active and passive defenses erected around an information system. Communication is important because somebody is about to break your security. During the time of the penetration test, alarm bells should ring, processes would be put into motion, and, if communication has not occurred, and appropriate permissions to perform these tests have not been obtained, law enforcement authorities may be contacted to investigate. Now wouldn't that be an embarrassment if your PCI-driven penetration test, planned for months, had not been approved by your chief information officer (CIO)?

Moreover, PCI DSS dives deeper into penetration testing details. These penetration tests must include the following:

- 11.3.1: Network-layer penetration tests

- 11.3.2: Application-layer penetration tests

Indeed, limiting to network layer tests is shortsighted, but this list still leaves a gap of nontechnical penetration testing via social engineering. Admittedly, most skilled penetration testing teams will perform such nontechnical testing as well, but not mentioning it explicitly in PCI official documents seems like a minor oversight.

COMMON PCI VULNERABILITY MANAGEMENT MISTAKES

It is worthwhile to point out a few common mistakes that organizations make while working toward satisfying the vulnerability management requirements.

We hinted at the first mistake when we described the password example. It is in focusing only on the technical assessment means (which are indeed easier and more automatic) and omitting the process-based mistakes and issues. In particular, for PCI DSS, it applies to testing only the technology controls but not checking for policy controls such as security awareness, presence of plans and procedures, etc. Thus, people often focus on the technical vulnerabilities and forget all the human vulnerabilities, such as susceptibility of many enterprise IT users to social engineering, and other lapses of corporate controls. The way to avoid this mistake is to keep in mind that even though you use a scanning vendor, your credit-card data might still be pilfered, and addressing the "softer" part of security is just as critical.

Another commonly "lost and forgotten" thing is application-level vulnerabilities, which is not only about open ports and buffer overflows in network-exposed server code. It is also about all the Web applications – from a now-common cross-site scripting and SQL injection flaws to cross-site request forgery to more esoteric flaws in Flash code and other browser-side languages.

Similarly, client-side applications including all the recent Internet Explorer versions (and, frequently, Firefox versions as well), MS Office, and Adobe weaknesses lead to many a government agency falling victim to malicious hackers. What is in common with those "newer" vulnerabilities? Scanning for them is not as easy to automate as finding open Telnet ports and overflows in Internet Information Services (IIS), which was the staple of vulnerability scanning in the late 1990s and early 2000s. PCI requirements refer to such weaknesses but, still, more attention seems to be paid to the network-level stuff exposed to the Internet. The way to avoid this mistake is to keep in mind that a lot of hacking happens on the application layer and to use internal authenticated scanning to look for such issues inside your in-scope network. Such scanning does not have to be performed by the ASV, but if you follow our guidance above, you hopefully picked an ASV that offers internal and authenticated scanning and not just external, mandatory ASV scanning.

Recent Qualys research into Laws of Vulnerabilities [9] shows that attention is not paid to client-side issues. If you limit the scope of analysis to core OS vulnerabilities, the half-life drops to 15 days (which means that people patch those quickly!). On the other hand, if you limit it to Adobe and MS Office flaws, the half-life sharply rises to 60 days (which means people just don't care – and the current dramatic compromise rampage will continue). The data that supports that situation is shown in Figs 8.13 and 8.14.

Even when application-layer vulnerabilities are not forgotten, and patching and other remediation are happening on an aggressive schedule

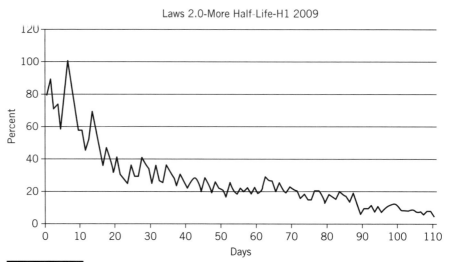

FIGURE 8.13 *Half-Life of Core Operating System Vulnerability. Source: Qualys Laws of Vulnerabilities research*

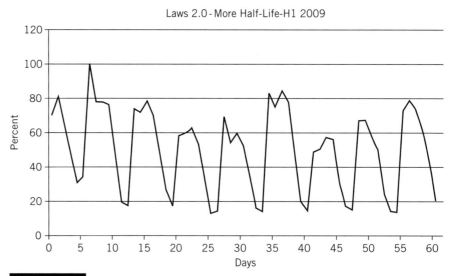

FIGURE 8.14 *Half-Life of Client Application Vulnerability. Source: Qualys Laws of Vulnerabilities research*

(nowadays, patching all servers within a "single day" time frame is considered aggressive, that is, what is done by "security leaders"), there is something else to be missed: vulnerability in the applications that were written in-house. Indeed, no vulnerability scanner vendor will have knowledge of your custom-written systems, and even if your penetration-testing consultant or an internal "red team" will be able to discover some of them during an annual penetration test, a lot of application code can be written in a year (and thus a lot more vulnerability introduced). The way to avoid this mistake is to train your software engineering staff to use secure programming practices to minimize the occurrence of such flaws, as we discussed in a previous section on Requirement 6 (the detailed coverage of it goes well beyond the scope of this book). While having a good application tester on staff is unlikely, assessing the security of the homegrown application needs to be undertaken more frequently than once a year. Obviously, initial focus on Web-based and Internet-exposed applications is a must.

The last mistake we mention is misjudging the list of in-scope systems or "scoping errors." Indeed, modern, large-scale, payment processing systems are complicated and have many dependencies. Avoiding this mistake is not easy: the only way to find all the systems that might need to be scanned and protected is to have your internal staff (who know the systems best) work with an external PCI consultant or QSA (who knows the regulation best) to find out what should be in scope for your particular environment. Primarily, avoid these mistakes by knowing and being able to describe all the business processes that touch the card data. This will take care of the known, authorized locations of card data (which is very important!) and can give you more ideas on scope reduction and reducing card data storage and processing. In addition, even though data discovery technologies are not mandated by PCI, it is advisable to use them to discover other locations of card data, which are not authorized and are not known to be a part of legitimate business process. The latter can be either eliminated or documented and added to PCI DSS scope: these are the only two choices, and "ignored" is not one of them.

Keeping these mistakes in mind has the chance of making your PCI compliance experience a lot less painful.

CASE STUDY

The case studies below illustrate how vulnerability management for PCI is implemented in a few real-world organizations.

PCI at a Retail Chain

This case study covers how PCI Requirement 11 was dealt with at a large retain chain in the US Midwest. The Unnamed Retailer Inc did not perform any periodic network vulnerability scanning and didn't use the services of a penetration-testing firm, which put them in a clear violation of PCI DSS rules. Their IT security staff sometimes used the freeware tools to scan a specific system for open ports or sometimes for vulnerabilities, but all such efforts were ad hoc and not tied to any program.

Upon the approach of PCI DSS compliance deadline, the company had to start the scanning using the PCI-ASV every quarter. They chose to deploy a service-based vulnerability scanning from a major vendor. The choice of vendor was determined after a brief proof-of-concept study.

Initially, they suffered from having no information or no knowledge of their vulnerability posture to having too much since they decided to scan all the Internet-facing systems. Later, however, they reduced the scope to what they considered to be "in-scope" systems, such as those processing payments (few of those systems are ever visible from the internet, however) and those connected to such systems.

Later, their scanning vendor introduced a method to scan the internal systems, which was immediately used by the retailer. However, it turned out that finding the internal systems that are in-scope is even more complicated since many systems have legitimate reasons to connect to those that process credit-card transactions. For example, even their internal patch management system was deemed to be in-scope since it frequently connected to the transaction processing servers.

As a result, their route to PCI vulnerability management nirvana took a few months following a phased approach. Implementation followed the these routes:

1. All Internet-facing systems that can be scanned

2. A smaller set of Internet-facing systems that were deemed to be "in-scope"

3. A set of internal systems that either process payments or connect to those that do

4. From there, the company will probably move to scanning select important systems that are not connected to payment processing, but are still critical in its business.

Even though the organization chose not to implement the intrusion detection earlier, their QSA strongly suggested that they look at some options in this area. The company chose to upgrade their firewalls to Unified Threat Management (UTM) devices that combined the capabilities of a firewall and a network IPS. An external consultant suggested their initial intrusion prevention rule set, which the company deployed.

Overall, the project ended up with a successful, if longish, implementation of PCI Requirement 11 using a scanning service as well as UTM devices in place of their firewalls. The organization did pass the PCI assessment, even though they were told to also look at deploying a file integrity monitoring software, which is offered by a few commercial vendors.

PCI at an E-Commerce Site

This case study is based on a major e-commerce implementation of a commercial scanning service, a penetration testing by a security consultancy, and a host IPS and file integrity monitoring on critical servers.

Upon encountering PCI compliance requirements, Buy.Web Inc. has assessed their current security efforts, which include the use of host IPS on their demilitarized zone (DMZ) servers as well as periodic vulnerability scanning. They realized that they needed to additionally satisfy the penetration-testing requirements and file integrity-checking requirements to be truly compliant. Their IT staff performed an extensive research of file integrity monitoring vendors, and chose one with the most advanced centralized management system (to ease the management of all the integrity-checking results). They also contracted a small IT security consultancy to perform the penetration testing for them.

In addition, the team used its previously acquired log-management solution to aggregate the host IPS and file integrity checking, to create a single-data presentation and reporting interface for their PCI assessors. Overall, this project was a successful illustration of a mature security program that needed to only "fill the gaps" to be PCI compliant.

SUMMARY

To conclude, the PCI DSS document covers a lot of activities related to software vulnerabilities. Let us summarize what areas are covered since such requirements are spread over multiple requirements, even belonging to multiple sections. Table 8.3 covers the vulnerability management activities that we covered in this chapter.

As a result, PCI allows for a fairly comprehensive, if a bit jumbled, look at the entire vulnerability landscape, from coding to remediation and mitigation. Thus, you need to make sure that you look for all vulnerability-related guidance while planning your PCI-driven vulnerability management program. While focusing on vulnerability management, don't reduce it to patch management – do not forget custom applications written in-house or by partners. You need to have an ongoing program to deal with discovered

Table 8.3 Vulnerability Management Activities in PCI DSS

Vulnerability-Related Activity Prescribed by PCI DSS	Requirement
Secure coding guidance in regular and Web applications	6
Secure software deployment	6
Code review for vulnerabilities	6
Vulnerability scanning	11
Patching and remediation	6
Technologies that protect from vulnerability exploitation	5, 6, and 11
Site assessment and penetration testing	11

vulnerabilities. Wherever you can, automate the remediation of discovered vulnerabilities and focus on what you cannot. Finally, make sure that you recheck for fixed vulnerabilities after they are reported to be fixed.

REFERENCES

[1] Qualys website. www.qualys.com [accessed 12.07.09].
[2] Williams AT, Nicolett M. Improve IT security with vulnerability management. Gartner research note, May 2, 2005. www.gartner.com/DisplayDocument?doc_cd=127481 [accessed 8.8.09].
[3] Prioritized Approach for PCI DSS 1.2. www.pcisecuritystandards.org/education/prioritized.shtml [accessed 12.07.09].
[4] Validation Requirements for Approved Scanning Vendors (ASV). PCI Council. www.pcisecuritystandards.org/.../pci_dss_validation_requirements_for_approved_scanning_vendors_ASVs_v1-1.pdf [accessed 8.8.09].
[5] Qualys PCI Vulnerability Report [accessed 21.07.09].
[6] Technical and Operational Requirements for Approved Scanning Vendors (ASVs). PCI Council www.pcisecuritystandards.org/.../pci_dss_technical_and_operational_requirements_for_approved_scanning_vendors_ASVs_v1-1.pdf [accessed 8.8.09].
[7] Qualys Criteria for PCI Pass/Fail Status. www.qualys.com/products/pci/qgpci/pass_fail_criteria/ [accessed 12.07.09].
[8] Security Scanning Procedures. Version 1.1. PCI Council, 2006.
[9] Qualys Laws of Vulnerabilities Research. http://laws.qualys.com [accessed 12.07.09].

Logging Events and Monitoring the Cardholder Data Environment

When most people think about information security, the idea of blocking, deflecting, denying, or otherwise stopping a malicious hacker attack comes to mind. Secure network architecture, secure server operating systems, data encryption, and other security technologies are deployed to actually shield your assets from that evil influence that can steal your information, commit fraud, or disrupt the operation of systems and networks.

Indeed, the visions of tall castle walls, deep moats, or more modern armor and battleships pervade most people's view of warfare as well as information security. However, there is more to warfare (and more to security!) than armor and shields. No, we are not talking about attacks and counter-attacks because we don't really do that in the field of information security. We are talking about the other keystone of ancient as well as modern (and, likely, future!) warfare: intelligence. Those archers who glance from the top of the castle walls and modern spy satellites that glance down to Earth are no less mandatory to winning (or "not losing," as we have it in the field of information security) the war than fortifications and armored divisions.

In fact, security professionals often organize what they do in security into the following:

- Prevention

- Detection

- Response

"Prevention" is what covers all the blocking, deflecting, denying, or stopping attacks. Notice that it includes the actual blocking of a live attack (such as running a network intrusion prevention system [IPS]) as well as making sure that such an attack cannot take place (such as deploying a patch management system). However, what happens if such prevention measures actually *fail* to prevent or block an attack? Wouldn't it be nice to know that when it happens?

This is exactly where "detection" comes in. All the logging and monitoring technologies, whether relevant for Payment Card Industry Data Security Standard (PCI DSS) or not, are things that allow you to *know*. Specifically, know that you are attacked, know that prevention measure gave way, and know that an attacker has penetrated the network and is about to make it out with the loot.

As any self-respecting security guidance, PCI DSS guidance mandates not just prevention but detection in the form of logging, alerting, and monitoring. Let's discuss all these in detail.

PCI REQUIREMENTS COVERED

Contrary to popular belief, logging and monitoring are not constrained to Requirement 10 but, in fact, pervade all 12 of the PCI DSS requirements; the key areas where logging and monitoring are mandated in PCI DSS are Requirement 10 and sections of Requirement 11.

WHY LOGGING AND MONITORING IN PCI DSS?

As we mentioned previously, for those who are used to thinking of security as prevention or blocking, the benefits of monitoring might need to be spelled out explicitly, Before we go into describing what security monitoring measures are prescribed by PCI, we will do exactly that.

So, why monitor?

First comes situational awareness. It simply means knowing what is going on in your network and on your systems and applications. Examples here are Who is doing what on that server?, Who is accessing my network?, or What is that application doing with card data? In addition, system logging helps you know not only what is going on but also what was going on; a vital component needed for investigations and later incident response.

Next comes new threat discovery, which is simply knowing the bad stuff that is happening. This presents one of the major reasons to collect and review logs as well as to deploy intrusion detection systems (IDSs).

Third, logging helps you to get more value out of the network and security infrastructure, deployed for blocking and prevention. For example, using firewall logs for intrusion detection – often explained and justified, but not as commonly used – is an example of that.

What is even more interesting is that logging and monitoring controls (notice that these are considered security "controls" even though they don't really "control" anything) allow one to measure security and compliance by building metrics and trends. This means that one can use such data for a range of applications, from a simple "Top users by bandwidth" report obtained from firewall logs, all the way to sophisticated tracking of card data movements and use.

That is exactly why most regulations, industry mandates, and even "best practices" frameworks (International Organization for Standardization [ISO], COBIT, ITIL) call for logging and monitoring. Of course, PCI DSS is not an exception!

Last, but not least, if the worst does happen, then you would need to have as much data as possible during your incident response process: you might not use it all, but having a reliable log, assessment trail, and network capture data from all affected systems is indispensable for a hectic postincident environment.

Requirements 10 and 11 are easily capable of inflating PCI compliance costs to the point of consuming the small margins of card transactions. No one wants to lose money to be PCI compliant. Therefore, the ability to meet the requirements above all must make business sense. Nowhere else in PCI compliance does the middle ground of design philosophy come into play more than in the discipline of monitoring, but this is also where minimizing the risk can hurt most.

Finally, assuming that you've designed your PCI environment to have appropriate physical and logical boundaries through the use of segregated networks and dedicated application space as we described in Chapter 4, "Building and Maintaining a Secure Network," you should be able to identify the boundaries of your monitoring scope. If you haven't done this part, go back to Requirement 1 and start over!

LOGGING AND MONITORING IN DEPTH

System and network logs, one of the key sources of monitoring data, are often called the "untapped riches." The now-famous humorous security calendar proclaims "Logfiles: The Data Center Equivalent of Compost: Let'em Rot." [1] Others are not as loud about it and quietly choose to follow this maxim and ignore logs – at their own peril – altogether. Many organizations, whether under PCI DSS or not, still think of security as blocking and denying and leave monitoring and logging aside, despite their importance.

On the other hand, as computer and Internet technology continues to spread and computers start playing an even more important role in our lives, the records that they produce, such as logs and other traces, start to play a bigger role. From firewalls and routers to databases and enterprise applications, to wireless access points and Voice over Internet Protocol (VoIP) gateways, logs are being spewed forth at an ever-increasing pace. Both security and other information technology (IT) components not only increase in numbers but also often come with more logging enabled out of the box. An example of this trend includes Linux operating system as well as Web servers, both commercial and open-source, that now ship with increased levels of logging out of the box. All those systems, both legacy and modern, are known to generate copious amounts of logs, assessment trails, records, and alerts. In addition, such additional monitoring methods as network packet capture, database activity monitoring (DAM), and special-purpose application monitoring are becoming common as well. And all this data begs for constant attention!

WARNING

A log management problem is to a large extent a data management problem. Thus, if you deal with logs (and deal with them you must – and not only due to PCI DSS mandate), you'll deal with plenty of data.

With logs, it is much better to err on the side of keeping more – in case you'd need to look at it later. This is not the same as saying that you have to keep every log message, but retaining more log data is safer.

But this is easier said than done. Immense volumes of monitoring data are being generated on payment card processing networks. In turn, it results in a need to manage, store, and search all this data. Moreover, such review of data needs to happen both reactively – after a suspected incident – and proactively – in search of potential risks and future problems. For example, a typical large retailer generates hundreds of thousands of log messages per day amounting to many terabytes per year. An online merchant can generate millions of various log messages every day. One of America's largest retailers has more than 60 TB of log data on their systems at any given time. Unlike other companies, retailers do not have the option of not using logging due to PCI DSS.

> **NOTE**
>
> Even though we refer to "retailers," PCI is not only about retailers but also about anyone who "stores, processes, or transmits" credit- or debit-card numbers in the course of his or her business.

To start our discussion of PCI logging and monitoring requirements, Table 9.1 shows a sample list of technologies that produce logs of relevance

Table 9.1 Log-Producing Technologies, Monitored Using Their Logs

Type	Example Logs
Operating Systems	Linux, Solaris syslog, Windows Event Log
Databases	Oracle, Structured Query Language Server assessment trails
Network infrastructure	Cisco routers and switches syslog
Remote access	Virtual private network logs
Network security	Cisco PIX firewalls syslog
Intrusion detection and preventions	Snort network intrusion detection system syslog and packet capture
Enterprise applications	SAP, PeopleSoft logs
Web servers	Apache logs, Internet Information Server logs
Proxy servers	BlueCoat, Squid logs
E-mail servers	Sendmail syslog, various Exchange logs
Domain Name System (DNS) servers	Bind DNS logs, MS DNS
Antivirus and antispyware	Symantec AV event logs, TrendMicro AV logs
Physical access control	IDenticard, CoreStreet
Wireless networking	Cisco Aironet AP logs

Table 9.2 Technologies Commonly Monitored *Not* Using Logs

Type	How to Monitor?
Databases	Oracle, Structured Query Language Server database activity monitoring
Enterprise applications	SAP, PeopleSoft application monitoring

to PCI. Though this list is not comprehensive, it is likely that the readers find at least one system that they have in their cardholder data environment and for which logs are not being collected, much less looked at, and that is not being monitored at all.

In addition, Table 9.2 shows a few of the technologies not commonly monitored using logs.

NOTE

Table 9.2 is not a full list; everybody has some esoteric and not so esoteric applications and devices that produce logs that are not covered in this table. In any case, if these devices are included in a payment card environment, it is likely that these device logs need to be collected, stored, and analyzed to satisfy PCI Requirement 10 as well as others.

NOTE

An astute reader notices that databases are present in Tables 9.1 and 9.2. How can that be? The reality of database security monitoring is such that even though logs (namely, assessment tables) are available in all major commercial and free, open-source databases, they are rarely used for monitoring. The most common reason for such neglect of logs in the database realm is due to a measurable performance impact that logging incurs on a high-performance production database. As a result, other mechanisms, such as dedicated security agents or IDS-like network sniffing appliances, are used to monitor database activity.

Many companies and government agencies are trying to set up repeatable log collection, centralization, and analysis processes and tools.

Despite the multitude of log sources and types, people typically start from network and firewall logs and then progress upward on the protocol stack as well as sideways toward other nonnetwork applications. For example, just about any firewall or network administrator will look at a simple summary of connections that his or her Cisco ASA (or older PIX) or Checkpoint firewall is logging. Many firewalls log in standard syslog format, and such logs are easy to collect and review.

For example, here is a Juniper firewall log message in syslog format:

```
NOC-FWa:   NetScreen   device_id=NOC-FWa   system-notification-
00257(traffic): start_time="2007-05-01  19:17:37" duration=60
policy_id=9  service=snmp  proto=17  src  zone=noc-services
dst  zone=access-ethernet  action=Permit  sent=547  rcvd=432
src=10.0.12.10  dst=10.2.16.10  src_port=1184  dst_port=161
src-xlated ip=10.0.12.10 port=1184
```

And, here is the one from Cisco ASA firewall device:

```
%ASA-6-106100:   access-list   outside_access_in   denied   icmp
outside/10.88.81.77(0) -> inside/192.10.10.246(11) hit-cnt 1
(first hit)
```

Reviewing network intrusion detection system (NIDS) or IPS logs, although "interesting" in case of an incident, is often a very frustrating task since NIDS would sometimes produce "false alarms" and dutifully log them. Still, NIDS log analysis, at least the postmortem kind for investigative purposes, often happens right after firewall logs are looked at.

As a result, organizations deploy their log management infrastructure for compliance, security, or operational uses; the value of such information for security is undeniable, and logs can, in most cases, be easily centralized for analysis.

Even though system administrators always knew to look at logs in case of problems, massive server operating system (both Windows and Unix/Linux variants) log analysis didn't materialize until more recently. Collecting logs from Windows servers, for example, was hindered by the lack of agentless log collection tools, such as Lasso, that only emerged in the last year or two. On the other hand, Unix server log analysis was severely undercut by a total lack of unified format for log content in syslog records.

Web server logs were long analyzed by marketing departments to check on their online campaign successes. Most Web server administrators would also not ignore those logs. However, because Web servers don't have native log forwarding capabilities (most log to files stored on the server itself), consistent centralized Web log analysis for both security and other IT purposes is still ramping up.

For example, the open-source Apache Web server has several types of logs. The most typical among them are *access_log* that contains all page requests made to the server (with their response codes) and *error_log* that contains various errors and problems. Other Apache logs relate to Secure Sockets Layer (SSL) (*ssl_error_log*) as well as optional granular assessment logs that can be configured using tools such as ModSecurity (which produces an additional highly-detailed *audit_log*).

Similarly, e-mail tracking through e-mail server logs languishes in a somewhat similar manner: people only turn to e-mail logs when something goes wrong (e-mail failures) or horribly wrong (external party subpoenas your logs). Lack of native centralization and, to some extent, complicated log formats slowed down the e-mail log analysis initiatives.

Even more than e-mail, database logging wasn't on the radar of most IT folks until last year. In fact, IT folks were perfectly happy with the fact that even though Relational Database Management Systems (RDBMSs) had extensive logging and data access assessment capabilities, most of them were never turned on – many times citing performance issues. Oracle, Microsoft Structured Query Language (SQL) Server, IBM DB2, and MySQL all provide excellent logging, if you know how to enable it, configure it for your specific needs, and analyze and leverage the resulting onslaught of data. In the context of PCI DSS, database monitoring is often performed not using logs but instead using a separate software called DAM.

What's next? Web applications and large enterprise application frameworks largely lived in a world of their own, but now people are starting to realize that their log data provides unique insight into insider attacks, insider data theft, and other trusted access abuse. Additionally, desktop operating system log analysis from large numbers of deployed desktops will also follow.

PCI RELEVANCE OF LOGS

Before we begin with covering additional details on logging and monitoring in PCI, one question needs to be addressed. It often happens that PCI Qualified Security Assessors (QSAs) or security consultants are approached by the merchants: what exactly must they log and monitor for PCI DSS compliance? The honest answer to the above question is that there is no list of what exactly you must be logging due to PCI or, pretty much, any other recent compliance mandate. That is true despite the fact that PCI rules are more specific than most other recent regulations, affecting information security. However, the above does not mean that you can log nothing.

The only thing that can be explained is what you *should* be logging. There is no easy "MUST-log-this" list; it is pretty much up to individual assessor, consultant, vendor, engineer, and so forth to interpret – not simply "read," but interpret! – PCI DSS guidance in your own environment. In addition, when planning what to log and monitor, it makes sense to start from compliance requirement as opposed to end with what PCI DSS suggests. After all, organization can derive value from using it, even without regulatory or industry compliance.

So, which logs are relevant to your PCI project? In some circumstances, the answer is "all of them," but it is more likely that logs from systems that handle credit-card information, as well as systems they connect to, will be in-scope. Please refer to the data flow diagram that was described in Chapter 4, "Building and Maintaining a Secure Network," to determine which systems actually PCI DSS requirements apply to all members, merchants, and service providers that store, process, or transmit cardholder data. Additionally, these requirements apply to all "system components," which are defined as "any network component, server, or application included in, or connected to, the cardholder data environment." Network components include, but are not limited to, firewalls, switches, routers, wireless access points, network appliances, and other security appliances. Servers include, but are not limited to, Web, database, authentication, Domain Name System (DNS), e-mail, proxy, and Network Time Protocol (NTP). Applications include all off-the-shelf and custom-built applications, including internally facing and externally facing Web applications.

By the way, it is important to remind you that approaching logging and monitoring with the *sole* purpose of becoming PCI compliant is not only wasteful but can actually undermine the intent of PCI DSS compliance. Staring from its intent – cardholder data security – is the way to go, which we advocate.

The following are a few common uses for log information, besides PCI DSS compliance:

- Threat detection: Even before PCI times in the 1990s, host intrusion detection system (HIDS) looked at assessment trails and logs in search of patterns and strings in logs and raised alerts upon seeing them. Today, hunting for signs of hacking attempts (as well as successes in the form of "compromise detection") in logs is just as useful.

- Incident response and troubleshooting: When a system is hacked, logs are the most informative, accessible, and relatively easy to analyze (compared to full disk images) form of incident evidence.

- Audit: IT auditors as well as PCI assessors commonly ask for logs from in-scope systems.

- E-discovery: Although some say that a possibility of a subpoena or an e-discovery requests provides a compelling reason to not have logs, in reality, hiding one's head in the sand is unlikely to work in this case.

- IT performance management and troubleshooting network is slow? Looking at logs will help find out why.

- Network management: Although log pundits might argue on whether a Simple Network Management Protocol (SNMP) trap is a kind of log record, logs are useful for many bandwidth management and network performance measurement tasks that are common in IT.

- Other compliance: Just about every recent regulatory compliance or "best practices" framework touches on assessment logs, now we are ready to dive into the specifics of PCI and logging.

LOGGING IN PCI REQUIREMENT 10

Let's quickly go through Requirement 10, which directly addresses logging. We will go through it line by line and then go into details, examples, and implementation guidance.

The requirement itself is called "Track and monitor all access to network resources and cardholder data" and is organized under the "Regularly monitor and test networks" heading. The theme thus deals with both periodic (test) and ongoing (monitor) aspects of maintaining your security; we are focusing on logging and monitoring and have addressed periodic testing in Chapter 8, "Vulnerability Management." More specifically, it requires a network operator to track and monitor all access to network resources and cardholder data. Thus, both network resources that handle the data and the data itself are subject to those protections.

Further, the requirement states that logging is critical, primarily when "something does go wrong" and one needs to "determine the cause of a compromise" or other problem. Indeed, logs are of immense importance for incident response. However, using logs for routine user tracking and system analysis cannot be underestimated. Next, the requirement is organized in several sections on process, events that need to be logged, suggested level of details, time synchronization, assessment log security, required log review, and log retention policy.

Specifically, Requirement 10.1 covers "establish[ing] a process for linking all access to system components (especially access done with administrative privileges such as root) to each individual user." This is a very interesting requirement indeed; it doesn't just mandate for logs to be there or for a logging process to be set, but instead it mentions that logs must be tied to individual persons (not computers or "devices" where they are produced). It is this requirement that often creates problems for PCI implementers because many think of logs as "records of people actions," while in reality they will only have the "records of computer actions." Mapping the latter to actual flesh-and-blood users often presents an additional challenge. By the way, PCI DSS Requirement 8.1 mandates that an organization "assigns all users a unique ID before allowing them to access system components or cardholder data, which" helps to make the logs more useful here.

NOTE

Question: Do I have to manually read every single log record daily to satisfy PCI Requirement 10?

Answer: No, automated log analysis and review is acceptable and, in fact, recommended in PCI DSS.

Next, Section 10.2 defines a minimum list of system events to be logged (or, to allow "the events to be reconstructed"). Such requirements are motivated by the need to assess and monitor user actions as well as other events that can affect credit-card data (such as system failures).

Following is the list from the requirements (events that must be logged) from PCI DSS:

- 10.2.1: All individual user accesses to cardholder data

- 10.2.2: All actions taken by any individual with root or administrative privileges

- 10.2.3: Access to all audit trails

- 10.2.4: Invalid logical access attempts

- 10.2 5: Use of identification and authentication mechanisms

- 10.2.6: Initialization of the audit logs

- 10.2.7: Creation and deletion of system-level objects

As can be seen, this covers data access, privileged user actions, log access and initialization, failed and invalid access attempts, authentication and authorization decisions, and system object changes. It is important to note that such a list has its roots in IT governance "best practices," which prescribe monitoring access, authentication, authorization change management, system availability, and suspicious activity. Thus, other regulations, such as the Sarbanes–Oxley Act and IT governance frameworks such as COBIT, have very similar lists of events that need to be logged.

NOTE

We hope that in the future, such a list of system events will be determined by the overall log standards that go beyond PCI. There are ongoing log standard projects such as Common Event Expression (CEE) from MITRE [2] that have a chance to produce such a universally accepted (or at least, industry-accepted) list of events in the next 2 to 3 years.

Table 9.3 is a practical example of the list on the previous page.

Moreover, PCI DSS Requirement 10 goes into an even deeper level of detail and covers specific data fields or values that need to be logged for each event. They provide a healthy minimum requirement, which is commonly exceeded by logging mechanisms in various IT platforms.

Table 9.3 Logging Requirement and How to Address Them

Requirement Number	Requirement	Example Type of a Log Message
10.2.1	All individual user accesses to cardholder data	Successful logins to processing server (Unix, Windows)
10.2.2	All actions taken by any individual with root or administrative privileges	Sudo root actions on a processing server
10.2.3	Access to all audit trails	Execution of Windows event viewer
10.2.4	Invalid logical access attempts	Failed logins (Unix, Windows)
10.2.5	Use of identification and authentication mechanisms	All successful, failed, and invalid login attempts
10.2.6	Initialization of the audit logs	Windows audit log cleaned alert
10.2.7	Creation and deletion of system-level objects	Unix user added, Windows security policy updated, database created

Such fields are as follows:

- 10.3.1: User identification

- 10.3.2: Type of event

- 10.3.3: Date and time

- 10.3.4: Success or failure indication

- 10.3.5: Origination of event

- 10.3.6: Identity or name of affected data, system component, or resource

As shown, this minimum list contains all the basic attributes needed for incident analysis and for answering the questions: when, who, where, what, and where from. For example, if you are trying to discover who modified a credit-card database to copy all the transactions with all the details into a hidden file (a typical insider privilege abuse), you would need-to-know all the above. Table 9.4 summarizes the above fields in this case.

Requirement 10.4 addresses a commonly overlooked but critical requirement: a need to have accurate and consistent time in all of the logs. It seems fairly straightforward that time and security event monitoring would go hand in hand as well.

Table 9.4 PCI Event Details

PCI Requirement	Purpose
10.3.1: User identification	Which user account is associated with the event being logged? This might not necessarily mean "which person," only which username
10.3.2: Type of event	Was it a system configuration change? File addition? Database configuration change? Explains what exactly happened
10.3.3: Date and time	When did it happen? This information helps in tying the event to an actual person
10.3.4: Success or failure indication	Did he or she try to do something else that failed before his or her success in changing the configuration?
10.3.5: Origination of event	Where did he or she connect from? Was it a local access or network access? This also helps in tying the log event to a person. Note that this can also refer to the process or application that originated the event
10.3.6: Identity or name of affected data, system component, or resource	What is the name of the database, system object, and so forth which was affected? Which server did it happen on? This provides important additional information about the event

System time is frequently found to be arbitrary in a home or small office network. It's whatever time your server was set at, or if you designed your network for some level of reliance, your systems are configured to obtain time synchronization from a reliable source, like the NTP servers.

A need to "synchronize all critical system clocks and times" can make or break your incident response or lead to countless hours spent figuring out the actual times of events by correlating multiple sources of information together. In some cases, uncertainty about the log timestamps might even lead a court case to be dismissed because uncertainly about timestamps might lead to uncertainty in other claims as well. For example, from "so you are saying you are not sure when exactly it happened?" an expert attorney might jump to "so maybe you are not even sure what happened?" Fortunately, this requirement is relatively straightforward to address by configuring an NTP environment and then configuring all servers to synchronize time with it. The primary NTP servers can synchronize time with *time.nist.gov* or other official time sources, also called "Stratum 1" sources.

Stratum 1 time sources are those devices acquiring time data from direct sources like the atomic clocks run by various government entities or Global Positioning System (GPS) satellites. Local hardware, in fact, is considered Stratum 1; it gets time from its own CMOS. Stratum 2 gets its time from Stratum 1 and so on. For purposes of PCI compliance, Stratum 2 is sufficient to "prove" time, as long as all systems in the PCI environment synchronize their clocks with the Stratum 2 source via the network. Obviously, having reliable power and network is critical to this sort of approach.

Security of the logs themselves is of paramount importance for reasons similar to the above concerns about the log time synchronization. Requirement 10.5 states that one needs to "secure audit trails so they cannot be altered" and then clarifies various risks that need to be addressed.

Because it is a key issue, we will look at the security of monitoring data and logs in the next section.

MONITORING DATA AND LOG SECURITY ISSUES

Although PCI is more about being compliant than about being hacked (well, not directly!), logs certainly help to answer this question. However, if logs themselves are compromised by the attackers and the log server is broken into, they lose all values for either security or compliance purposes. Thus, having assured log confidentiality, integrity, and availability (CIA) is a requirement for PCI as well as a best practice for other log uses.

First, one needs to address all the CIA of logs. Section 10.5.1 of PCI DSS covers the confidentiality: "Limit viewing of audit trails to those with a job-related need." This means that only those who need to see the logs to accomplish their jobs should be able to. What is so sensitive about logs? One of the obvious answers is that authentication-related logs will always contain usernames. Although not truly secret, username information provides 50 percent of the information needed for password guessing (password being the other 50 percent). Why give possible attackers (whether internal or external) this information? Moreover, because of users mistyping their credentials, it is not uncommon for passwords themselves to show up in logs. Poorly written Web applications might result in a password being logged together with the Web Uniform Resource Locator (URL) in Web server logs. Similarly, a Unix server log might contain a user password if the user accidentally presses "Enter" one extra time while logging in.

Next comes "integrity." As per Section 10.5.2 of PCI DSS, one needs to "protect audit trail files from unauthorized modifications." This one is blatantly obvious; because if logs can be modified by unauthorized parties (or by anybody), they stop being an objective assessment trail of system and user activities.

However, one needs to preserve the logs not only from malicious users but also from system failures and consequences of system configuration errors. This touches upon both the "availability" and "integrity" of log data. Specifically, Section 10.5.3 of PCI DSS covers that one needs to "promptly back-up audit trail files to a centralized log server or media that is difficult to alter." Indeed, centralizing logs to a server or a set of servers that can be used for log analysis is essential for both log protection and increasing log usefulness. Backing up logs to CDs or DVDs (or tapes, for that matter) is another action one has to perform as a result of this requirement. One should always keep in mind that logs on tape are not easily accessible and not searchable in case of an incident.

Many pieces of network infrastructure such as routers and switches are designed to log to an external server and only preserve a minimum (or none) of logs on the device itself. Thus, for those systems, centralizing logs is most critical. Requirement 10.5.4 of PCI DSS states the need to "copy logs for wireless networks onto a log server on the internal LAN."

To further decrease the risk of log alteration as well as to enable proof that such alteration didn't take place, Requirement 10.5.5 calls for the "use file integrity monitoring and change detection software on logs to ensure that existing log data cannot be changed without generating alerts." At the same time, adding new log data to a log file should not generate an alert because log files tend to grow and not shrink on their own (unless logs are rotated or archived to external storage). File integrity monitoring systems use cryptographic hashing algorithms to compare files to a known good copy.

The issue with logs is that log files tend to grow due to new record addition, thus undermining the utility of integrity checking. To resolve this difficulty one should note that integrity monitoring can only assure the integrity of logs that are not being actively written to by the logging components. However, there are solutions that can verify the integrity of growing logs.

The next requirement is one of the most important as well as one of the most overlooked. Many PCI implementers simply forget that PCI Requirement 10 does not just call for "having logs" but also for "having the logs and looking at them." Specifically, Section 10.6 states that the PCI organization must, as per PCI DSS, "review logs for all system components *at least daily*. Log reviews must include those servers that perform security functions like IDSs and AAA servers (e.g., RADIUS)."

Thus, the requirement covers the scope of log sources that need to be "reviewed daily" and not just configured to log and have logs preserved or centralized. Given that a Fortune 1000 IT environment might produce gigabytes of logs per day, it is humanly impossible to read all of the logs. That is why a note is added to this requirement of PCI DSS that states that "Log harvesting, parsing, and alerting tools may be used to achieve compliance with Requirement 10.6." Indeed, log management tools are the only way to go to satisfy this requirement.

The final Requirement 10.7 deals with another hugely important logging question – log retention. It says to "retain audit trail history for at least one year, with a minimum of three months online availability." Unlike countless other requirements, this deals with the complicated log retention question directly. Thus, if you are not able to go back 1 year and look at the logs, you are in violation. Moreover, PCI DSS in its updated version v1.1 got more prescriptive when a 1-year requirement was added explicitly.

So, let us summarize what we have learned so far on logging in PCI:

- PCI Requirement 10 calls for logging specific events with a predefined level of details from all in-scope systems.

- PCI calls for tying the actual users to all logged actions.

- All clocks and time on the in-scope systems should be synchronized.

- The CIA of all collected logs should be protected.

- Logs should be regularly reviewed; specific logs should be reviewed at least daily.

- All in-scope logs should be retained for at least 1 year.

Now, we are ready to dig deeper to discover that logs and monitoring "live" not only within Requirement 10 but in all other PCI requirements.

LOGGING AND MONITORING IN PCI – ALL OTHER REQUIREMENTS

Although many people think that logs in PCI are represented only by Requirement 10, the reality is more complicated: logs are in fact present, undercover, in all other sections. We will now reveal where they hide in other sections. Table 9.5 highlights some of the places where logging requirements are implied or mentioned. The overall theme here is that logging and log management assists with validation and verification of many other requirements.

Table 9.5 Logging and Monitoring across PCI DSS Requirements

	Domain	Requirement	Logging Relevance and Recommendations
1	Build and maintain a secure network	Install and maintain a firewall configuration to protect cardholder data	Enable firewall logging, review logs for access violations, use of risky protocols, device configuration changes, accesses to critical network segments
2	Build and maintain a secure network	Do not use vendor-supplied defaults for system passwords and other security parameters	Review logs to look for insecure services, additional services starting on servers, as well as password changes upon server deployment
3	Protect cardholder data	Protect stored cardholder data	Review the logs related to key management to verify that the requirements (such as key changes) are being followed
4	Protect cardholder data	Encrypt transmission of cardholder data across open, public networks	Look at firewall, virtual private network logs to verify that only secure network communication is used
5	Maintain a vulnerability management program	Use and regularly update antivirus software	Verify that antivirus software is updated by looking at antivirus logs; also look for detection and mitigation failures that might indicate that malware is present on the network
6	Maintain a vulnerability management program	Develop and maintain secure systems and applications	Make sure that custom applications written or customized for your environment also provide logging. Watch logs of system update and software distribution servers to make sure that patches are being deployed when needed on all relevant servers
7	Implement strong access control measures	Restrict access to cardholder data by business need-to-know	Verify that such access is indeed limited by reviewing the access logs

Continued

	Domain	Requirement	Logging Relevance and Recommendations
Table 9.5		Logging and Monitoring across PCI DSS Requirements *Continued*	
8	Implement strong access control measures	Assign a unique ID to each person with computer access	Perform log correlation to detect ID sharing in violation of this requirement; review logs indicating changes to users' privileges; verify password changes based on authentication systems logs, and so forth. Look for administrator and root accounts that can sometimes be shared (and are rarely removed from systems)
9	Implement strong access control measures	Restrict physical access to card-holder data	Collect, analyze, and review physical access control system logs
10	Regularly monitor and test networks	Track and monitor all access to network resources and cardholder data	Covered above; this is the main logging and monitoring requirement
11	Regularly monitor and test networks	Regularly test security systems and processes	Monitor intrusion detection/prevention systems and file integrity checking
12	Maintain an information security policy	Maintain a policy that addresses information security	Make sure that logging and monitoring are represented in your security policy as well as operational standards, procedures, and management reports

Now, let's dive deeper into the role of logs to further explain that logs are not only about the Requirement 10. Just about every claim that is made to satisfy the requirements, such as data encryption or antivirus updates, can make effective use of log files to actually substantiate it.

For example, Requirement 1, "Install and maintain a firewall configuration to protect cardholder data," mentions that organizations must have "a formal process for approving and testing all external network connections and changes to the firewall configuration." However, after such a process is established, one needs to validate that firewall configuration changes do happen with authorization and in accordance with documented change management procedures. That is where logging becomes extremely handy, because it shows you what actually happened and not just what was supposed to happen.

Specifically, seeing a message such as this Cisco ASA appliance record should indicate that someone is likely trying to modify the appliance configuration.

```
%ASA-5-502103: User priv level changed: Uname: jsmith From:
privilege_level1 To: privilege_level2
```

Or this message indicates a failure to complete configuration update:

```
%ASA-5-111004: 10.1.1.1 end configuration: FAILED
```

Other log-related areas within Requirement 1 include Section 1.1.6.

"Justification and documentation for any available protocols besides Hypertext Transfer Protocol (HTTP), SSL, Secure Shell (SSH), and virtual private network (VPN) where logs should be used to watch for all events triggered due to such communication."

Section 1.1.7: Justification and documentation for any risky protocols allowed (for example, File Transfer Protocol [FTP]), which includes the reason for use of protocol and security features implemented, where logs help to catalog the user of "risky" protocols and then monitor such use.

The entire Requirement 1.3 contains guidance to firewall configuration, with specific statements about inbound and outbound connectivity. One must use firewall logs to verify this; even a review of configuration would not be sufficient, because only logs show "how it really happened" and not just "how it was configured."

Similarly, Requirement 2 talks about password management "best practices" as well as general security hardening, such as not running unneeded services. Logs can show when such previously disabled services are being started, either by misinformed system administrators or by attackers.

For example, if Apache Web server is disabled on an e-mail server system, a message such as the following should trigger an alert because the service should not be starting or restarting.

```
[Sun Jul 18 04:02:09 2004] [notice] Apache/1.3.19 (Unix) (Red-
Hat/Linux) mod_ssl/2.8.1 OpenSSL/0.9.6 DAV/1.0.2 PHP/4.0.4pl1
mod_perl/1.24_01 configured — resuming normal operations
```

Further, Requirement 3, which deals with data encryption, has direct and unambiguous links to logging. For example, the entire subsection 3.6, shown below in an abbreviated form, implies having logs to verify that such activity actually takes place.

"3.6: Fully document and implement all key management processes and procedures for keys used for encryption of cardholder data, including the following:

3.6.1: Generation of strong keys

3.6.2: Secure key distribution

3.6.3: Secure key storage

3.6.4: Periodic changing of keys

3.6.5: Destruction of old keys"

Specifically, key generation, distribution, and revocation are logged by most encryption systems, and such logs are critical for satisfying this requirement.

Requirement 4, which also deals with encryption, has logging implications for similar reasons.

Requirement 5 refers to antivirus defenses. Of course, to satisfy Section 5.2, which requires that you "Ensure that all antivirus mechanisms are current, actively running, and capable of generating audit logs," one needs to see such mentioned logs.

For example, Symantec AntiVirus might produce the following log record that occurs when the antivirus software experiences problems and cannot continue scanning, thus putting you in violation of PCI DSS rules.

```
Product: Symantec AntiVirus - Error 1706. AntiVirus cannot
continue.
```

Thus, unless you are monitoring for such event records, you cannot be in compliance.

So, even the requirement to "use and regularly update antivirus software" will likely generate requests for log data during the assessment, because the information is present in antivirus assessment logs. It is also well-known that failed antivirus updates, also reflected in logs, expose the company to malware risks because antivirus without the latest signature updates only creates a false sense of security and undermines the compliance effort.

Requirement 6 is in the same league: it calls for the organizations to "Develop and maintain secure systems and applications," which is unthinkable without a strong assessment logging function and application security monitoring.

Requirement 7, which states that one needs to "Restrict access to cardholder data by business need-to-know," requires logs to validate who actually had access to said data. If the users who should be prevented from seeing the data appear in the log files as accessing the data usefully, remediation is needed.

Assigning an unique ID to each user accessing the system fits with other security "best practices." In PCI, it is not just a "best practice"; it is a requirement (Requirement 8 "Assign a unique ID to each person with computer access").

Obviously, one needs to "Control addition, deletion, and modification of user IDs, credentials, and other identifier objects" (Section 8.5.1 of PCI DSS). Most systems log such activities.

For example, the message below indicates a new user being added to a PIX/ASA firewall.

```
%ASA-5-502101: New user added to local dbase: Uname: anilt
Priv: 1 Encpass: 56Rt8U
```

In addition, Section 8.5.9, "Change user passwords at least every 90 days," can also be verified by reviewing the logs files from the server to assure that all the accounts have their password changed at least every 90 days.

Requirement 9 presents a new realm of security – physical access control. Even Section 9.4 that covers maintaining a visitor log (likely in the form of a physical log book) is connected to log management if such a visitor log is electronic. There are separate data retention requirements for such logs: "Use a visitor log to maintain a physical assessment trail of visitor activity. Retain this log for a minimum of three months, unless otherwise restricted by law."

Requirement 11 addresses the need to scan (or "test") the in-scope systems for vulnerabilities. However, it also calls for the use of IDS or IPS in Section 11.4: "Use network intrusion detection systems, host-based intrusion detection systems, and intrusion prevention systems to monitor all network traffic and alert personnel to suspected compromises. Keep all intrusion detection and prevention engines up-to-date." Intrusion detection is only useful if monitored.

Requirement 12 covers the issues on a higher level – security policy as well as security standards and daily operational procedures (e.g., a procedure for daily log review mandates by Requirement 10 should be reflected here). However, it also has logging implications because assessment logging should be a part of every security policy. In addition, incident response requirements are also tied to logging: "Establish, document, and distribute security incident response and escalation procedures to ensure timely and effective handling of all situations" is unthinkable to satisfy without effective collection and timely review of log data.

Thus, event logging and security monitoring in PCI DSS program goes much beyond Requirement 10. Only through careful data collection and analysis can companies meet the broad requirements of PCI.

TOOLS FOR LOGGING IN PCI

At this stage, we went through all of the PCI guidelines and uncovered where logging and monitoring are referenced. We now have a mammoth task ahead – how to address all those requirements? Let's quickly go back and review what we learned, both in Requirement 10 and beyond.

- We need to make sure that we log specific events with a predefined level of detail from all in-scope systems.

- PCI calls for tying the actual users to all logged actions.

- All time on the in-scope systems should be synchronized.

- The CIA of all collected logs should be protected. In addition, auditing access to audit logs is also essential.

- Logs – and other monitoring data – should be regularly reviewed; specific logs should be reviewed at least daily. Automation of such review is not only acceptable but desirable, because manual review is guaranteed to fail (on high-volume networks).

- All in-scope logs should be retained for at least 1 year, with live availability for 3 months.

- In-scope systems include at least all systems that directly process credit-card data (such as PAN and other private cardholder information), including underlying operating systems as well as data processing applications, systems that store such data, network infrastructure for networks where such data is transmitted, and systems that protect any of the above (such as firewalls, NIDS, and Internet Protocol Security [IPS]). This also includes systems not specifically segregated from these processing servers and applications.

Let's analyze the above requirements and needs to determine what kind of tools we might need to develop or procure.

First, let's note that if we are talking about a single server and a single piece of network gear such as a router, there might be no need for automation and tools. One can easily configure logging and then look at the logs (measuring a few pages of text a day or more, in case more comprehensive assessing is performed), as well as save a copy of said logs to make sure that one can go back a year and review the old logs if needed. However, this approach fails miserably and dramatically when the number of systems grows from 1 to, say, 10. In reality, a large e-commerce site or a whole chain of stores might easily have thousands of in-scope systems, starting from mainframes with customer databases down to servers to complex network architectures (including classic LANs, WANs, wireless networks, and remote access systems with hundreds of remote users) to point of sale (POS) systems and all the way down to wireless card scanners. A handheld wireless card scanner is "a credit-card processing system" and thus is in-scope for PCI compliance.

Looking through recent media headlines, such as credit card compromises at BestBuy and other "brick and mortar" retailers, one learns that credit-card information has indeed been stolen this way.

Once it has been accepted that manual review of logs is not feasible or effective, the next attempt to satisfy the requirements usually comes in the form of scripts written by system administrators, to filter, review, and centralize the logs as well as makeshift remote logging collectors (usually limited to those log sources that support syslog, which is easy to forward to another system).

For example, one might configure all in-scope Unix servers to log a single "log server" and then write a Perl script that will scan the logs for specific strings (such as "fail*," "attack," "denied," "modify," and so forth) and then send an e-mail to the administrator upon finding one of those strings. Another script might be used to summarize the log records into a simple "report" that highlights, for example, "Top Users" or "Top IP Addresses." A few creative tools were written to implement various advanced methods of log analysis, such as rule-based or stateful correlation.

Such "solutions" work well and do not require any initial investment. Other advantages of such "homegrown" approaches are as follows:

- You are likely to get exactly what you want because you design and build the tool for your environment.

- You can develop tools that have capabilities not offered by any commercial tool vendor.

- The choice of platform, development tools, analysis methods, and everything else is yours alone.

- You can later customize the solution to suit your future needs.

- There is no up-front cost for buying software and even hardware (if you are reusing some old unused servers, which is frequently the case for such log analysis projects).

- Many system administrators say that "it is fun to do."

What makes it even easier is the availability of open source and freeware tools to address some of the pieces of log management for PCI. For example, Table 9.6 summarizes a few popular tools that can be (and in fact, have been) used in PCI log management projects.

However, if an author's extensive experience with logging and monitoring is any indication, most if not all projects of this type, no matter how well thought-out and no matter how well funded, will fail.

Table 9.6	Logging Tools Useful for PCI DSS			
Origin	**Tool**	**License**	**Purpose**	**Satisfied PCI Requirement**
BalaBit IT	syslog-ng	Open source	General purpose syslog replacement, reliable, and secure log transfer	Multiple sections of Requirement 10 and others; enabling infrastructure
Project LASSO	Project LASSO	Open source	Remote Windows event collection	Windows logging centralization; enables analysis of Windows logs covered by Requirement 10
Various	Stunnel, OpenSSH, FreeS/WAN	Open source	Secure data (including log) transfer	Log protection sections in Requirement 10
Various	MySQL, PostgreSQL	Open source	Data (including log) storage	Log retention section of Requirement 10
Various	Swatch, logwatch, logsentry	Open source	Small scripts for log filtering, alerting, and simple monitoring automation	Automated log review in Requirement 10
Risto Vaarandi	SEC	Open source	Log correlation and rule-based analysis	Automated log review in Requirement 10 on a more advanced level
OSSEC team	OSSEC	Open source	Log analysis	Automated log review in Requirement 10 on a more advanced level
OSSIM team	OSSIM	Open source	Log analysis and correlation across logs and other information sources	Automated security monitoring across various systems

One reason for it is the scalability of such custom tool. It might work great in a laboratory but fall completely flat on its face in a production environment due to data volume, complexities of infrastructure, and so forth. Log analysis or security monitoring system needs to be capable to handle volume, not only live flow but also storage. A lot of log tools work well on 10 MB of logs, but then again, so does a human brain. When you move to terabyte volumes, a lot of simple things start to require engineering marvels. Is it as hard as getting the Linux kernel (the pinnacle of open-source engineering) to achieve high performance? Probably not as hard, but the logging tool developer needs to be both a log expert and a performance expert.

In addition, the question is also whether this tool will scale with your organization or will it require a complete redesign and then rewrite when your environment grows and/or your needs change? Such efforts are usually a big drain on IT teams because people who might be doing things critical to maintaining a well-oiled "IT machine," all start writing code instead – and often not the most secure and efficient code at that.

Next, management often likes to point out that such an approach doesn't pass "the bus test" (namely, there is no satisfying and credible answer to the question, "What do we do if the smart guy who wrote this wonder of log analysis technology gets run over by a bus?").

And the final, most terrifying reason: ongoing maintenance of such tools is what deals a mortal blow to many in-house log analysis projects. System vendors change, log formats change, often without notice and without documents (provided they did have documents in the first place) thus leading to log analysis system failures with subsequent gaps in PCI-compliance log review or, worse, log collection or retention. We are aware of more than one case where a large corporation abandoned a well-built in-house log analysis tool (with capabilities superior to those of commercial vendors at the time) after spending literally millions of dollars for that reason alone: efforts to update the tool levied a heavy "tax" on team's productivity.

Thus, many people turn to commercial vendors when looking for solutions to PCI logging and monitoring challenges. On the logging side, commercial log management solutions can aggregate all data from the in-scope entities, whether applications, servers, or network gear. Such solutions enable satisfying the log data collection, monitoring, analysis, data protection, and data retention. (Why do we keep saying "retention" where some people would have used to term "storage?" It is important to note that "retention" usually implies making sure that data is stored.) Vendors also help with system configuration guidance to enable optimum logging (sometimes for a fee as "professional services"). Advantages of such an approach are obvious: on day 1, you get a supported solution as well as a degree of certainty that the vendor will maintain and improve the technology as well as have a roadmap for addressing other log-related organization needs beyond PCI compliance.

On the negative side of acquiring a PCI logging solution from a vendor sits a landmine of "unmet requirements." It might happen that what was bought and deployed doesn't match what was imagined and needed. Many factors contribute to such a situation: starting from aggressive vendor sales tactics ("overselling") to insufficient onsite testing and to not thinking about the needs before talking to vendors. Without a doubt, if you "don't know what you need," it is unlikely that you'd buy "exactly what you need."

Fortunately, there are simple things you can do to avoid the pitfall of unmet requirements when acquiring a log management solution.

- Review PCI logging guidance such as this book (as well as the standard itself) to clarify the standard's requirements.

- Consider how a log management solution would work in your environment.

- Define the need by talking to all the stakeholders in your PCI project and have the above information in mind.

Look through various commercial log management such as LogLogic (www.loglogic.com), ArcSight (www.arcsight.com), Splunk (www.splunk.com), or others to "case the joint" and to see what is out there. Congratulations! You are ready to talk to vendors. Here are a few additional questions to ask the vendor:

- Can your tool collect and aggregate 100 percent of all log data from all in-scope log sources on the network?

- Are your logs transported and stored securely to satisfy the CIA of log data?

- Are there packaged reports that suit the needs of your PCI projects stakeholders such as IT, assessors, maybe even Finance or Human Resources? Can you create the additional needed reports to organize collected log data quickly?

- Can you set alerts on anything in the logs to satisfy the monitoring requirements?

- Does the tool make it easy to look at log data on a daily basis? Can the tools help you prove that you are by maintaining an assessment trail of log review activities? (Indeed, it is common for the assessors to ask for a log that shows that you review other logs and not for the original logs from information systems! Yes, log analyst activities need to be logged as well – if this is news to you then welcome to the world of compliance!)

- Can you perform fast, targeted searches for specific data when asked? Remember, PCI is not about dumping logs on tape.

- Can you contextualize log data (say for comparing application, network, and database logs related to an in-scope system) when undertaking forensics and other operational tasks?

- Can you readily prove, based on logs, that security (such as antivirus and intrusion prevention), change management (such as user account management), and access control policies mandated by the PCI requirements are in use and up-to-date?

- Can you securely share log data with other applications and users that are involved in various compliance initiatives?

LOG MANAGEMENT TOOLS

Let's take a more detailed look at the capabilities of a typical log management solution, a common choice for security monitoring for PCI DSS. The first thing to mention is that such solutions make logs useful for security, IT performance monitoring, system and network troubleshooting, investigations, assessment, and, obviously, compliance such as PCI DSS.

For example, real-time alerting is useful primarily as a threat detection measure. To provide such data protection measures, companies should implement a log management solution that enables administrators to set alerts on all applications, devices, and system logs. This enables them to provide evidence that the infrastructure has been configured properly and that misconfigured or vulnerable systems are not providing a backdoor for intruders or malicious insiders. Alerts can provide administrators with early warning of misuse and attacks, allowing them to isolate and fix the problem before damage occurs or data is lost, and of various data access policies and processes not being followed.

NOTE

Alerts are only useful if there is a process and personnel in place to intake, analyze, and respond to alerts on a timely basis. In other words, if nobody is wearing a pager or looking for e-mail alerts, they are next to useless.

Securing the CIA of log data is explicitly mentioned in the PCI requirements above; thus, it is crucial to any implementation of a log management tool. This not only serves to reduce the risk of this vital information leaking by means of logs (confidentiality) and prevents it from being altered or lost thereby reducing its relevance, immutability, and forensic quality (integrity) but also makes sure that log data is there when you need it (availability). It is hardly possible to say which is the most important and thus the CIA triad lives on.

A need to be able to use logs to address all those PCI requirements brings us to access management and change management. Although two different areas with little overlap, both access and change managements are critical to meeting PCI compliance requirements as well as other regulations and IT governance frameworks, such as ITIL, COBIT, or various ISO guidance documents. Strong access and change control measures ensure that only authorized users can access or take action on critical data. The PCI standard mandates that companies maintain a complete record of access (both failed and successful), activity, and configuration changes for applications, servers, and network devices. Logs are that record. Thus, such log data allows IT to set up alerts to unusual or suspicious network behavior and provide information to assessors with complete and accurate validation of security policy enforcement and segregation of duties.

Further, a log management solution allows administrators to monitor who has permission to access or make changes to devices and applications in the network. It also enables administrators to create a complete assessment trail across devices and protect network resources from unauthorized access or modifications. An effective log management tool supports centralized, automated storage of collected data for faster, more reliable data retrieval during an assessment or while investigating suspicious behavior.

You probably remember that PCI compliance necessitates ongoing monitoring of network activity (see Requirement 11 and others) to validate that processes and policies for security, change and access management, and user validation are in place and up-to-date.

Logging and monitoring allow for fast problem isolation and thorough analysis when something goes (reactive analysis) or is about to go wrong (proactive analysis). Ongoing and automated log monitoring gives administrators greater insight into the PCI environment at all times so that unusual user activity, unauthorized access, or even risky insider behavior can be identified – and stopped – immediately.

In light of the above, the components of an effective log management solution are as follows:

- Collection and aggregation of 100 percent of all log data from in-scope enterprise data sources including firewalls, VPN concentrators, Web proxies, IDSs, e-mail servers, and all the other systems and applications mentioned and implied in the PCI standard

- Creation of reports that organize the log data quickly and automatically so that administrators can deliver detailed network activity information and proof of compliance to assessors

- Setting of alerts based on changes to individual devices, groups of devices, or the network, to minimize network downtime and loss of data due to malicious attacks, security breaches, insider misuse, or performance issues

- Fast data retrieval from securely stored, unaltered raw log files; immutable logs are critical in litigation and attestation

- Integration with existing network management and security solutions to reduce maintenance and administration and leverage existing architecture

- The ability to contextualize log data (comparing application, network, and database logs) when undertaking forensics and other operational tasks

OTHER MONITORING TOOLS

It is critical to remember that the scope of security monitoring in PCI DSS is not limited to logs because system logs alone do not cover all the monitoring needs. Additional monitoring requirements are covered by the following technologies (as well as process requirements that accompany them):

- Intrusion detection or intrusion prevention; mandated by PCI Requirement 11.4 "Use intrusion detection systems and/or intrusion-prevention systems to monitor all traffic in the cardholder data environment"

- File integrity monitoring; mandated by PCI Requirement 11.5 "Deploy file-integrity monitoring software to alert personnel to unauthorized modification of critical system files, configuration files, or content files"

We will cover the critical issues related to these technologies in the section below.

INTRUSION DETECTION AND PREVENTION

NIDS and IPSs are becoming a standard information security safeguard. Together with firewalls and vulnerability scanners, intrusion detection is one of the pillars of modern computer security. When referring to IDSs and IPSs today, security professional typically refers to NIDS and network IPS. As we covered in Chapter 4, "Building and Maintaining a Secure Network," the former sniffs the network, looking for traces of attacks, whereas the latter sits "inline" and passes (or blocks) network traffic.

NIDS monitors the entire subnet for network attacks against machines connected to it, using a database of attack signatures or a set of algorithms to detect anomalies in network traffic. See Fig. 9.1 for a typical NIDS deployment scenario.

On the other hand, network IPS sits at a network choke point and protects such a network of systems from inbound attacks. To simplify the difference, IDS alerts whereas IPS blocks. See Fig. 9.2 for a typical network IPS deployment.

The core technology of picking "badness" from the network traffic with a subsequent alert (IDS) or blocking (IPS) is essentially similar. Even when intrusion prevention functionality is integrated with other functions to be deployed as so-called Unified Threat Management (UTM), the idea remains

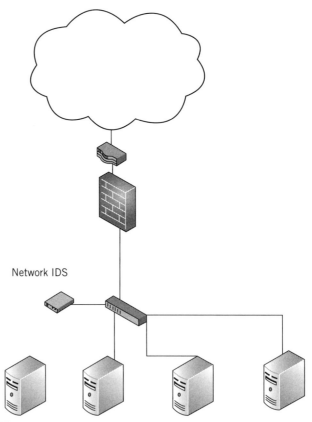

FIGURE 9.1 *Network Intrusion Detection Deployment*

the same: network traffic passes through the device with malicious traffic stopped, suspicious traffic logged, and benign passed through.

Also important is the fact that most of today's IDS and IPS rely upon the knowledge of attacks and thus require ongoing updates of signatures, rules, attack traces to look for, and so forth. This is exactly why PCI DSS mandates that IDS and IPS are not only deployed but also frequently updated and managed in accordance with manufacturer's recommendations.

In the context of PCI, IDS and IPS technologies are mentioned in the context of monitoring. Even though IDS can only alert and log attacks while IPS adds blocking functionality, both can and must be used to notify the security personnel about malicious and suspicious activities on the cardholder data networks. Below we present a few useful tips for deploying IDS and IPS for PCI DSS compliance and card data security.

Despite the domination of commercial vendors, the free open-source IDS/IPS Snort, now developed and maintained by its corporate parent, Sourcefire,

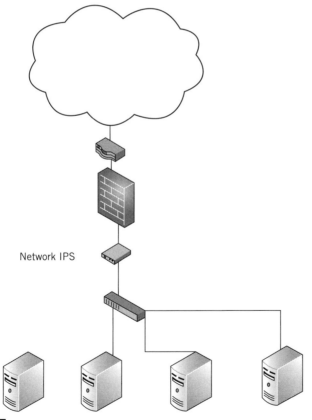

FIGURE 9.2 *Network Intrusion Prevention Deployment*

is likely the best IDS/IPS by the number of deployments worldwide. Given its price (free) and reliable rule updates from Sourcefire (www.sourcefire .com), it makes a logical first choice for smaller organizations; it shouldn't be taken off the shortlist even for larger organizations seeking to implement intrusion detection or prevention.

Although a detailed review of IDS and IPS technologies and practices goes well beyond the scope of this book, we would like to present a few key practices for making your PCI-driven deployment successful.

First, four key facts about IDS and IPS, which are also highlighted in the PCI standard:

1. IDS or IPS technology must be deployed as per PCI DSS. If another device includes IDS or IPS functionality (such as UTM mentioned above), it will likely qualify as well.

2. IDS and IPS need to "see" the network traffic in cardholder; for IDS, it needs to be able to sniff it and for IPS, to pass it through. An IDS box sitting in the closet is not PCI compliance (and definitely not security!).

3. IDS and IPS must be actively monitored by actual people, devoted (full-time, part-time, or outsources) to doing just that. PCI DSS states that systems must be set to "alert personnel to suspected compromises."

4. IDS and IPS rely on updates from the vendor; such updates must be deployed, or the devices will lose most of its value. PCI does highlight it by stating to "Keep all intrusion-detection and prevention engines up-to-date."

The above four facts define how IDS and IPS are used for the cardholder requirement. Despite the above knowledge, IDS technologies are not the easiest one to deploy, especially in light of the number 3 consideration above. PCI DSS-driven IDS deployments suffer from a few of the common mistakes covered below.

First, using an IDS or an IPS to protect the cardholder environment and to satisfy PCI DSS requirement is impossible without giving it an ability to see all the network traffic. In other words, deploying an NIDS without sufficient network environment planning is a big mistake that reduces, if not destroys, the value of such tools. Network IPS, for example, should be deployed on the network choke point such as right inside the firewall leading to cardholder network, on the appropriate internal network segment, or in the De-Militarized Zone (DMZ). For the shared Ethernet-based networks, IDS will see all the network traffic within the Ethernet collision domain or subnet and also destined to and from the subnet but no more. For the switched networks, there are several IDS deployment scenarios that use special switch capabilities such as port mirroring or spanning. When one or more IDS devices are deployed, it is your responsibility to confirm that they can "cover" the entire "in-scope" network.

Second, even if an IDS is deployed appropriately, but nobody is looking at the alerts it generates, the deployment will end in failure and will not lead to PCI compliance. It's well known that IDS is a "detection" technology, and it never promised to be a "shoot-and-forget" means of thwarting attacks. Although in some cases, the organization might get away with dropping the firewall in place and configuring the policy, such a deployment scenario never works for intrusion detection. If IDS alerts are reviewed only after a successful compromise, the system turns into an overpriced incident response helper tool, clearly not what the technology designers had in mind. Even with IPS, a lot of suspicious indicators are not reliable enough to be blocked automatically, thus monitoring is just as critical as with IDS.

PCI DSS Requirement 12.5.2 does state that an organization needs to "Monitor and analyze security alerts and information, and distribute to appropriate personnel." Still, despite this, many organizations deploy IDS and develop a no response policy. As a result, their network IPS is deployed, it "sees" all the traffic, and there is somebody reviewing the alert stream. But what is the response for each potential alert? Panic, maybe? Does the person viewing the alerts know the best course of action needed for each event? What alerts are typically "false positives" – alerts being triggered on benign activity – and "false alarms" – alerts being triggered on attacks that cannot harm the target systems – in the protected environment? Unless these questions are answered, it is likely that no intelligent action is being taken based on IDS alerts – a big mistake by itself, even without PCI DSS.

The fourth and final mistake is simply not accepting the inherent limitations of network intrusion protection technology. Although anomaly-based IDSs might detect an unknown attack, most signature-based IDS will miss a new exploit if there is no rule written for it. IDS and IPS must frequently receive vendor signature updates, as mandates by the PCI DSS. Even if updates are applied on a schedule, exploits that are unknown to the IDS vendor will probably not be caught by the signature-based system. Attackers may also try to blind or evade the NIDS by using many tools available for download. There is a constant battle between the technology developers and those who want to escape detection. IPS/IDS are becoming more sophisticated and able to see through the old evasion methods, but new approaches are constantly being developed by attackers. Those deploying the NIDS technology should be aware of its limitations and practice "defense-in-depth" by deploying multiple and diverse security solutions.

Thus, IDS/IPS is a key monitoring technology for PCI DSS and data protection; however, when deploying it, many pitfalls need to be considered if it were to be useful for PCI compliance and security.

INTEGRITY MONITORING

In the prehistoric days of security industry, before all the current compliance frenzy and way before PCI DSS, the idea of monitoring key system files for changes was invented. As early system administrators engaged in an unequal battle with hackers who compromised almost every server connected to the Internet, the idea of a quick and easy way for verifying that system files was not modified and thus not subverted by hackers seemed like a god-send.

Indeed, just run a quick "scan" of a filesystem, compute cryptographic checksums, save them in a safe place (a floppy comes to mind – we are talking 90s here, after all), and then have a "known good" record of the system files. In case of problems, run another checksum computation and compare the results; if differences are found, then something or someone has subverted the files.

That is exactly the idea of integrity checking and monitoring. The tools such as the pioneering tripwire (now developed by its corporate parent, Tripwire, Inc) have matured significantly and offer near real-time checks, an ability to revert to the previous version of the changed files, as well as a detailed analysis of observed changes across a wide range of platforms for servers, desktops, and even network devices.

NOTE

Question: What is the difference between host intrusion detection and integrity monitoring?

Answer: Many different types of applications are labeled as host-based intrusion detection. In general, the distinction is that with IDS, the end goal is the detection of malicious activity in a host environment, whereas an integrity monitoring system aims to provide visibility into all kinds of change. Detecting malicious change or activity is a big part of an integrity monitoring system but that is not the entire motivation behind its deployment.

As we mentioned, PCI DSS mandates the use of such tools via Requirement 11.5. Namely, "Deploy file-integrity monitoring software to alert personnel to unauthorized modification of critical system files, configuration files, or content files; and configure the software to perform critical file comparisons at least weekly."

This means that the tools must be deployed on in-scope systems, key files need to be monitored, and comparisons are to be run at least weekly.

Indeed, knowing that the server has been compromised by attackers a week after the incident is a lot better than what some recent credit-card losses indicate. For example, TJX card theft was discovered *years* after the actual intrusion took place, causing the company some massive embarrassment.

On the tools side, although Tripwire rules the commercial file integrity monitoring, its open-source clone is also of the best known free, open-source tools. Free tripwire is even included with some Linux and Unix operating systems.

Some of the challenges with such tools include creating a list of key files to checksum. Typically, relying on integrity checking tool vendor default (or even "PCI DSS-focused") policy is a good idea. Here is an example list of such files for a typical Linux server:

- Configuration files in /etc directory

- All system executables (/bin,/usr/bin, /usr/sbin, and other possible binary directories)

- Key payment application executable, configuration, and data files

- Log files /var/log (these require a special append-only mode in your integrity monitoring)

Also, just as with IDS and IPS, a response policy in case of breach of integrity is essential.

Finally, let's review our suggestions on monitoring and logging policy for PCI DSS.

TOOLS

On a more detailed level, here are some sample PCI-related reports and alerts for log review and monitoring.

Alerts used for real-time monitoring of in-scope servers are as follows:

- New account created
- New privileges added to a user account
- Firewall rules change
- Multiple failed logins
- Critical system restarted
- Antivirus protection failed to load
- Malware detected
- Logs created or log subsystem started
- Log collection failed from an in-scope system

Reports used for daily review of preanalyzed data are as follows:

- Risky firewall traffic
- All traffic other than that allowed by PCI
- Software update activities
- User account changes on servers (e.g., additions, deletions, and modifications)
- Login activity on in-scope servers
- User group membership changes
- Password changes on in-scope servers and network devices
- All administrator/root activities on in-scope servers
- Log review activities on a log management solution

By now the reader should be convinced that it is impossible to comply with PCI requirements without log data management processes and technologies in place. Complete log data is needed to prove that security, change management, access control, and other required processes and policies are in use, up-to-date, and are being adhered to. In addition, when managed well, log data can protect companies when compliance-related legal issues arise (e.g., when processes and procedures are in question or when an e-discovery process is initiated as part of an ongoing investigation). Not only does log data enable compliance but also allows companies to prove that they are implementing and continuously monitoring the processes outlined by the requirements.

COMMON MISTAKES AND PITFALLS

Additionally, we will present a few common mistakes noted in PCI DSS-driven logging implementations.

- Logging in the PCI DSS is not confined to Requirement 10. As we discussed above, all the requirements imply having a solid log management policy, program, and tools.

- Logging in PCI is not only about log collection retention; Requirement 10.6 directly states that you need to review, not just accumulate logs.

- Log review in PCI does not mean that you have to read the logs yourself; using automated log management tools is not only allowed but suggested.

- A careful review of what is in-scope must be performed. Otherwise, one creates a potentially huge issue for the organization in terms of having what is thought of as a solid PCI program, but then suffering a data breach and getting fined due to missing a wireless POS system or some other commonly overlooked but clearly in-scope systems. (Well, at least it becomes clear after your organization is fined.)

- Your logging tools purchased and deployed for PCI compliance are almost certainly useful for other things ranging from other compliance mandates (see the above example of PCI and Sarbanes–Oxley) as well as operational, security, investigative, incident response, and other uses.

CASE STUDY

Next, we present two of the case studies that illustrate what is covered in this chapter.

The Case of the Risky Risk-Based Approach

This case study covers deployment of a log management solution to satisfy PCI requirements at a large retail chain in the Midwest. Bert's Bazaar, an off-price retailer servicing the Midwest and southern US states, decided to deploy a commercial log management solution when their PCI assessor strongly suggested that they need to look into it. Given that Bert has a unique combination of a large set of in-scope systems (some running esoteric operating systems and custom applications) and an extreme shortage of skilled IT personnel, they chose to buy a commercial solution without seriously considering an in-house development. So, they progressed from not doing anything with their logs directly to running an advanced log management system.

The project took a few months following a phased approach. Bert's IT staff decided to implement it from the outside based on their risk assessment. They started from their DMZ firewalls and then progressed with feeding the following logs into a log management system, while simultaneously defining alerts and running reports from vendor's PCI compliance package.

Their project proceeded as follows:

1. All Internet DMZ firewalls

2. Select internal firewalls that control access to payment processing systems

3. DMZ front-end processing servers – operating system only

4. Other payment processing servers – operating system only

5. Databases that are involved in payment processing

6. Actual payment processing applications from all involved servers

A few things need to be said about the above approach. One common piece of technology conspicuously missing from the list is network intrusion detection. The reason is that the organization chose not to implement it due to resource shortage (even though modern NIDS have improved, they still require people to provide care and feeding). The sequence is based on both their risk assessment and the complexity of log collection. The former led them to focus on the outside threat first, whereas the latter delayed some of the log collection efforts: it is much easier to forward Cisco PIX firewall logs to an analysis server, but a database logging configuration, collection, and analysis present a significant challenge (due to multiple factors from affecting performance to grabbing logs from a database itself in a secure and reliable manner).

Overall, the project is a successful implementation of PCI logging requirements by using a commercial logging solution. The organization did pass the PCI assessment with flying colors and was commended on their comprehensive approach to logging. In addition, the security team built a case that their PCI logging implementation actually addresses a few other compliance mandates (such as US Sarbanes–Oxley Act) because PCI DSS goes into higher-level details while covering essentially the same areas of IT governance. At the same time, a log management tool also bolstered its operational capabilities and overall IT efficiency.

The Case of Tweaking to Comply

This case study is based on a major e-commerce implementation of an off-the-shelf log management technology in combination with in-house developed tools to address a unique need alongside PCI compliance. Upon encountering PCI compliance requirements, Wade's Webbies developed its own set of scripts to go through a Web server and payment application's server logs to identify hacking and fraud attempts. Such scripts were very useful but proved to be onerous to operate, update, maintain, and trouble-shoot. Additionally, a few key IT staffers who helped develop the solution departed to join a consulting company.

Thus, IT management decided to pick a commercial log management application, which will have to work together or integrate with their previous scripts (that still delivered unique value to the organization); they would use a vendor's collection and analysis log management infrastructure but retain an ability to look for fraud using their own methods.

Their log management project proceeded as follows:

1. Web server logs from DMZ Web servers

2. Operating system logs from the same Web servers

3. Custom payment processing application logs

4. Network logs from the DMZ (firewall, router)

The project approach was driven by the preexisting log analysis solution. Although the vendor solution was being deployed, they were adapting their scripts to run based on the log management vendor's API. Such API provided access to preanalyzed as well as raw log data and allowed the organization to retain a large part of the effort spent on developing the scripts. At the same time, such API capability allows the users of the tools to take advantage of the vendor's advanced log management technology as well as regular updates and customer support.

Overall, this project was a successful illustration of a combined approach of using a homegrown and commercial solution and thus achieving combined benefits.

SUMMARY

In conclusion, the authors would like to stress a few points that were covered as well as leave readers with a few thoughts about how PCI logging fits into the bigger picture of IT governance and risk management. Despite the fact that this book is about PCI DSS, we do not recommend that you embark on a log management project or on a security monitoring project solely for PCI DSS. Taking control of your logs is useful for a huge number of IT and information security goals; thus doing logs "just for compliance" is akin to using an expensive and powerful tool as a hammer. Overall, a common scenario observed by the authors is "buy for compliance [such as PCI], use for all the needed purposes." We recommend that the organizations that are subject to PCI DSS use the motivating power of PCI DSS to acquire the needed tools and then proceed to using them for solving all the problems in the whole IT security realm.

REFERENCES

[1] Sourcefire Security Calendar, www.ranum.com/security/computer_security/calendar/ [accessed 13.07.09].
[2] Common Event Expression (CEE), http://cee.mitre.org [accessed 13.07.09].

CHAPTER 10

Managing a PCI DSS Project to Achieve Compliance

Information in this chapter

You have determined that your organization needs to comply with the Payment Card Industry Data Security Standard (PCI DSS) and, looking at the requirements, you are not sure where to start. Should you jump in and go through the 12 PCI DSS requirements one at a time ensuring that the requirements are in place? Or should you first figure out at what level you need to validate your compliance? How will you make sure that your fellow associates are on board with the changes you are proposing so that you can efficiently comply with PCI DSS? Is senior management on board? How about the IT department that will actually be doing most of the work? How will you make the compliance effort come together? After putting the plan together, how will you ensure that your fellow associates have the training and information in front of them to help keep your company from falling out of compliance? Putting together a comprehensive plan will allow you to manage your compliance project efficiently and, in the end, achieve and maintain PCI DSS compliance as well as efficiently validate it.

This chapter will answer your questions about how to achieve compliance. You will learn how to justify putting in the effort and figure out if you need to comply at all. Once you know you have to comply with PCI DSS, we will explore how you will bring all the players to the table to help build and enforce the compliance plan. You will read about tips on how to budget your time and resources so that you can achieve compliance quickly. Once you have your plan in place, you will need to get the message out to your staff and ensure they receive the right training to make sure your organization does not fall out of compliance. By the end of this chapter, you should have a clear plan on where to start with your own PCI DSS compliance efforts and the steps you will need to plan a program to meet compliance.

JUSTIFYING A BUSINESS CASE FOR COMPLIANCE

One of the first steps of any compliance plan is to justify putting in the effort. You must first figure out if you need to comply with the PCI DSS regulation and also figure out if you have overlap from other compliance plans already in place. Once you know compliance is a must, you need to figure out at what level you need to validate. Depending on the card brand's program you review, PCI DSS compliance mandates apply to up to four different groups depending on volume and the medium by which you accept payments. The biggest question should be, "What is the cost of noncompliance?" Because compliance with the PCI DSS is mandatory, you will be hit with fines today depending on the level of merchant you are, and ultimately your credit-card processing capabilities could be terminated. The fines that are rolling down to merchants today should provide concrete numbers for the total amount of annual fines you can expect. The primary motivation should come from facing living through a breach. If you have never had the opportunity to manage through a major breach, ask around in your industry. There are plenty of individuals that can help you frame your message properly such that you can make a positive impact and get the funding and support from the top that you need.

Figuring Out If You Need to Comply

Your first step with any compliance effort should be figuring out if you need to comply with a regulation. Regardless of the state of the economy, no company wants to waste time putting in measures that you are not required to have. Once you have figured out if you need to comply and what your validation requirements are, you will be in a good position to make your case to management.

NOTE

If you know you have card data in your environment, then you will have to comply with PCI DSS, but are you a merchant or a service provider? Many merchants offer ancillary services to franchisees or even to other local companies to defray the costs of running their payment processing network. By doing this, many merchants end up being service providers and have slightly different reporting requirements for each card brand. If you are accepting payments from any third party (like a franchisee), you are most likely a service provider. Consult with your acquiring bank or a Qualified Security Assessor (QSA) to clarify this before you go too far down your compliance project path!

Compliance Overlap

Once you determine that you have to comply, you need to look at the other compliance plans you have in place (if any). One sure way to fast track your PCI DSS compliance program is to leverage investments made for other compliance or security initiatives. Compliance and information security initiatives often overlap (as shown in Fig. 10.1) because most of the regulations are based on good business and security practices. So, pull out your Health Insurance Portability and Accountability Act (HIPAA) of 1996 and Sarbanes–Oxley (SOX) compliance plans, and figure out which components you can reuse for your PCI DSS compliance plan. You might find that you are already

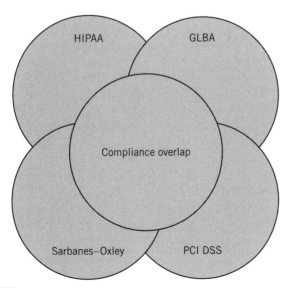

FIGURE 10.1 *Leveraging Compliance Overlap*

in compliance but need to document that the measures you have in place are consistent with the PCI DSS regulations. For more information on how common compliance initiatives overlap, see Chapter 14, "PCI and Other Laws, Mandates, and Frameworks."

The best place to start to figure out how to leverage your other compliance efforts is to set up a meeting with the team leaders from that project. You need to get an idea of how the project performed and how it was accepted by management. The main point is to find out what the other teams have done in their compliance effort and see what elements you can bring over into your PCI DSS compliance plan. For example, HIPAA and PCI DSS both have rules regarding encrypting data. Can you use your encryption policy and procedure from HIPAA for PCI DSS compliance? That answer will come as you talk to your HIPAA compliance team leaders and review the policy and procedure to see if it already fits the PCI DSS encryption requirements found in Requirements 3.4 through 3.6. Your company policy for HIPAA compliance should mandate that you have encryption in place as you transmit protected health information across public networks like the Internet. PCI DSS Requirement 4 mandates the encryption of cardholder data as it moves across public networks. In this case, you do not need to recreate the wheel; you might just need to reclassify what type of data is required to be encrypted. Any efforts spent in leveraging your existing regulatory compliance will help to shorten the time it will take for you to become PCI DSS compliant.

NOTE

To help your organization determine how many new policies and procedures you will have to put in place to become PCI DSS compliant, complete Self-Assessment Questionnaire D (SAQ-D) in the early part of planning your compliance program. SAQ-D is a good tool to help demonstrate what compliance you already have and can show what you need to do to become compliant. SAQ-D can be downloaded from the PCI Security Standards Council (PCI SSC) Web site at www.pcisecuritystandards.org/saq.

The Level of Validation

Now that you are on your way to planning your PCI DSS compliance project, you need to figure out at which level you need to validate. Unlike other regulations that present you with an all or nothing stance on how to validate your compliance, PCI DSS validation levels are based on how many credit-card transactions a merchant processes or a service provider processes/stores as well as on other related items you already read in Chapter 3, "Why Is PCI

Here?" The more transactions that are processed, the more validation activities you may have to perform.

For most organizations, validation consists of passing quarterly security network scans and completing an SAQ. If you process transactions in the millions, you need to have a QSA to validate your PCI DSS compliance through an on-site assessment. Remember, the five individual card brands set the enforcement requirements for PCI DSS, not the council. It is possible (by volume, but level reciprocity will make the merchant a Level 1 across the board) to be a Level 1 American Express merchant, a Level 2 Master-Card merchant, and Level 3 Visa Merchant all at the same time! To help you determine your merchant or service provider level, you can review the information in Chapter 3, "Why Is PCI Here?" Keep in mind, card brands frequently alter their programs, so before you go too far into this process, visit the links in Chapter 3 to get the most recent levels from each of the card brands. Or better yet, call your acquirer(s) and ask them to help you determine your level.

What Is the Cost for Noncompliance?

The question that should be answered during your justification process is: "What is the cost for not complying with PCI DSS?" In all cases, the costs (assuming the worst) associated with a breach far outweigh the costs of being compliant. Can your organization afford the fines and penalties, bad media press, and damage to its reputation? Breaches cost more during recessions as companies face dwindling or flat growth while doing everything possible to protect their cash reserves.

Your risk managers will tell you that the three things you can do with a risk is to resolve the issue, transfer the risk, or ignore the risk. The way PCI DSS states its 12 requirements – the only way to truly deal with the elements – is to resolve the issue or transfer the risk. Transferring the risk might mean that you outsource or bring in a managed service to deal with that requirement. Therefore, when you transfer the risk, you are still dealing with it indirectly. Ignoring the risk in PCI DSS is not an option. Even one noncompliant item in a Report on Compliance (ROC) or SAQ means you do not comply with PCI DSS. If you are compromised and found to be not compliant with PCI during the investigations, the fines are steep.

NOTE

Breach fines are calculated in different ways depending on the situation. Visa's Account Data Compromise Recovery (http://usa.visa.com/merchants/operations/adcr.html) program describes how Visa fines compromised merchants. They calculate fines based on the number and type of records lost. Your acquirer may be able to give you more information if you are interested in how the formula is calculated. MasterCard, in comparison, has an unpublished, but known process whereby the size of the fine is largely based on fraud rates and amounts from cards affected by your breach.

Penalties for Noncompliance

Did you know that every quarter (if you are a Level 1 to 3 Visa or MasterCard merchant) your acquiring bank is telling Visa and MasterCard if you have validated compliance? Both card brands are now actively fining merchants for noncompliance, but the amounts vary widely depending on your level. Let's take a minute to review the current fines that merchants of Level 1 to 3 can expect to receive.

Visa Compliance Acceleration Program (CAP) Fines:

- Level 1 merchants:
  - $25K each month for noncompliance ($300K/year)
  - Tiered interchange penalties, meaning that every transaction will cost you slightly more to process, potentially costing companies millions

- Level 2 merchants:
  - $5K each month for noncompliance ($60K/year)

MasterCard Fines:

- Level 1 and 2 merchants:
  - Quarterly escalating fines of $25K, $50K, $100K, and $200K ($375K/year)
  - Resets to $25K on the quarter following the $200K fine

- Level 3 merchants:
  - Quarterly escalating fines of $10K, $20K, $40K, and $80K ($150K/year)
  - Resets to $10K on the quarter following the $80K fine

While you may never find either of these programs detailed on the card brand's respective Web sites (Visa: www.visa.com/cisp/, MasterCard: www.mastercard.com/sdp/), your acquiring bank will have all the information relevant to your situation. Reach out to your acquirer first, then use the figures here (or the ones provided by your acquirer) to assist in your cost analysis. This information was obtained through previous online publications (in Visa's case) and through customer relationships (for both), and are subject to change at any time. Remember, fines come from both Visa and MasterCard now.

If you suffer a breach and your organization is found to be out of compliance with PCI DSS, the penalties can be severe. Theoretically, the organization could be forbidden to store, process, or transmit credit-card information. A more likely result would be stiff penalties from the card brands used to recoup the costs associated with fraud and becoming a Level 1 merchant for one reporting period, thus dramatically increasing your compliance costs. Each case is handled individually on its merits. With the advent of new privacy laws in different states, you might be required to notify your customers of a breach and provide them with credit reporting services. Once notifications go out, your organization's reputation will be dragged through the media and blogging community. Looking at what it takes to comply, it should be easy to see how and why you need to put together your PCI DSS compliance plan.

BRINGING THE KEY PLAYERS TO THE TABLE

Once you have justified your compliance effort, it is vital that you bring all the players to the table to ensure that you are successful in becoming compliant. You need the correct corporate sponsorship, otherwise senior management could reject any plan you put together. You need to look at your organization from the top down and identify each of the key people who are necessary to put the plan together, forming your compliance team. You need to identify the key members of your team to tackle components of the compliance plan and keep the project moving.

Compliance plans can be won or lost based on the participants you bring in to help you with the project. It is vital to bring the correct people to the table. Look hard at the people you bring into your team, as they will make putting together the compliance plan either a success or a failure. Remember what noncompliance can bring – failure is not an option.

WARNING

Be sure to get a good understanding of the current workload of the members you would like to invite to be a part of your compliance team. Many times, people are enthusiastic to be a part of a new project, but realistically they do not have the time to work on it. At the end, team members miss meetings or deadlines, which may impact deadlines associated with your compliance project.

Obtaining Corporate Sponsorship

Management sponsorship is a critical success factor for any compliance effort. If senior management does not support the process, support from the staff will also be lacking. Why should they comply if your manager does not? As the leader of your compliance effort, you need to first work with your senior managers to make them aware of the issues and let them understand the justification of why they need to comply with PCI DSS. Make them understand the cost of noncompliance, and they will back you up as soon as they realize that the company could be in jeopardy for not complying. Start at the top, because the earlier you gain support from the CEO, the faster you will get support from the Vice President and other senior management.

NOTE

Try to schedule a lunch meeting outside the office with the company CEO or other senior manager, where you would have his or her full attention, devoid of any distractions. Help him or her to understand the cost of noncompliance.

Attempt to get a senior manager on your compliance team. When other employees in the company hear that he or she is part of the team, the entire project will get more support, which will help drive home the fact that the compliance effort is vital for the organization.

Forming Your Compliance Team

Your compliance team is the focal point of your compliance project and is responsible for the success of the project plan. The best time to create your team is after you have received corporate sponsorship. Many times people who heard about the compliance project from a manager and want to participate will approach you. You need to get a good mix of people on the team to make the most impact. The PCI DSS has 12 requirements that can touch different departments in your company, so be sure to include at least one person from each of those functional areas. For example, PCI DSS requires you to build and maintain a secure network; therefore, if you do not get a team member involved from networking, you cannot be sure that a firewall is installed or maintained going forward.

Roles and Responsibilities of Your Team

Your compliance team will help set the pace and scope of your compliance project. The selection of participants will make the project a success, but it is important to make it clear from the beginning what each team member is responsible for by assigning them roles and responsibilities. You will need your team to assist in the following ways:

- Work with managers and other team members to set the scope of the compliance project

- Select leaders for each of the areas where you need compliance

- Analyze information needed for the compliance plan

- Work with senior management to ensure that the end result is compliance

Getting Results Fast

The best way to ensure a successful project and gain the respect from all levels of your organization is to get results fast (or at least score a few quick wins). As you are planning your compliance plan, you need to identify some low-level compliance issues that are relatively easy to fix and have your team tackle those first. People want to see results, and the faster you can show them results, the more confidence they will have in the project. If it takes you months to get the first item addressed, people might wonder if the organization will ever be compliant and become complacent about the effort as a whole, derailing all your efforts up to this point. Getting results early keeps the momentum and support moving in a positive direction for your entire project.

Notes from the Front Line

To give you a good example of how important it is to select the right team members, here is a real-world story of the first time Karen was on a compliance team.

Karen was approached by her manager, Christina, to help with the PCI compliance effort. Christina felt that Karen's knowledge would be an asset to the team. The team leader sent out a meeting request for the 10 team members, and Karen was excited to help make a difference in her organization. She showed up at the first meeting on time, ready to do what was necessary–even if it meant having to put in overtime to get the job done. That first meeting did not go so well. The team leader was 10 min late and only half of the team members showed up for the meeting.

During the meeting, Karen began to realize that none of the other senior managers were briefed on the compliance project, and some even wondered whether they needed to comply with these new regulations. Even though there was no senior management support, the team leader knew the company needed to get into compliance or face trouble. When Karen asked about the missing team members, the team leader thought that it was probably due to the lack of support from upper management.

After weeks of meetings, false starts, and many extra hours, the compliance team finally had senior management involved and then the wheels started to turn. The entire team showed up for a meeting for the first time, but they had to start over from the beginning. Karen and the team leader soon realized that the meeting lacked the right people for the areas need to become compliant.

After a few more weeks, the right people did get involved with the team, and miraculously senior management support was still there. The project took off like a wild fire. Karen's team did a gap analysis and figured out what needed to be fixed and hit the ground running. After months of trying to put the team together, once Karen's company had the team in place, they were able to knock out the entire project in 3 weeks. Just like the expression needing the right tool for the right job, you definitely need the right team for any compliance project you are attempting to pull off.

BUDGETING TIME AND RESOURCES

In order for your project to be a success, you need to ensure that it is managed correctly and that it does not take too long to complete. As important as it was for your team to get some results early on, you must continue to make sure that you set expectations, goals, and milestones. Figure out early on how you will manage the time and resources of your team and you will have a successful compliance project.

Setting Expectations

Setting expectations is a key factor when budgeting time and resources within your team. From the first stages of your compliance project, your team needs to know what to expect from you, other team members, and management. If this project is a priority one, the team needs to know that all other tasks are secondary until the compliance plan is in place. You also need to be sure you set the right expectations with management, so they know what to expect with the compliance plan.

Management's Expectations

Knowing from the beginning what management expects out of this effort should be one of your first tasks. Before you bring the team together, you should talk to senior management to make sure you understand what they expect out of the project and the timeline in which the project must be completed. Be sure you understand the criticality of the compliance effort to the organization, as that will help you get a pulse on the project itself.

Once expectations (and the appropriate management sign-off) of the compliance project are in place, you need to document them and share them with all the members of your team. By having all the team members of the compliance project working from the same set of expectations, you are one step closer to having a successful project. If management feels that the project needs to be done in 4 weeks but the team actually needs 8 weeks to complete the tasks, be sure to set the correct expectations.

Establishing Goals and Milestones

Once a timeline is in place, it is important to set goals for the team on when key items should be complete. You want to make it very clear when project items are due and when parts of the compliance plan need to be in place.

Start by listing the goals of the project and assign those goals to team members. Make it clear when goals need to be met, as some will have prerequisites that must be finished before you can move on to the next task. Having goals in place will keep the project moving in the right direction. Set up milestones for success and publish your plan to everyone involved to keep them up-to-date on the project's status.

A good way to keep your time and resources managed is by using project planning software such as Microsoft Project, which allows you to create Gantt charts that map resources to goals (see Fig. 10.2). Gantt charts give

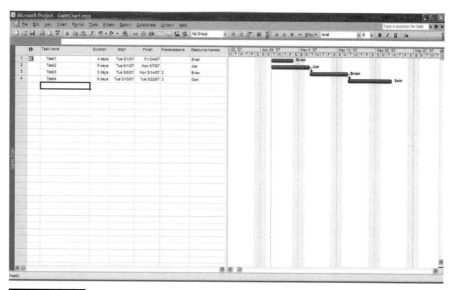

FIGURE 10.2 *Example of Gantt Chart*

you a way to easily report on your compliance project. If an item slips or is completed early, the chart will adjust and keep your project in line with the project timeline.

If you don't have Microsoft Project, some open-source equivalents are as follows:

- GanttProject: www.ganttproject.biz/

- OpenProj: http://openproj.org/openproj

- OpenWorkbench: www.openworkbench.org/

A Web-based equivalent is:

- Gantter: www.gantter.com/

Having Status Meetings

The key to keeping your project on time is to have weekly (or daily if needed) team status meetings. The meetings should include your compliance team members and each should report on what they have accomplished in the past week and what they will be working on in the next week. These meetings also give team members a chance to compare notes and bounce ideas off each other if they are stuck on a problem.

You should also have status update meetings with senior management on a regular basis. Depending on the length of your project, the meetings should be, at a minimum, once per month. During these meetings, you can go over your goals and milestones, and show how the project is progressing. It will also give the senior managers a chance to give their input on the project and reinforce the support you need from them.

Be prepared to hand out copies of your working project plan Gantt chart. It will give a clear picture to your senior management team of where you are in the process and who is working on what issues. It is a good idea to send these charts to the managers beforehand to give them time to review the progress so that they can determine the guidance and support you will need.

EDUCATING STAFF

Training can make or break any compliance project. From the first meeting, ensure there is a training component to make all members aware of how the project will run and make sure they have all the necessary information to move forward with their part of the compliance project. Also, when your compliance program is in place, you need to make sure that part of that program includes training. Actions and plans to meet PCI DSS requirements must be maintained after they have been developed. The only way to do this is through a series of reminders and recurring training classes for your organization's employees. Having a training program in place from day 1 will go a long way in keeping your organization compliant after you have completed your compliance plan.

Training Your Compliance Team

When your compliance team meets for the first time, you should review common information for all members. Items should include the following:

- An overview of the PCI DSS
- An overview of the PCI DSS compliance effort for your organization
- Why your organization is going through the process
- A review of the project plan itself at a high level to share goals and milestones
- A review of any elements the team might be submitting (i.e., how a policy should be written or status reports)

You could even use this book's Table of Contents as a guide for your training, making sure that you pull out the relevant portions for the teams you are working with.

Training your compliance team will help them understand how the plan came together and how to execute it to make your organization compliant. It will also get all members on the same page about what PCI DSS is and why your organization is going through the effort. You want to remove all myths around the project and level the playing field for your team members, so they can be successful in making your organization compliant.

Training the Company on Compliance

After your project is complete and you deem your organization to be compliant, you need to make sure the rest of the company knows that you need to maintain a level of compliance. You do not want to have a violation in the first week because an employee did not know about the need for compliance.

You need to put together a corporate compliance training program for all new employees and for existing employees to complete annually, which acts as a refresher course and also gives you a chance to present any information that has changed over the past year.

Setting Up the Corporate Compliance Training Program

Be sure to set up your corporate compliance training program as an element of your compliance plan. Get the human resources department involved early on in the process to make sure that all employees of your organization receive the training. Many times you can leverage existing programs, like your current new employee orientation, to train existing employees.

NOTE

Keep your compliance training program upbeat and fun. Although security might be boring to most of your employees, it is fundamental to the success of your compliance efforts. One idea would be to have prizes at your training classes and offer them to people who get answers right during a question and answer session. People will be more likely to want to attend the training class if they can win a dinner, movies, or a gift card to any number of retail stores.

The compliance training program is more than just creating a one-time training class for your employees. The following elements should be incorporated for a successful program:

- Create a new hire training class that all new employees are required to attend. It can be as simple as handing out this book to your new hires, and making sure they understand the content by asking questions about PCI, or as complicated as bringing in a trainer to develop a program for you. The initial training will need to be comprehensive, potentially derived from this book's Table of Contents. Work with your human resources department to see if this training class can be injected into an existing orientation program, or be sure you are a part of the process, so your training team is notified about new hires.

- Create an intranet Web site that outlines key elements from the compliance training, so employees have a good source to review information.

- Create a series of reminders to help keep the compliance effort on the minds of the employees. Good ideas for this are awareness posters, articles in your company's newsletter, and even compliance days where you can make a fun event around being PCI DSS compliant.

- Create a recurring annual training program for employees to make sure they are reminded about what they need to do to comply. Recurring training should update your employees on new developments (for example, in 2009, we saw MasterCard change both validation requirements and add fines), changes in PCI DSS, or covering specific areas that your company struggles with. The recurring training program can work either as a live training class or as a Web-based training class that they can take when time permits. Either way the training is presented, it should be required to keep your organization in compliance.

With the right training programs in place, you can be sure that from the first meeting of your compliance team to the annual recurring training for your associates, your compliance efforts will have a lasting effect on your organization.

NOTE

One of the greatest tools in any compliance awareness program is the use of posters. With the use of posters, you can get the message out quickly. The posters you put out should have simple messages that grab people's attention. For PCI DSS compliance, simple phrases such as, "Ensure your Anti-Virus is Up to Date" or "Keep all Cardholder Data Under Lock and Key" will get the message to your employees quickly. Compliance posters are also a great way to get that first big result. You can create and put these posters up in the first part of your compliance planning efforts to give a kick-start to the project. When senior managers are walking around the office, they will see the posters and see that you are taking the compliance project seriously.

PROJECT QUICKSTART GUIDE

Putting a compliance plan together for PCI DSS can seem like an overwhelming task. You are probably asking yourself where to start. Whom do you get involved? When do you look at the PCI DSS SAQ? This section will get you pointed in the right direction and give you the first step toward getting your organization compliant with PCI DSS.

The Steps

We know how to plan a project to meet compliance, but when it comes to PCI DSS, what are the specifics you should be looking at to become compliant quickly and efficiently? For an overview of the steps, see Fig. 10.3.

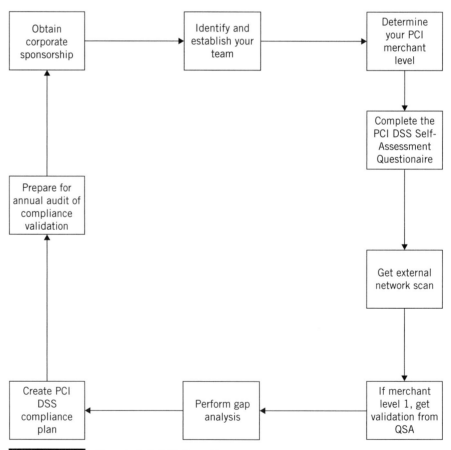

FIGURE 10.3   *Steps to PCI DSS Compliance*

Step 1: Obtain Corporate Sponsorship

Once you have corporate sponsorship, you will have the backing for all the steps of your compliance project plan. Be sure to meet with these members of your organization first to get the sign-off and acceptance that your company needs to be PCI DSS compliant. Remember, you need to make sure you get support from the highest level possible in your organization. Getting the backing from senior managers will help to ensure that the rest of the employees will be willing to work with you on getting compliant with PCI DSS.

Step 2: Identify and Establish Your Team

This is a critical step because it could make or break your compliance project. You need to be sure to select your team members from the appropriate areas of your company. Include the business leaders that have to worry about PCI DSS compliance and also the techies in the trenches who are setting up your networks. Having a good mix of key players will help your project succeed.

You should choose leaders for each of the 12 requirements of PCI DSS. If you break PCI DSS up into each requirement, you will be in a better position to complete your effort in a timely and concise manner. You should also set up a training class during your first team meeting to review what PCI DSS is, why your company has to comply, and the initial plan of what needs to be done to get into compliance.

Step 3: Determine Your PCI Level

You need to know what your PCI merchant or service provider level is, which will tell you how you need to validate compliance with PCI DSS. Talk with your team members who are from the business side and figure out how many transactions you perform. Or, if you are a merchant, call your acquirer(s). Then, refer to the card brand's Web sites to help you figure out your organization's level.

Knowing your level will set the stage for what exactly you need to do to comply as each level has different requirements for validating compliance. It is important that you determine this early on in the process because as you get closer to Level 1 (or Level 2 for MasterCard merchants), your compliance effort will take longer and involve more resources. If you are not at Level 1 from the start, you want to periodically review how many transactions you are processing – especially if you are on the border. If you slip to another level, you may also slip out of compliance.

Step 4: Complete a PCI DSS SAQ-D

You need to complete SAQ-D (or the most appropriate one for your business, but most will use SAQ-D) in one of your first compliance meetings because the results of the questionnaire will give you clear guidance on how compliant your organization already is or is not with PCI DSS. The questionnaire can be found at the PCI SSC Web site: www.pcisecuritystandards.org/saq/. If you answer "No" to any of the questions, you are not in compliance. The questions on the questionnaire map directly to the requirements of the PCI DSS. When your organization has the questionnaire complete, it will indicate not only if you are compliant with PCI DSS, but what you need to do to become compliant.

Step 5: Set Up Quarterly External Network Scans from an Approved Scanning Vendor

Compliance with PCI DSS requires a quarterly network scan from an Approved Scanning Vendor (ASV), but Level 4 Visa, MasterCard, and Discover merchants may not have to submit their scans to their acquirer. All externally exposed Internet Protocol (IP) addresses must be scanned for vulnerabilities by an ASV, which means performing your own external scans will not make you compliant. The PCI SSC maintains a list of ASVs at www.pcisecuritystandards.org/pdfs/asv_report.html. For more information, see Chapter 8, "Vulnerability Management."

At the end of the network scan, the ASV is required to provide you with a report that will show you if your Internet-facing network is PCI DSS compliant. If they discover a vulnerability of a high-enough severity, they will typically point you in the right direction toward a remedy.

WARNING

You must select your ASV from the list that is maintained by the PCI SSC. If you do not use an approved vendor, any results you have, no matter how good they appear to you or your organization, can invalidate your PCI compliance efforts. Remember that you must have clean, quarterly external scans, except for initial PCI DSS compliance where all you need is a recent, passing scan and documented policies and procedures requiring quarterly scans. Submitting scans with vulnerabilities that must be fixed for compliance proves you are not compliant with PCI.

Step 6: Get Validation from a QSA

This step is only required if you are at a merchant level that requires this (currently, Levels 1 and 2) or your acquiring bank mandates it. You want to engage the QSA to help you with Step 7 below. PCI Assessments are an annual process, where all components that are a part of how your company stores, processes, and transmits cardholder data are assessed. You can find a list of QSAs at www.pcisecuritystandards.org/pdfs/pci_qsa_list.pdf.

Step 7: Perform a Gap Analysis

After your team has gone through the SAQ, the network scan results, and potentially the reports from your QSA, they now must prepare a document that lists out the gaps in your compliance effort. Your gap analysis document will set the stage for the creation of your compliance plan. To assist with your gap analysis, you should put together a worksheet that lists each requirement and indicates whether you are compliant or not. You can also use the worksheet to initially assign the requirement to a compliance team member.

Step 8: Create PCI DSS Compliance Plan

Following the steps above, you now have the steps needed to create your PCI compliance plan. As discussed throughout this chapter, you should take all these elements and bring them into your compliance plan. Your plan should include the gaps that are standing in the way of your PCI DSS compliance efforts and what your organization plans to do to stay compliant year after year. Once all the gaps are closed, your compliance plan will be the live document that ensures you stay compliant with PCI DSS.

Step 9: Prepare for Annual Assessment of Compliance Validation

To maintain compliance, you should start over at Step 1 and begin the process again every year. The good news is that most of what you need to do is already complete, and you are mainly validating that you are still PCI DSS compliant.

PCI SSC NEW PRIORITIZED APPROACH

For those companies that feel lost among the mountain of remediation that needs to be done, the PCI SSC may have some help for you. In early 2009, the Council released a Prioritized Approach for PCI DSS (www.pcisecuritystandards.org/education/prioritized.shtml) [1]. While the approach provides guidance to those individuals responsible for steering a PCI compliance project to completion, it needs to be customized for each organization to most efficiently meet your needs. At the above URL, there are two documents available for download.

NOTE

How can you use the PCI Prioritized Approach to make PCI DSS easy for you?

- Use the document to *plan your PCI project* from current state to compliant and secure state

- Use sheet for *ongoing planning* of the next steps and identifying weak areas/next area to handle

- Use Excel sheet to *track status* and *create a report* of compliance status for senior managers

The PDF document describes the approach and gives some background on why the approach was created, it describes objectives, and it outlines the six milestones in their plan. The other document is a Microsoft Excel spreadsheet that contains the entire PCI DSS with a milestone number next to each requirement. Most companies that use this tool will add more columns to it to bring in their assessment data and will change the milestones to be in line with their particular project milestones. If you have no milestones defined, use these as a reference. Remember, you will probably need to adjust the milestones to fit more appropriately into your company's current compliance plan.

SUMMARY

Planning a project to meet compliance can be so overwhelming that you wind up having false starts or not begin the project at all. Your compliance efforts do not have to end this way. By putting together a good compliance project plan, you will have what it takes to make your organization PCI DSS compliant.

From the start of your project, you need to take a close look at why you need to become PCI DSS compliant. Simply figuring out if you need to comply can save you weeks of time and effort that could be devoted to other compliance initiatives. Once you determine that you must comply, spend time understanding your current level, type of company (merchant or service provider), and what exactly you have to do to validate your compliance. Once you know your level, either you will have a QSA perform an assessment against your company or you will fill out one of the four SAQs relevant to your business model. The Council's Web site has information on all four SAQs, and what must be submitted for compliance validation purposes (www.pcisecuritystandards.org/saq/). You also need to figure out what is the cost to your organization for noncompliance. Can your organization afford the risk? With the new legislation and fines coming down pike, nearly all situations will yield a firm "No."

Once you determine that you need to be PCI compliant and cannot afford the risk of noncompliance, you need to bring all the players to the table. You first want to obtain senior manager (C-Level) sponsorship to get the backing you need to complete the project. The corporate sponsorship process will also help you form your compliance team. Your compliance project starts by getting your team together and working through the planning process.

You must guide your team in the right direction and help them budget their time and resources effectively. First, you need to set expectations with your team and management about what the compliance effort entails. At this point, you can set up goals and milestones to help keep the project on a timeline and define when the project should be completed. It is important to have status meetings with your team and management during the process to keep everyone informed and moving forward.

As you start your compliance planning project, make sure that your team members get the correct training by providing an overview of what PCI DSS is and why your organization is going through this compliance effort. You should also train all the employees in your company, so they know what it takes to be compliant and to stay compliant. Setting up a corporate compliance training program will have a lasting effect on your organization – not only in keeping PCI compliant but also keeping your workforce thinking about security at all times.

Then, we outlined the nine steps you should take to become PCI DSS compliant. If you go through each of these steps, you will complete the first round of your compliance effort. Knowing that you are PCI compliant will help allay the fears of noncompliance by management. If you find yourself still needing a place to start, you can try out the new PCI SSC Prioritized Approach to compliance. Remember, the information provided may not directly apply to your organization, so you must customize it to make it effective.

At the end of your compliance effort, congratulate the team and encourage them to continue to keep your organization PCI DSS compliant.

REFERENCE

[1] PCI Security Standards Council. Prioritized Approach for DSS 1.2. www.pcisecuritystandards.org/education/docs/Prioritized_Approach_PCI_DSS_1_2.pdf; 2009 [accessed 29.07.09].

Don't Fear the Assessor

The title of this chapter might shock you a little bit. Why? Have you noticed that the words "audit" and "auditor" in reference to Payment Card Industry Data Security Standards (PCI DSS) are copiously missing from this book? That's because the correct terms are "assessment" and "assessor" when referring to PCI DSS. While your Qualified Security Assessor (QSA) may be a CPA, it is not a requirement, and most QSAs are not. The procedures an assessor uses to validate your compliance with PCI DSS are called the Security Assessment Procedures (not the Auditing Procedures). It's amazing what the change of a word will do to get you a more complete assessment. Imagine if your Internal Audit Group changed their name to the Primary Assessment Group, and everyone changed their title to Assessor.

Sure, it's a psychology trick, but part of the goal here is to use the right terminology with sound advice to follow it. Your internal audit group should be involved in your PCI DSS program from a self-assessment perspective, but remember, PCI DSS is assessed, and you work with assessors.

Whether it's your first on-site assessment or your first external vulnerability scan, it's pretty easy to find gaps to compliance. And while this may not be the case for you, you should have a plan in place to deal with this if it happens. This may happen because you interpreted a requirement slightly different from an assessor, or it may be that you simply missed something that an experienced assessor would catch. When things go wrong, it's easy to blame the assessor. Having the right attitude can make all the difference. Generally, assessors should not allow you an easy pass. If they do not properly report gaps in your PCI DSS compliance, they can lose their QSA status. In addition, your company will be dragged through the mud after the breach as yet another example showing how ignoring PCI and only paying lip service to it will get you not only breached, but also fined by the card brands.

REMEMBER, ASSESSORS ARE THERE TO HELP

When dealing with on-site assessors or approved scanning vendors (ASV), most people fit into one of following three groups.

1. Some people are intimated by assessors. They see assessors as people with a lot of power, and they hope that they will say and do the right things, avoiding the pain of a gap.

2. Some people look at assessors as their enemy. They believe that they must wrestle with the assessor and hopefully win in the end.

3. Some people treat the assessor like a consultant whom they've brought in to help bring their company into compliance. They respect the assessor's opinions and keep the assessor in the loop as they work out solutions.

While it might surprise you, the last group will get the most out of their assessor and will have the best overall experience. They will quickly be able to bring their company into compliance with the least amount of hassle, and they will usually gain quick upper management support for funding required to resolve the issues identified during the assessment.

As hard as it might be to believe, assessors are there to help you. After all, you are the one paying for their services. It's important to know how to work well with assessors so that your assessment will go smoothly and efficiently, and ensure that you get your money's worth. A good assessor will go over your company's systems, practices, and policies with a fine-toothed comb, and tell you what you can do to improve your security. Hopefully, your primary goal in becoming PCI compliant is to have your company become more secure and decrease the likelihood of card data theft or loss. When you realize that assessors provide you with a valuable service and that you're both on the same team working towards a common goal, you will have the right attitude. Remember that assessors have moral and professional obligations to follow the guidelines and procedures they've been given for the assessment, despite the fact that you are paying for their services. It is not appropriate to ask them to compromise those obligations, just for that reason. The assessor's integrity is more important to them than your fee. Assessors are trained and likely have performed many assessments, and they can give you great advice on what you can do to bring yourself into compliance.

When you choose your assessor, interview them! This assessment is probably one of the most important projects you will embark on this year. Getting out of the gates with the wrong assessor will make your pain so much greater. First, set up an interview with someone from your prospective assessor. Understand their methodology, and how they will strive to ensure you are not one of the companies that exited their assessment process thinking they were compliant, only to find out (sometimes days) later that they had been breached, and their assessor did a poor job (sadly, there are some example of this very event, which are being discussed in the media at this very time). Good assessors will bring a team of at least two QSAs to every engagement to make sure that you get the most accurate result. Good assessors will come on-site and will not just interact with you via email. Have you ever tried to explain to someone how to build a replica Millennium Falcon out of Lego® blocks over the phone or, worse, email? Of course not. So don't expect your assessor to get a good view of your infrastructure over the phone, either. Finally, you get what you pay for! You don't always need to choose the most expensive bid, but if you get bids of $20K and $200K from the exact same scope, something is not right. Don't get stuck in an apples-to-oranges comparison. You will end up with prune juice every time.

When you have the right attitude you will find ways to use your assessor to improve the security of your company. Seasoned assessors have a wealth of knowledge, even outside of payment security, and can be leveraged when bridging gaps in compliance. They have seen many technologies, policies, and practices that others have put in place to mitigate risks, and they should be able to give you choices to help you meet requirements that work best for your situation. For example, if cost is your main concern, an assessor may know of a low cost or open source tool that you can use to comply with certain requirements. On the other hand if time is more important, the assessor may know of a solution that is quick to set up that will bring you into compliance. As you work on your remediation, it's important to keep your assessor in the loop. This way he or she can give opinions on what you've chosen to do and can give further advice. It will also likely make your next assessment much easier for both parties involved.

Don't forget the old business adage-pick any two of the following when asking someone to provide you with a good or service: good, fast, or cheap!

Balancing Remediation Needs

Do your homework when looking at ways to bridge compliance gaps. Depending on the problem you're trying to solve, there may be open source tools, managed solutions, off-the-shelf software, or hardware appliances to consider. When looking at products and services that can help bring you into compliance, there are usually four main factors that you should consider.

1. Effectiveness: Will the solution you're looking at really solve the problem and allow you to pass your next assessment? If it won't, it should be ignored.

2. Cost: Normally cost is a factor in any decision made by a business. Sometimes decisions are based solely on initial cost, but costs of maintaining should also be considered. While one product or service is cheaper up front, it may end up costing your organization much more in the long run.

3. Time to Install: You probably want to get into compliance quickly. If you're not in compliance you may be facing fines but will definitely have gaps in your security begging for a hacker to exploit.

4. Time to Maintain: Many times, the time used to maintain a product will be the most expensive part of adding it to your organization. It may end up that a solution you choose will be more expensive in the long run, because it takes a lot of time to maintain (i.e., purchasing a log management solution instead of outsourcing the management to a managed service provider).

Depending on your exact situation, some of these may be more important than others, but they should all be considered when choosing a solution.

How FAIL == WIN

In some cases, failing an assessment ends up being a huge win for the security of your company. In many organizations, the security staff (or security minded IT staff) would like to put certain security measures in place, but have been blocked by upper management because of cost. Remember, upper management's job is to help the company make money, not spend money. Even after you have done a careful cost-benefit analysis and have determined that the benefits outweigh the costs, upper management may still say no. A failed assessment may be the perfect time to help them to say "yes." If the assessor is requiring that you add something to comply with PCI DSS, you can use that as leverage with upper management to get it put into place.

Again, submit a cost-benefit analysis, adding the cost of noncompliance to the total cost. Let them know that the assessor says you will not be compliant without that measure.

DEALING WITH ASSESSORS' MISTAKES

Assessors are human. Assessors make mistakes. Although this does not happen often, there is a right way to deal with it when it does. The first thing to do is to talk to the assessor and have him or her explain how he or she came to his or her conclusion. Many times someone misunderstood a requirement or believed a compensating control mitigated a problem, but the assessor doesn't agree. Having good open dialogue about what you believe is a mistake, will often solve the problem quickly.

Many assessors find their roots in security (some find it in auditing, which can, on occasion, make this more difficult). Sometimes an assessor will "make up" a requirement because it just makes good sense, but when you ask the assessor to show you where in the PCI DSS that requirement exists, they will realize their mistake. Notice how that last sentence was phrased. Ask them to "show you where the requirement is in PCI DSS," don't ask them to "PROVE IT!"

Before you go to the step in the next paragraph, consider why you think the assessor made a mistake. Is it because you personally have an attachment to a particular system or control? Was the assessor rude? Have you tried to fix the issue the assessor identified with no success? Or was he or she trying to sell you something that his or her company happens to offer? Assessors make mistakes, but don't assume that because an assessor feels a certain way that he or she is alone on an island where no other assessor would dare sail. Before pushing back on the assessor, ask yourself this: "If I were breached tomorrow, could this be a cause?" If it is, don't waste time bullying the assessor. Take some time to research and look up the issue;

NOTE

You may feel like you have compensating controls in place to solve a problem but the assessor doesn't agree. If the assessor does not agree with the control and you are a merchant, try working with your acquirer (sorry, service providers, you do not have this option). If your acquirer chooses to accept the risk, they can absolutely do so. Most acquirers will side with an assessor, so be sure if you want to go down this route that you present a good case. Most of the time it's easier to follow the requirement exactly than to try to get a mitigating control to fix the problem.

don't argue because you happen to dislike his or her advice or don't want to deploy a particular technology or change a certain "bad habit" of your organization. Use that energy to fix the issue and close the issue that an attacker may use to break into your system.

In some cases, you may need to push back on your assessor. Pushing-back is when you challenge an assessor's results. When you push back, be polite. Simply explain to the assessor your point of view and why you believe there was a mistake. If the assessor disagrees, ask him to explain his reasoning. If the assessor has explained why you didn't pass and you don't agree with his reasoning, you may need to talk to his manager or a practice lead about the situation. Explain your situation to the manager and why you think a mistake was made. Most of the time, the manager will talk to the assessor to get his side of the story before coming to any conclusions. If the assessor's manager agrees with the assessor, you will need to fix the problem to be validated as compliant.

Sometimes an assessor or an ASV will report a false positive. This is when an assessment shows you have a vulnerability such as a missing patch or vulnerable system that really is not there. This seems to happen more with remote scans, as they have less access to systems. Any good assessor or ASV knows how to keep false positives to a minimum. When you do get a false positive, your ASV should be able to work through it with you; many have a mature, automated process for dealing with scan mistakes and other false positives. They may want to get more details from you so they can verify it as a false positive, and then fix the system so the error does not come back in the future.

WARNING

Don't forget, you get what you pay for! Most scanning engines are based on either Qualys (www.qualys.com/) or Nessus (www.tenablesecurity.com/), but not all ASVs will produce the same results. Interview your ASV and ensure that they are involved in the process, not just setting you up in a database for scans. You may need help in interpreting the results or addressing false positives, and those features may cost more.

Some ASVs only run automated tools with very little human checking. This generally works well most of the time, but sometimes the scans can be complicated, and a false positive may end up in a report. If you get a report listing a serious vulnerability, first act as if it's true and see if there's something you can do to remedy the problem quickly. Depending on the situation, it may be a good idea to do some tests on your own. You already have a scanning solution on-site for the internal scans mandated by Requirement 11.2, so use it against the target in the external scan report. Depending on the type of vulnerability that was reported, you may be able to do some manual testing. For example, if your report says that a patch is missing, you may want to manually check the system to validate the finding. If you are unable to find the vulnerability after your testing, it may be time to challenge your scanning vendor's findings and report it as a false positive. They should do additional tests to determine why the false positive happened, and fix the problem or remove this finding from your final PCI scan report.

PLANNING FOR REMEDIATION

A good rule of thumb when doing remediation is that it should be as transparent as possible, so that it has a minimal impact on the business. Sometimes business or user impact is impossible to avoid. For example, implementing a much stricter password policy or disabling group accounts may have an effect on how people perform their jobs. For the most part, patches and system updates should be transparent to users. The more transparent your remediation, the fewer problems you're likely to have implementing it. As you plan your remediation process, always keep transparency in mind.

The first thing you should do in planning for remediation is review your gap analysis with your assessor. Your gap analysis describes the difference from where you are now to where you should be to be compliant. Ask your assessor which risks he considers high priority. For example, if the assessor feels that you have urgent risks that could easily be exploited at any time, you would want to work to remedy those first. In a few cases, an assessor will find a risk that is being actively exploited. In this case, the assessor should let you know as soon as he finds the problem and not wait until the rest of the assessment is done. This would then become your top priority, and you should follow your company's incident response plan. See Fig. 11.1 for a visual representation of this process.

Now that you have your results and understand what needs to be done to comply with PCI DSS, it's time to prioritize your risk. With the help of your assessor, work to determine which problem can be exploited easiest and can cause the most damage. These are the ones that should be fixed first. If there are not any "gaping holes," the conversation should turn to the items that you can address that will (1) get you some quick wins, and (2) give you the biggest bang for your compliance buck. There are many tools that can be

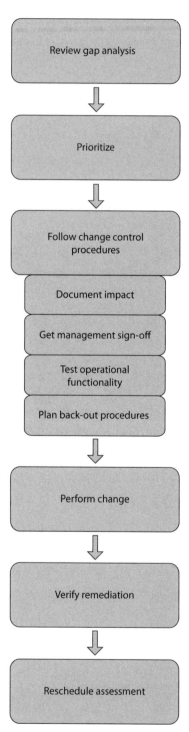

FIGURE 11.1 *Remediation Process*

used to help you classify risks, including the many vulnerability-aggregating Web sites. Here are some that you might find useful.

- Common Vulnerability and Exposures (CVE): This is a well respected, and much referred to, listing of vulnerabilities in products. Many products use CVE numbers to reference vulnerabilities (http://cve.mitre.org/).

- National Vulnerability Database: This is supported by the Department of Homeland Security and has a great database of many types of vulnerabilities (http://nvd.nist.gov/).

- Open Source Vulnerability Database (OSVDB): This community-run database of vulnerabilities will give you a lot of great information on a vulnerability, including references, ways to test your system, and how to mitigate the problem (www.osvdb.org).

- Security Focus Bugtraq: A well-organized site that will give you a lot of information including what versions are affected, an overview of the problem, and examples of exploits. It uses Bugtraq IDs (bids) which are supported in many products (www.securityfocus.com/bid/).

- Secunia: A Danish computer security company that lists and prioritizes vulnerabilities (http://secunia.com/).

Fun Ways to Use Common Vulnerability Scoring System

The Common Vulnerability Scoring System (CVSS) is a standard for scoring vulnerabilities that has become more widely used. ASVs must use CVSS scores instead of PCI scores starting June 30, 2007 for any vulnerabilities that have a CVSS score. Most vulnerability databases will list CVSS scores, which are great in helping you to determine the impact of a vulnerability. There are some vulnerabilities that may not have a CVSS score, but NIST provides a tool to help you calculate them, which can be found at http://nvd.nist.gov/cvss.cfm?calculator.

For example, let's say that your report shows that you don't have your credit card area physically secured. Because this is not a specific vulnerability with a specific system, there won't be a CVSS score for it, but you can use CVSS to help you determine the priority.

In this example, we'll use a physical security issue to show you how this works. While this system is mainly for computer security issues, it works pretty well for physical vulnerabilities, as well.

Jeff is the afternoon manager for Teri's Tapas To Go, a small tapas bar near midtown Manhattan. When Teri built out the location, she found certain constraints as to where electric and telecommunications wiring could be placed. Thus, she has a fax machine near the bathroom to receive faxes containing orders with cardholder data on them. Because the fax machine is not visible by Jeff (or any employee) unless she is in front of the counter, she cannot closely monitor it. Often, Teri's staff are busy with customers and are not watching the fax machine. If they are too busy, they may not hear the fax machine and therefore delay in checking for new orders. Anyone passing by the bathroom could easily grab a fax.

On the calculator page, Teri would start with the Base Scoring Metrics. This gives her a base CVSS score to work from.

Related exploit range is where an attacker would have to be to be able to exploit this vulnerability. If an attacker can compromise the system over the Internet or some other remote means, then it would be remote. In our case, with the credit card area not being physically secured properly, it would be *local*.

Attack complexity is how difficult the attack is to pull off once an attacker has found the vulnerable target. If the attack requires other factors to be in place for it to work, it may make it complex. In our case, we'll say that this is *low* complexity. Once an attacker knows where the credit card data is, it's easy for them to get to it.

The level of authentication needed is if an attacker must be authenticated to pull off an attack. This means that there is some test to verify who the user is that must be bypassed to attack the system. An example would be something like a fake badge to get access to the fax machine. In this case, an attacker would not because the fax machine is in a public area, so the level will be *not required*.

Confidentiality impact describes how the exploit will affect the confidentiality of data in question. In our case, if they can access cardholder data by walking into a protected area and wheeling a file cabinet with all cardholder data in it out the door, it would be complete. Normally a heavy filing cabinet is pretty safe, but since Teri has faxes coming in with cardholder data and there is little to no protection of that data once it hits the fax machine. In this case the confidentiality impact could be Partial (as in you are not getting ALL of the cardholder data), or Complete (as in you did get the complete card number). For illustration purposes, we'll choose *partial*.

Integrity impact describes how the attack will impact the integrity of data. In our case, it's not likely that integrity will be compromised, so we'll use *none*.

Availability impact describes the measure of how the availability of systems and data is affected. Because the attacker can walk off with a fax, the data is no longer available, so we'll mark that as *partial*.

The Impact value weighting allows you to give more weight to confidentiality, integrity, or availability. In our case, the biggest problem will be confidentiality, because the attacker just walked off with cardholder data, so we will chose Weight confidentiality. At this point if we click Update Scores, we will get a base score of 3.7.

Next we will do the temporal score metrics.

Availability of an exploit lets you to determine if an exploit is actually available or not. In our case, we'll say that a functional exploit exists since the attack would work much of the time, but there may be times when one of Teri's employees would catch somebody.

The type of fix available allows us to specify if there is currently any way to remediate the problem. We'll say that Teri has asked employees to keep an eye on the fax machine, which is a *temporary* fix until she finds a better home for the fax machine.

Level of verification that the vulnerability exists allows us to specify how sure we are the vulnerability is actually present in the system. In our case, we know that the vulnerability exists so we'll choose *confirmed*.

Finally, we arrive at the environmental score metrics section. Here we will score the kind of damage that will happen.

Organization specific potential for loss allows you to specify the physical impact the attack could have on your systems. In our case, one credit card number stolen on a fax won't bankrupt Teri, so we'll say it has *low* (light loss) potential for loss.

The percentage of vulnerable systems allows us to choose how many of our systems are vulnerable to this attack. In Teri's case, this is her only fax machine so we'll say all choose *high* (76 to 100 percent).

Now that we're done, we click the Update Scores button and get an overall score of 3.9.

There are many ways to prioritize risks – more than we could review in the scope of this book. Don't spend a huge amount of time and effort prioritizing risks, since in the end they all need to be fixed. But it's good to have a general idea.

PLANNING FOR REASSESSING

While you are working through your gap assessment, include your assessor! Not only can he or she give advice on how to mitigate some risks and bring yourself into compliance, but he or she can also help you to set realistic completion dates. As you run into roadblocks, he or she can help you adjust the dates and remediation plan, and be there to support you through the process.

After this is done and everything is in place, plan to reassess yourself. We provide some self-assessment tips in Chapter 13, "You're Compliant, Now What?" Validate that the gaps are closed to save time and money with your assessor. Provided you included your assessor during the remediation process, your reassessment should be quick and painless. Then you will finally be able to have your PCI DSS compliance party!

SUMMARY

Don't feel bad if your first assessment does not end in a compliant report. Instead, use it to your advantage to better your company's security posture. Work with your assessors instead of against them. Remember you and your assessor are on the same team and the process of assessing should feel like a partnership. By following your assessor's recommendations, your assessment should be less painful and go by quickly. You should involve your assessor as you work to bridge your compliance gaps. The more you involve your assessor, the easier your reassessment will be.

The Art of Compensating Control

Few payment security professionals can find a hotter Payment Card Industry Data Security Standards (PCI DSS) topic than compensating controls. They often look like this mythical compliance accelerator used to push PCI compliance initiatives through completion at a minimal cost to your company with little or no effort.

Compensating controls are challenging. They often require a risk-based approach that can vary greatly from one Qualified Security Assessor (QSA) to another. There is no guarantee that a compensating control accepted today will also work one year from now, and the evolution of the standard itself could render a previous control invalid.

The goal of this chapter is to paint a compensating control mural. After reading this chapter, you should know how to create a compensating control, what situations may or may not be appropriate for compensating controls, and what land mines you must avoid as you lean on these controls to achieve compliance with the PCI DSS.

WHAT IS A COMPENSATING CONTROL?

In the early years of the PCI DSS, and even one author's experience under the CISP program, the term compensating control was used to describe everything from a legitimate work-around for a security challenge to a shortcut to compliance. If you are considering a compensating control, you must perform a risk analysis and have a legitimate technological or documented business constraint before you even go to the next step. Companies being assessed will present more documented business constraints for review based on the current economic situation. Just remember the word *legitimate* and the phrase *perform a risk analysis* before proceeding to the next step. "Bob" being on vacation is not a legitimate constraint, and an armchair review of the gap and potential control is not a risk analysis. QSAs should ask for documentation during a compliance review, and having it ready to go will make sure that you are efficiently using their time. If they do not, you can bet that your assessment is not thorough.

If you think that compensating controls are easy, please read the note below.

NOTE

The compensating control polygon has four specific points that must be met. For a compensating control to be valid, it must

1. Meet the intent and rigor of the original PCI DSS requirement;

2. Provide a similar level of defense as the original PCI DSS requirement;

3. Be "above and beyond" other PCI DSS requirements (not simply in compliance with other PCI DSS requirements); and

4. Be commensurate with the additional risk imposed by not adhering to the PCI DSS requirement.

For an example of a completed compensating control, review Appendix C of the PCI Security Assessment Procedures.

An example of a valid control might be using extra logs for the *su* command in UNIX to track actions executed under a shared root password. In rare cases, a system may not be able to use something like *sudo* to prevent shared administrator passwords from being used. Keep in mind, this is not a license to use shared passwords everywhere in your environment.

Nearly every system has the ability to use something like *sudo*, or "Run As" which is free or built into your OS, or a commercial variant if your platform requires this.

As stated earlier in this section, before immediately running down the compensating control route, be sure that you have done your research and make sure that you legitimately meet all of the requirements for a compensating control. Five years ago, compensating controls were relied on because most platforms did not have readily available solutions to certain components of the PCI DSS. That's not true today. As a rule of thumb, if the operating system can meet the patching requirements in 6.1, it will probably have everything you need available for it (possibly in later versions) to comply with PCI DSS.

WHERE ARE COMPENSATING CONTROLS IN PCI DSS?

Compensating controls are not specifically defined inside PCI but are instead defined by you (as a self certifying merchant) or your QSA. That's where the trouble starts!

Thankfully, the PCI Council provides an example of a completed compensating control in Appendix C of the PCI DSS, as well as a blank template to fill out. Appendix B provides all the guidance they feel necessary to design a compensating control.

WARNING

Pay close attention to sub-bullets A to C under list item 3. In our experience, this is where most companies go wrong.

As long as you have met the requirements in Appendix B for a compensating control, you should be able to build that control into your environment and satisfy PCI DSS. Compensating controls are ultimately accepted by acquirers or the card brands themselves (if applicable), so even after putting all of this information together you could face the rejection of your control and a significant amount of expense re-architecting your process to fit the original control. This is where an experienced QSA can really help you to ensure that your control passes the "Sniff Test." If it smells like a valid control, it probably will pass. If you need examples, look later in this chapter under the section titled "Funny Controls You Didn't Design."

WHAT A COMPENSATING CONTROL IS NOT

Compensating controls are not a shortcut to compliance. In reality, most compensating controls are actually harder to do and cost more money in the longrun than actually fixing or addressing the original issue or vulnerability.

Imagine walking into a meeting with a customer who has an open, flat network, with no encryption anywhere to be found (including on their wireless network, which is not segmented either). Keep in mind, network segmentation is not required by PCI, but it does make compliance easier. Usually in this situation, assessors may find a legacy system that cannot be patched or upgraded, but now becomes in-scope. Then the conversation about compensating controls starts. Now imagine someone in internal assessing telling you not to worry because they would just get some compensating controls. Finally, imagine they tell you this in the same voice and tone as if they were going down to the local drug store to pick up a case of compensating controls on aisle five.

Compensating controls were never meant to be a permanent solution for a compliance gap. Encryption requirements on large systems were made unreasonable early in this decade. Not only was there limited availability of commercial off-the-shelf software, but also it was prohibitively expensive to implement. For Requirement 3.4 (Render PAN, at minimum, unreadable anywhere it is stored), card brands (largely Visa at the time) were quick to point out that compensating controls could be implemented for this requirement, one of those being strong access controls on large systems.

For mainframes, assessors would typically do a cursory walk through the controls and continue to recommend an encryption solution at some point for those systems. At one point, compensating controls were deemed to have a lifespan, meaning that the lack of encryption on a mainframe would only be accepted for a certain period of time. After that, companies would need to put encryption strategies in place.

Compensating control life spans are never materialized. Compensating controls can be used for nearly every single requirement in the DSS – the most notable exception being permissible storage of sensitive authentication data after authorization. There are many requirements that commonly show up on compensating control worksheets, Requirement 3.4 being one of them.

Even with no defined life span, compensating controls are not an eternal free pass. Part of the process during every annual assessment is to review all compensating controls to ensure that they meet the four requirements as currently defined by the PCI Security Standards Council, remembering that the requirements can change between versions of the standard, the original business or technological constraint still exists, and it proves to be effective in the current security threat landscape. If certain types of attacks are on the rise and a certain compensating control is not effective in resisting those attacks, it may not be considered OK on your next assessment.

To further cloud the situation, it is up to the QSA performing the assessment to decide to accept the control initially, but the acquiring bank (for merchants) has the final say. Substantial documentation and an open channel of communication to your acquirer is essential to ensure money is not wasted putting together controls that ultimately do not pass muster.

Don't get discouraged, though! Compensating controls are still a viable path to compliance even considering the above caveats and descriptions of why you may not want to use them.

The authors would not be true security professionals if there were not a fun story or two based on experiences coaching companies or individuals to better security. No names will be used, and the details will be altered to protect those who were most likely being forced to try the old "Push Back on the Assessor" routine. We hope you enjoy reading them as much as we enjoyed listening to them.

FUNNY CONTROLS YOU DIDN'T DESIGN

Some of the most cherished stories and experiences come from customers and vendors that had the right intentions, but never seemed to follow the basic doctrines listed above on how good compensating controls are made. By the way, if you read this and think, "Hey! He is talking about ME!?", I'm not. Pinky swear.

Before one of the authors was heavily involved in PCI, he or she did some IT assessing for a bank that was owned by his or her employer. He or she knew the drill of responding to assessor findings. They usually start with a meeting, bringing all the key stakeholders together to mull over a spreadsheet listing all the findings. Findings are separated out in the "To Fix" pile, and the "To Push Back" pile, each item being assigned to an expert to push back on the assessors. "We don't need that control because of a control over here," or "This gap does not apply to our environment," are the common phrases heard in these meetings. Eventually, a happy (potentially unhappy) medium is established, and the assessment is closed out.

The same process is often applied to PCI, and the compensating control "Cha Cha" commences.

Before we poke fun at the following examples, please understand that we are only illustrating a point. At no time were these suggestions made by people who didn't understand both the requirement and the capabilities of the technology in question. These people were professionals, and based on their credentials and experience, they should have known better.

Encryption has always been a hotly debated topic. Our favorite failed compensating control for Requirement 3.4 comes from a vendor that called an author late one afternoon. They brought in their product team and tried to convince him that RAID-5 was essentially an equivalent to encryption. Their argument stated you could not take any one drive and reconstruct useful data that could be considered compromise worthy; thus, their product should be considered valid to sell to companies as encryption.

If one drive (probably damaged) falls off of a truck during transport, the technology does prevent someone from reconstructing all the data that was on that system. If the system was large enough, chances are that the data on the drive may not provide any use to nefarious individuals either. But that's not really the goal of the requirement, is it? Physical theft prevention is covered in other areas of the standard. The point of the requirement is to render the data unreadable anywhere that it is stored. RAID may render the data unreadable on one physical drive, but it does not render it unreadable in any other circumstance. A simple compromise of one area of the system could lead to the access and theft of massive amounts of unencrypted data.

Speaking of encryption, disk-only encryption inside data centers is not very useful either, unless additional user credentials are tied to the decryption process. Another favorite was a vendor that offered PCI compliance through an encryption appliance that was completely transparent to the operating system. So basically, the vendor was only protecting the data as it sat on disk, in a secured facility, with gates, cameras, and Buck, the not-so-friendly security guard that looks like a hiring manager gave a night shift and a Taser to the ex-bouncer of a dance club. If applications sat on disk drives housed in the unlocked part of a post office, then anyone could see the value here. Until then, the solution only focuses on the physical media and nothing else.

Encryption is really not the big problem with Requirement 3, key management is. Once companies figure out that encryption technologies are available for their platforms, they realize that key generation and management is a whole different problem.

NOTE

One vendor, who apparently thought a severe case of weekend-itis had firmly set in, made a case for using the COBOL Random Number Generator (RNG) to spit out 16 digits (technically 128 bits of data) for use as an encryption key. People can come up with some really creative ideas when the fear of failing an assessment looms.

Yes, they were trying to be random and they will end up with a 128-bit key. Anyone with a basic knowledge of encryption will quickly find the problem with that approach. Not that COBOL's RNG is less than R, but that you have eliminated a giant section of possible key space! A 128-bit key generated in that manner is the equivalent of (approximately) 53 bits of encryption, thus making it computationally feasible to brute force that key, meaning 50 computers could do it in less than 1 year.

HOW TO CREATE A GOOD COMPENSATING CONTROL

We've spent quite a bit of time setting up this section. We talked about what compensating controls are, what they are not, and some of the best misguided attempts to create them. Before we discuss the examples, please remember that these examples should be used for illustrative purposes only. We have over simplified the scenarios for brevity, and things are rarely this simple in the corporate world. Ultimately, compensating controls must be approved first by a QSA, or barring that, your Acquiring Bank. I know I don't like it when someone brings an article about PCI to an interview during an assessment, so please don't do that with this one. Now let's walk through a couple of examples of how one might create a good compensating control.

Here's a common compensating control that QSAs will define and implement at a customer. A Level 1, brick and mortar retailer with 2,500 stores has some systems in their stores that do not process cardholder data. These systems are a high risk to this customer's cardholder environment because they may access both the Internet through a local firewall and the corporate intranet and webmail system, and users log-in to that machine with the default administrator account. Store managers and retail operations claim that the systems are required for day-to-day business because each store is empowered to customize their operations to better fit the local market. The corporation believes this drives innovation and helps them maintain a competitive edge over their peers. See Fig. 12.1 for a simplistic view of the network.

If the retailer chooses not to segment the network, all of the systems in the store are now in-scope, and they must meet all of the applicable requirements of the PCI DSS. Doing this will add significant expense to the IT infrastructure, and will probably force a call center to be staffed up to manage the volume of calls that will come in for things like password maintenance.

What do you do? Do you crush the retailer aspirations to innovate by telling them they must deploy active directory to these machines, lock them down

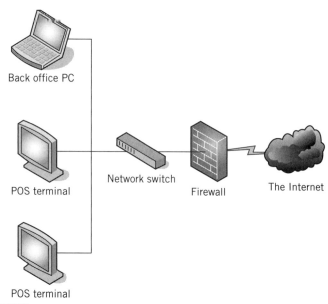

FIGURE 12.1 *Flat Store Network*

Department of Defense tight, and staff a call center? That is one option. But, if you made that recommendation, then you missed something important – understanding the business and limiting the impact that your compliance recommendations make. Instead, consider this compensating control.

Any number of network components could be used to create some segmentation in this environment. Let's say that we have a virtual local area network (VLAN) aware switch at the location that can have access lists (ACLs) tied to it. Why not create a new VLAN for just the point of sale (POS) network? Then create some ACLs around it to make it look like it is segmented behind a firewall. Now the threat of the in-store PC is effectively mitigated provided that the ACLs are appropriately secure. See Fig. 12.2 for an example of what that might look like.

NOTE

"Wait a second," you might say. "ACLs? Those are not supposed to be used for compliance with PCI!" They most certainly can be used for compliance as we discussed in Chapter 4, "Building and Maintaining a Secure Network." Requirement 1.3.6 only refers to external connections, not internal connections. Using ACLs internally is perfectly acceptable. For an extra boost in security, use a reflexive access list (RACL) that will basically look and feel like a stateful inspection firewall.

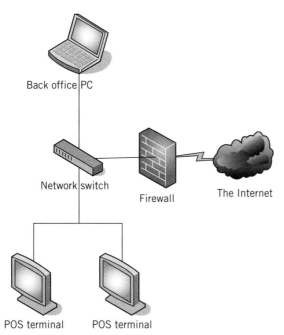

Back office PC

Network switch

Firewall

The Internet

POS terminal   POS terminal

FIGURE 12.2 *VLAN with ACLs Segmenting the Store Network*

"But my store networks are different in every store," you say. "I can't just slap something in there like that and expect it to work globally!" If this is the case, is your store support group is overloaded with break-fix calls? Maybe this could be an opportunity to shore this up and make each store based on a consistent footprint.

Barring that, how about this twist?

Let's say that you are running a Windows XP variant as the operating system powering your POS. You are already required to put some kind of anti-virus and malware removal tools on there. Most of those come with software-based firewalls that could be administered remotely. Deploying firewall capabilities to the POS itself could be viewed as appropriate segmentation depending on the policy attached to that firewall. It is neither a transparent solution, nor is it very pretty, but it works.

The first solution aforementioned is really less of a compensating control and more of a way to reduce the scope of PCI. The best thing you can do for your company is reduce the scope of PCI (or any compliance initiative) to the bare minimum required, and then manage that subset of your infrastructure. The second truly is a compensating control. It meets the original intent and rigor of the original PCI requirements and provides a similar level of defense as the original requirements (reduce the vulnerability to payment systems), goes above and beyond the base requirements of PCI (firewalls are not required on devices that do not leave the premises), and it is most definitely commensurate with the additional risk imposed by not meeting the original requirement.

Take a closer look at those two suggestions. The first may be "free" to your company depending on what is already in place! You will need to adjust business process and prepare your IT community to deal with the change, but you may not need to spend any hard dollars rolling this solution out (unless your equipment cannot do this in the first place). The second suggestion, which is actually the compensating control, requires capital outlay for software licensing and training or consulting to build out the environment. Upon rollout, things will break that will result in potential losses to the business.

WARNING

Without fail, companies that push major changes to large environments often face some kind of error upon the final rollout. Keep in mind, large environments always vary just a little bit among locations. Be sure to have a solid contingency and rollback plan.

Are you starting to get the hang of this thing? How about another example?

A Service Provider has a large mid-tier UNIX, like Solaris or AIX, installation that runs critical areas of the payment process, including long-term data storage. For various reasons, encrypting the data is not an option on these machines. How do we make this service provider compliant with PCI Requirement 3.4?

This is a real-world example that comes up frequently. Encryption implementations have come a long way since early in this decade. The words "my platform does not have a solution for encryption" is no longer valid for platforms that can comply with PCI. When presenting the following control to customers, it is shocking how fast they find a way to encrypt their data.

Most mid-tier UNIX operating systems have the ability to switch from discretionary access control (DAC) to mandatory access control (MAC). MAC will cause that mid-tier UNIX machine to act like a mainframe using RACF/ACF2, and managing those controls is now a massive chore for whoever is charged with it. Converting the appropriate systems to MAC, and potentially adding some segmentation could effectively render cardholder data unreadable and meet PCI Requirement 3.4.

Things are never that easy. Security professionals inside companies love the idea of converting to MAC as it allows us to have more granular control over the systems and their data. Practical ones know that converting an existing system requires so much effort that the costs outweigh the benefits. This is a perfect example of how a compensating control might look good on paper (it's only three words when you use the acronym! "Convert to MAC!"), but in reality would be much easier to just meet the implied requirement to encrypt that data.

One more example, and then it's time for you to get creative!

A medium-sized retailer with less than 500 stores is struggling with Requirement 10.2.1 to log "all individual accesses to cardholder data." All of their data is stored in a large DB2 database that runs on a mainframe. They run massive batch processes at regular intervals, and their space constraints prevent logging every single access to a row. Do you tell them to go back to their board for a Capital Expenditure (CapEx) request to buy lots and lots of drive space to store logs?

Before we proceed, consider the intent of the requirement. Reliable logs are valuable in investigating a breach quickly. Without them, it may take forensic examiners days, or even weeks, to determine the source of a breach. Once the source has been identified and analyzed, forensic companies must attempt to determine how many card numbers may have been exposed. If there are no logs, the assumption is that everything could be exposed, meaning that fines will add up pretty quickly.

The idea is not necessarily to make a log record that includes every single card number that is accessed, but to be able to identify which cards are accessed through the data contained in the logs. If we were to log the actual query performed against the database during a batch process, with knowledge of the date and time that the query was run and exactly what that query will do, we should then be able to determine, with reasonable certainty, which cards were accessed. Common batch processes run on a daily basis, usually using the data from the previous day to produce its output. If we must determine what could have been exposed from January 1 to January 8, we could look at the data that would have been accessed by that batch process during those days.

Logging the query, and all the other elements required by 10.3 about that action, would generate a reasonably accurate list of records that would use a fraction of the drive space required by creating an entry that has every single record exposed.

SUMMARY

What a pretty mural we have painted over the last several pages! Good compensating controls are the result of a marriage between art and science. We've discussed what compensating controls are, what they are not, some funny examples of how to go wrong, and three solid scenarios from which we created good controls.

Compensating controls are not the golden parachute of compliance initiatives. They require work to build effective ones that will pass the scrutiny of both a QSA and an Acquiring Bank (or card brand). Rarely do they yield lower cost and effort than simply meeting the original requirement. PCI DSS is based on many good (not best) standards of practice for security, and should be viewed as a baseline by which to operate, not a high water mark by which you aspire to be one day. Compensating controls may help you lower the bar of compliance in the short term, but remember, only you can prevent a security breach.

You're Compliant, Now What?

Congratulations, you passed! Your Report on Compliance (RoC) is filed or SAQ is completed, vulnerability scans come back clean, and compliance status is validated. You are DONE! Depending on where you were when you started, you may have worked long and hard to get here. So now you can kick back, relax, and enjoy your flight until you land at your next annual assessment, right? It would be great if it were that easy, but unfortunately it's not. Security (and PCI compliance in particular) requires constant vigilance, both for new controls deployment and for event monitoring. In this chapter, we will discuss how you can best spend your time now to ensure compliance in the future. First, we will discuss why you should think about security as a process instead of an event. We will then make suggestions on periodic review and training that should be happening in your organization. Last, we will outline some suggestions on performing a self-assessment on your own network.

SECURITY IS A PROCESS, NOT AN EVENT

And so is compliance, including Payment Card Industry Data Security Standards (PCI DSS) compliance which is intended to induce people to get to security.

Security is not something that can be achieved and then forgotten about. Contrary to some security vendor's claims and some management hopes, you cannot install a magical device on your network that will make you eternally secure. Security is a process of constantly assessing your risks then working to mitigate them to a reasonable level. These risks are ever-changing, so processes and technology to address them should be ever-changing as well.

One thing to keep in mind is that you were never 100 percent secure. Even if you've done everything to secure your systems, an attacker can still find ways in. In fact, it's actually very difficult to prove that you are secure, while it's relatively easy to prove that you are insecure. To prove that you are secure, you must prove that every possible threat (remember, these are constantly changing) is addressed. To prove insecurity, you only have to find one attack vector that allows you past the rest of the security controls in place. Thanks to more zero day attacks, that vector could be something you had not even considered. It could be an exploit known to only one attacker in the world; if that attacker decides to target your company, then despite all you have done it could successfully attack your network.

First, the more complex a system, the harder it is to secure. It is very difficult to have a system that's completely risk-free while actually doing something useful, like serve a Web page or allow a user to send an e-mail. In general, today's systems are very complex, and therefore hard to secure.

Second, risks, technologies, and your organization are changing constantly. New attacks are invented constantly. New technologies and software are implemented in your network on a regular basis. New people come to your company and current employees forget things from time to time. People need to be trained regularly.

Third, it's impossible to be PCI compliant without approaching compliance and security as a process. All of the requirements require some sort of maintenance. Logs need to be reviewed, systems and policies need to be updated, and security assessments need to be performed. These are all part of the security process that keeps your company as safe as possible from attack.

NOTE

All of the requirements mandate some sort of maintenance. Please remember that Your compliance is validated by a Qualified Security Assessor (QSA), but it is maintained by you and you alone. Validation is a moment when you feel like you accomplished something and you did. Compliance is an ongoing state of vigilance, as is security.

PLAN FOR PERIODIC REVIEW AND TRAINING

It's important to plan now for future review and training. Working with technology in an organization can get very hectic, and if you put off planning then you are far less likely to do it. It's important to review your security polices and practices often to verify they're actually in place. In fact, many of the PCI DSS requirements mention monthly, quarterly, and annual processes.

NOTE

Here are some examples from PCI DSS requirements and testing procedures that mention ongoing process:

- Requirement 1.1.6: "Requirement to review firewall and router rule sets at least *every six months*."

- Requirement 11.1: "Test for the presence of wireless access points by using a wireless analyzer at least *quarterly* or deploying a wireless IDS/IPS to identify all wireless devices in use."

- Requirement 11.2: "Run internal and external network vulnerability scans at least *quarterly* and after any significant change in the network."

- Requirement 3.4 testing procedure: "Verify that policies and procedures include a programmatic (automatic) process to remove, at least on a *quarterly* basis, stored cardholder data that exceeds business retention requirements, or, alternatively, requirements for a review, conducted at least on a quarterly basis, to verify that stored cardholder data does not exceed business retention requirements."

More examples are covered in the next section of this chapter called "PCI Requirements with Periodic Maintenance."

Many times companies write great policies but they never enforce them, and so they are never actually followed. Train your employees often so they are aware of your security policies and re-emphasize their importance so that employees are more likely to follow them.

NOTE

Perform training sessions that are brief and frequent. For example, a short 15-min reminder session several times a year will probably be better than an hour-long review session once per year. Here are some ideas of things you may want to review with employees at your organization:

- Passwords: What makes a good password? Remind them never to share their password with anyone for any reason. Warn them of common mistakes such as writing passwords on a post-it note and sticking on the computer monitor.

Continued

NOTE (Continued)

- Social Engineering: Don't let people fool you. Make policies for visitors clear to ensure that a malicious visitor won't leave with information they shouldn't have. Also, you could review polices for verifying an employee's identity when they make requests (such as password resets) over the phone or in some other non-face-to-face situation.

- Physical Access: Verify that everyone knows what a visitors badge looks like and knows what the company policies are with regards to where visitors are allowed to go and where they are not allowed to go.

- Correctly Storing and Destroying Sensitive Material: Help employees keep up-to-date with company polices that require sensitive data be destroyed. For example, it's important that employees are trained on destroying paper and electronic media that contains confidential data when it's not longer needed.

Your Information Technology (IT) staff also needs to be regularly trained on security. For example:

- Secure Coding Practices: Software engineers don't necessarily need to be security experts; however, it's important that they understand secure coding practices. For example, anyone working on a Web application should be aware of cross-site scripting (XSS) and Structured Query Language (SQL) injection bugs. Programmers should also be aware of unsafe functions that may be available in their language, and their safer alternative functions. Requirement 6.5 mandates this.

- Systems Training: Systems administrators should be kept up-to-date with secure practices that are related to the systems they administer. They should know how to securely install and configure these systems. Many of the Requirement 2 items mandate that.

Finally, security professionals at your company must be trained regularly. Depending on the size of your company, this may be a few or several employees. These people are responsible for securing your systems every day. They must receive periodic training to help them be aware of new technologies and new attacks.

Regularly review the PCI requirements and compare what is asked with what you have at that moment. Focus on the requirements that cause your company trouble. Set aside a day per month for your review. A good rule of thumb is to review all PCI requirements at least quarterly. Reviewing on this schedule should keep you in great shape for your quarterly scan and annual assessment as well as keep you up-to-date with any changes in the PCI requirements. Your self-assessment process can be as detailed as walking through the testing procedures of the PCI DSS, or reviewing Self-Assessment Questionnaire D.

PCI REQUIREMENTS WITH PERIODIC MAINTENANCE

PCI DSS has many requirements that mandate ongoing actions with varying outcomes. Some requirements have documentation outputs that are reviewed during your annual assessment, and other requirements actions are in fact the compliance activity. Finally, some requirements don't have an actual maintenance requirement, but there is documentation that must be updated before an assessment, so we'll cover those as well.

WARNING

Please, if you remember one thing from reading this entire book, let it be: you are never "done" with security. Also, while validating your PCI compliance is your QSA's task, maintaining compliance and data security is yours and yours alone.

Build and Maintain a Secure Network

Of the requirements in this domain that requires some kind of action, one in particular was updated for PCI DSS version 1.2. Requirement 1.1.6 formerly required a quarterly review of all firewall and router rules and configurations. In version 1.2, the requirement was changed to every 6 months. That means that when your annual assessment is due, you should have documentation from at least two of these reviews; that is what your QSA will be asking about. The reviews should be detailed enough to show that an engineer checked every item and validated that it was still needed.

Your assessor will also review documentation for two other requirements in this domain, and while they may not have to be updated through a formal process, many companies have failed parts of their PCI Assessment because they forgot to do something simple like update a configuration standard that referenced outdated, or known vulnerable software. Requirements 1.1 and 2.2 fall into this category. Be sure that during your normal review for Requirement 1.1.6, you review and update your firewall and router configuration standards for Requirement 1.1. Do the ruleset review first and note anything that is not in the standard, then go update the standard so that it matches what is in the ruleset. While it may seem overly picky, an assessor would be in the right if they noted outdated configuration standards for Requirement 1.1.

In addition, go back through all of your in-scope system types and ensure that their configuration is up-to-date for Requirement 2.2. Most companies fall short on this requirement when they reference out-of-date software packages or versions that have security vulnerabilities in them. For example, if your configuration standards still say to start with a stock build of Sendmail 8.9, an outdated and vulnerable version of Sendmail, you would not be able to pass that requirement.

Protect Cardholder Data

Requirement 3 has two key items to address, and one that may just need to have a fresh set of eyes. First off, Requirement 3.1 mandates that you create retention requirements for cardholder data. Requirement 3.1 has a quarterly requirement to purge old data by way of manual review or automated disposal process. Even if your process is 100 percent automated, take the time each quarter to make sure that the processes are in fact functioning correctly. During your assessment, expect your assessor to ask you to produce your oldest set of retained data. They will then check to make sure that it does not exceed the retention requirements set forth in the aforementioned review.

WARNING

Our guidance from Chapter 6, "Protecting Cardholder Data," still stands: It is usually easier to not store the data than to protect stored data. This is not a traditional way to think about data security, but it is one way of thinking about which is extremely useful for painless PCI DSS compliance.

Consider expanding that quarterly process to include a review of the actual requirements to retain data. The business, regulatory, and legal environments can easily change more than annually (maybe not all at the same time, but one of the three will happen at least more than annually), so use that time to be sure that you do not need to alter your data retention requirements. If you do, republish the information and perform a new review to make sure you are in compliance with your own policy.

NOTE

Time and time again, companies write policies in good faith and then completely ignore them when it comes time to execute. As an example, Matt works for a large, Level 2 merchant. His company's corporate policy is actually more restrictive than PCI, and requires that all security patches be installed within 10 days of release, and that cardholder data must be encrypted internally over the wire. When Matt's assessor was performing the assessment, she noticed that one process for the florist shop inside his stores did not encrypt the cardholder data over the wire. When Matt confronted the department responsible for the florist shop's systems, the response he got back was "Well, it's not a PCI requirement so we just did the minimum," thus completely ignoring the corporate policy. Usually you don't find that just one policy is violated – there tends to be many. This would be a clue for his assessor to dig deeper to ensure that policies requiring the minimum PCI requirement are actually being followed. Moral of the story? If you have a corporate policy that exceeds the base requirements of PCI, FOLLOW IT. There is a reason why that policy is in place!

Requirement 3.6 gives us an annual requirement for key rotation. All keys used for the encryption of in-scope data need to be rotated at least annually. Your assessor will first look at your key management processes and make sure that there is a requirement to rotate annually, and then will check your documentation to see if you actually did rotate the key annually. While you are doing that, take a look at the overall key management processes and procedures and ensure they are up-to-date for Requirement 3.6. Common gotcha's here include forgetting to update the key management processes when you change encryption technologies. That's a big, red flag for an assessor, and it is pretty easy to spot.

Maintain a Vulnerability Management Program

Vulnerability management is a task that is easily seen as ongoing. New vulnerabilities and viruses are found every day, and companies need to take the appropriate precautions to ensure that they are protected. Requirement 5.2 has one of those few pesky occurrences of the word "periodic" in it as a carryover from PCI DSS version 1.1. To comply with this requirement, you must perform periodic scans of your in-scope machines.

TOOLS

We cover the vulnerability scanning tools that help with external and internal network scanning in Chapter 8, "Vulnerability Management."

With the ever-changing landscape of attacks and malware, you should probably scan your systems at least once a month, and likely more frequently. More of the quality vulnerability vendors offer unlimited scanning; you can use freeware tools such as Nessus as well for internal scans and "unofficial" external scans (those not performed by an ASV). To determine how often you should scan your systems, perform a risk analysis of these systems and include elements such as the criticality of the systems, amount of processing power, business hours and uptime requirements, bandwidth, and the frequency by which you update your antivirus definitions. Such risk analysis is in fact prescribed in Requirement 12.1.2. (Security policy must "include an annual process that identifies threats, and vulnerabilities, and results in a formal risk assessment"). PCI DSS does not give you a time period for performing a full scan, but most assessors would probably accept as long as quarterly as an acceptable period if you were including on-demand scanning as well. It's a slippery slope with many variables, but more frequent scanning followed by the ongoing remediation is clearly better. If you do your homework, you can take your assessor on a journey through your logic, with documentation to back it up.

Security patches must be installed within 1 month of their release. Why the Council decided to change the verbiage from 30 days to 1 month in the new version is a mystery. This particular requirement will quickly ruffle the feathers of system administrators, and particularly those of mainframes and large databases. These systems have high availability requirements and typically are not brought down frequently to install patches. When looking at Requirement 6.1, be sure that the patches you are considering installing are actually security related. Only those patches must be installed according to this schedule. Alternatively, if you have a way to mitigate the vulnerability without installing the patch, do that. Since PCI DSS version 1.2, the note below Requirement 6.1 allows you to take a risk-based approach on your patches, and prioritize critical systems first. Then you can patch the remaining systems within 3 months (quarterly) instead of one.

NOTE

A good example of an action that could be used to mitigate a security vulnerability instead of deploying a patch is the Microsoft Graphics Rendering Engine vulnerability from early 2006 (www.microsoft.com/technet/security/Bulletin/MS06-001.mspx). In their notes, unregistering the DLL mitigates the vulnerability until the patch is deployed. This is acceptable for PCI DSS compliance.

Finally, be sure that you scan your public-facing Web applications at least annually, or after any changes for Requirement 6.6. Your assessor will review your policy and procedure documents, as well as review the output from processes like the above to make sure it is occurring as prescribed. If you do not want to go through this process, Requirement 6.6 allows you to use a Web application firewall in lieu of the above process. Most companies end up choosing a hybrid of the two. They may have a Web application firewall protecting their applications, and also perform an automated Web application security scanning as needed. Keep in mind that both scanning and Web application firewall monitoring are ongoing tasks; scanning is periodic while WAF management is continuous. Also, keep in mind that scanning is not terribly useful unless vulnerabilities found by the scanner are actually fixed!

Implement Strong Access Control Measures

Strong access controls are key to preventing unauthorized access to your data. While Requirement 7 does not specifically have a mandate to review access granted to cardholder data, consider adding it to your quarterly Sarbanes–Oxley review (or if you do not do these, review cardholder access quarterly). This will help to keep only those with a business or job-related requirement to access in-scope data part of the access groups that grant this type of privilege.

For those that do have a requirement to access in-scope data, be sure that users inactive for more than 90 days are disabled or removed (Requirement 8.5.5). To save time, build an automated process to do this, and assess the process quarterly. Be sure to document everything you find! While you are doing this, think back to the last time you changed your password. Did all systems you access force you to do it at least quarterly? If not, follow up on that now. Don't wait for your annual assessment to learn that your systems are not requiring quarterly password changes (Requirement 8.5.9).

Do you use off-site storage for tape backups or hard copy media? If so, be sure you visit it at least annually and review its security.[1] Some of these facilities have annual assessments performed and can provide the documentation to you upon request. If they do this, be sure you have a chance to review the methodology used by the assessment company, and it includes common security controls in the scope of the review. SAS-70 Type I and II assessment reports are often provided for this type of due diligence. If you receive this, be sure to insist on the Type II report as it has the most amount of detail, and carefully review its scope statement to make sure key areas were not left out of the review. You may want to do this in conjunction with your annual media inventory process for Requirement 9.1.1.

Finally, one of those requirements without a stated review period is Requirement 9.2. You developed procedures to visually distinguish identification provided to both visitors and employees. Make sure it is up-to-date, addresses all personnel, and is still accurate as part of the hire and fire process.

Regularly Monitor and Test Networks

Time for one of our more frequent periodic review elements is daily log review for Requirement 10.6. Chances are you don't have a team of people driving themselves insane by reading every log generated by every in-scope

---

[1] Some of the secure storage locations might not allow on-site visits because of their own security policies. All such issues need to be resolved contractually! In other words, before your use any outside storage provider for cardholder data, it is your responsibility to make sure that you would be able to satisfy PCI DSS requirements.

device. You most likely have some tools to collect, aggregate, normalize, and correlate these logs. As part of that process, the log management tool should be intelligent enough to find items that are not part of normal operations and create alerts to your staff for follow-up. Have your internal assessment group periodically assess this process to make sure it is working as designed. It is more important to review an ongoing process for log review and to make sure it is current and active than to review every single log manually.

Next comes Requirement 11. Almost all subrequirements under Requirement 11 have some kind of periodic action associated with them. Starting with Requirement 11.1, quarterly running a wireless analyzer at all of your locations to search for unauthorized wireless activity. As we discussed in Chapter 7, "Using Wireless Networking," doing a quarterly walk-through may not be the best idea from a resource and threat mitigation perspective. If you only have one location the logistics might work, but from a security protection perspective you are not doing everything you should. If you have chosen to deploy Wireless IDS/IPS technology instead, perform a quarterly asessment of the systems to ensure they are properly alerting and deploying defense and containment measures that you configured.

Next comes the quarterly scans. Requirement 11.2 requires that both internal and external scans are performed at least quarterly, with clean scans being the desired outcome for both of those operations. Save each of those clean quarterly scans in a special place because your assessor will need them as part of the on-site assessment review. Here is another requirement that can benefit from network segmentation as a scope reduction exercise. Companies are required to scan all in-scope internal systems, and all external IP Addresses. PCI DSS scoping instructions state that systems connected to networks that process cardholder data are in-scope for PCI DSS, even if they do not process or store cardholder data themselves. Thus, putting firewalls between these systems will reduce the amount of work you need to do for your internal scans. Externally, you can reduce the scope of your scans by air-gapping networks (meaning that the networks that process cardholder data externally are physically disconnected from ones that do not) or other strong segmentation techniques. Every situation is slightly different, so it is best to check with your QSA on which method works best for you.

Although those quarterly scans should address most of your vulnerabilities, you must also perform a deeper inspection of your systems and applications at least annually with a Penetration Test (Requirement 11.3). Two common mistakes companies make are forgetting to include applications (Requirement 11.3.2) and neglecting to perform the penetration test from an internal perspective as well as an external perspective. The penetration test is one of the most critical periodic requirements used by PCI DSS. The quality of your assessment will directly impact the likelihood of being caught up in a breach due to an external (or internal) attack. Your penetration test should include the following elements:

- Network attacks

- Application attacks

- Social engineering

- Modem penetration testing (if applicable)

- Wireless penetration testing (if applicable)

Once your test is performed, be sure to address any findings and have them rechecked to make sure your fixes worked.

Finally, Requirement 11.5 has two distinctly different periodic requirements to consider. The first is to perform critical file comparisons at least weekly, meaning that all in-scope machines (including the Point of Sale) should have some kind of file integrity monitoring run on its files. Whether you go with a commercial solution, or script something using a hashing utility like *sha5sum*, be sure that you run those comparisons at least weekly and for the second part of the review, follow up with any exceptions that come out of the process. The only reason an exception would be generated by the file integrity process is if you deployed a system update or patch and can track the exception back to a change control ticket, or if something bad was happening (maliciously or not) to the system. Both should be followed up on and closed appropriately.

Maintain an Information Security Policy

If you have not had enough with documentation, here's some more periodic requirements specifically for your information security policy and framework. Requirement 12.1 has two subrequirements with an annual review requirement, Requirement 12.1.2 mandating an annual risk assessment, and potentially as a part of that, Requirement 12.1.3 mandates a policy review. Your organization probably already performs some kind of annual risk assessment as a part of normal operations. You may be able to tag along with that, but be sure to include an assessment of risks relevant to PCI DSS. If you ignore all in-scope systems and don't include the risks associated with storing cardholder data, the risk assessment is not much help to your PCI efforts. Including your policies in the risk assessment might be a nice way to kill two birds with one stone. Be sure to update your policies to address findings in the risk assessment! Your assessor will look for this!

One of the more abstract requirements deals with daily operational security procedures (Requirement 12.2). This should include (but not be limited to) things like following up on log alerts, searching for new threats to systems, and checking on vulnerability data. Your assessor will want to see your definition of these items, and will want to see evidence that you are following the process.

Security awareness training is something that is often overlooked, but critical to maintaining a secure company (Requirement 12.6.1). You must demonstrate this ongoing educational process occurs at least annually and for all new hires. Limiting this type of training to only once per year will meet PCI DSS, but it is a bit too relaxed to be considered a security best practice. Find fun ways to engage your employees with security. Do demonstrations or exercises often. Consider posting things in break rooms or common areas where employees congregate. Add something to their pay stub. Or even involve them in a demonstration like "Find the Bad Guy" where you have an employee walking around with a fake badge, or maybe no badge at all. Offer prizes like Starbucks or iTunes gift cards. You will be amazed at how well this will improve the weakest link in your security: people.

None of us want to invoke an incident response policy, but like your will, it needs to be defined and planned incase something bad happens. Requirement 12.9.2 mandates annual testing of the incident response policy. Instead of hiring someone to steal something from your company, consider doing a table-top exercise whereby you simulate an incident, and walk through all the steps in your plan. This will help your employees understand their roles and will ferret out problems or gaps in the process. In addition to doing this, you must train your staff with security breach responsibilities so they have the specific skills needed to respond. This may include sending key employees to forensics training, or Continuing Professional Education (CPE) classes around breaches and their aftermath.

PCI SELF-ASSESSMENT

In addition to the elements called out earlier, take the time to review all of the requirements at least once before your assessor shows up. You should be going into an assessment by a QSA knowing that you will pass. Don't rely on the assessor to find all of your gaps. Instead, show your assessor that you have been compliant all year long. You'll be amazed at how much faster your assessment goes, and how much more confident your management will be when asked about your current PCI DSS posture.

The PCI Security Standards Council (www.pcisecuritystandards.org) provides some great documents to help you with your self assessment. For example, Self-Assessment Questionnaire D can help you to determine your company's current compliance level in a Yes or No format. You should periodically review these documents, and look for ways to improve your company's security posture.

CASE STUDY

You have read plenty of case studies in this book where someone made a mistake that lead to a breach. It's not that there are no GOOD programs in this world; it's just that we (should) learn from others mistakes. Those lessons will hopefully prevent us from walking off the proverbial cliff. However, in this chapter, we're turning the tables and presenting a case study where a company got it right. Not only right, but knocked it out of the park!

The Case of the Compliant Company

Peggy's Pad Thai Palace, a national Thai food chain, enjoyed quick success with its multiple brands and quality food. Peggy's vision was to create two sides to the business and started with a high-quality dining experience in freestanding restaurants. Once she had her recipes down, she figured out how to prepare something very close to the same quality and taste in a mass-produced way, and opened hundreds of stores in shopping malls across the country. Her success spread like a wildfire, and before she knew it, she was managing a billion-dollar enterprise with more than 3000 locations.

She began accepting credit cards in her mall locations 5 years ago, and quickly ascended through the levels to become a Level 1 merchant. Before she became a Level 1 merchant, she attended many conferences and seminars geared toward restaurateurs, and heard alarming stories about how people lost their restaurants because a hacker breached their point of sale systems and stole credit card data. Peggy was determined not to let that happen to her.

Peggy began investing in security soon after hearing these stories and had a full enterprise security assessment performed to see how she stood up against the ISO Standards on information security (17,799 at the time, 27,002 now). She further invested in a framework to address the gaps discovered during the assessment, and within 2 years had a mature ISO program, complete with compliance management. She hired a small staff of individuals to handle her information security and compliance needs, and after completing several internal assessments against PCI DSS, she set out to find a QSA.

Her QSA came on board during the next quarter, and was duly impressed at how organized her processes and systems were. Through segmentation and other scope reduction techniques, Peggy had reduced the scope to the POS Terminals and one additional machine per store, three machines at the corporate office, and a few routers and switches in between. Overall, it was less than 1 percent of her total infrastructure. She also was sure to complete internal preassessments before the QSA arrived, and had all the documentation built and ready to go.

Peggy approached compliance as a cost of doing business, and was sure that she invested in security to cover her compliance needs. Her company went into each assessment KNOWING the outcome would be positive, and never had an issue passing her compliance assessment, and building security best practices to cover security threats where PCI DSS did not.

SUMMARY

Security is fleeting. You've got it 1 min and it's gone the next, but there are some steps that can be taken to keep yourself as secure as possible. Working with management and employees, you can keep your company in a good position to combat many attacks now and in the future. Things you can do to maintain your security include keeping your policy up-to-date, periodically assessing your security, and periodic training.

Please remember that it really doesn't matter how many times the author team will say "security first!" If some organizations don't get security with all of its complexities and ignore it for years, "compliance first" becomes a real choice for them. At least they can understand it. And then later, "compliance first" becomes "compliance ONLY," "checklists" replace "risk awareness," "flowcharts" replace thinking about their threats and vulnerabilities. And then hackers get them!

Reading this chapter should have reminded you that maintaining ongoing PCI DSS compliance and data security is your job, not ASVs, not QSAs, not your bank's. It is yours and yours alone! You can't achieve security; it's a never-ending process; you must constantly be assessing and working to mitigate risks. Also, you should plan now to train and review the employees and IT staff regularly to keep them reminded of and up-to-date on company policies.

PCI DSS changes as well: review the PCI requirements regularly to keep yourself up-to-date.

But more often: systems and attacks change. Regularly assess your systems to ensure they are still PCI compliant and secure. Similarly, regularly review your policies to verify they are up-to-date and are working at your company.

PCI and Other Laws, Mandates, and Frameworks

Take a look at the information security and compliance landscape. Do you think Payment Card Industry (PCI) is the worst thing out there? It's not. If you don't believe that, rope in your legal team and ask them which of these information security regulations or laws stand to damage a company the most. In this chapter, we want to expand upon the idea that there is an overlap between security standards and laws – an idea introduced in Chapter 10, "Managing a PCI DSS Project to Achieve Compliance." In reality, most laws and regulations that deal with protecting information are closely tied back to good information security practices (notice the term was *good*, not *best*). As a company, if you focus on information security instead of compliance, your long-term costs are dramatically lower.

In this chapter, we will learn how PCI augments and supplements many of the other compliance initiatives that companies must address. Arguably, this section is quite U.S. centric, but our coverage of PCI as it relates to ISO 27000 is meant to take a more global approach without getting into every country's specific legislation – that's what your legal team does. Arguably, for those countries or municipalities that have data breach notification laws, you will see a corollary between your particular situation and the PCI and State Data Breach Notification Laws section in this chapter. In the Regulation

Matrix section at the end of this chapter, we will provide a small compliance matrix that will compare (at a high level) PCI to the other regulations we cover to illustrate the amazing amount of overlap that exists.

PCI AND STATE DATA BREACH NOTIFICATION LAWS

According to the National Conference of State Legislatures (www.ncsl.org), "forty-five states, the District of Columbia, Puerto Rico, and the Virgin Islands have enacted legislation requiring notification of security breaches involving personal information" [1]. That's right, only five states (Alabama, Kentucky, Mississippi, New Mexico, and South Dakota) have not enacted laws that fall into this class, but rest assured, they most likely will. These laws are primarily used as a vehicle to prosecute companies that are irresponsible with their residents' data. In most cases, the laws do not limit themselves to companies that have physical locations in their state, but instead focus on the resident. In other words, if you do not have a store in Montana, but someone from Montana does business with you and you lose their information, you are required to follow the process in their law (Mont. Code Section 30-14-1701 et seq., 2009 H.B. 155, Chapter 163). Neither author is a lawyer, so understand that you should perform a formal risk analysis (if you have not already) on these laws to understand what your liability is, and where they fall.

Dealing with this many institutions seems like a horrible prospect, especially if you ever spend time reading any of these regulations – they are an insomniac's saving grace! But there are some commonalities that most of the regulations share that are relevant for comparison with PCI.

Origins of State Data Breach Notification Laws

Most of the laws you see enacted today can point back to the infamous California Senate Bill 1386 (SB 1386) for their origins. SB 1386 became effective on July 1, 2003, and contained revolutionary legislation that helped to shape how companies globally dealt with information security breaches.

Before laws like SB 1386, data breaches were typically swept under the carpet and only those very close to the matter even knew something occurred. Your sensitive data was in the hands of a bad guy, and you never had a chance to defend against it because you didn't know a breach occurred! The only way you would know is if you decided to go finance a new car or home, and the finance people had the "sit-down" meeting where nothing good happens. Did you know that you owed $50K on another car in another state?

Identity theft is much more dangerous for individuals than a credit card breach. If your credit card is stolen, as long as you are on top of your finances and validate every transaction on your statement (i.e., catch it early), you will probably have no financial liability. If you wait, things may be different. But if someone opens a line of credit under your name with stolen information, it could take years to clear your name and restore your credit. SB 1386 was the first of many that intended to protect residents against this kind of identity theft going unnoticed.

Commonalities Among State Data Breach Laws

So with 48 (potentially) different laws that you have to deal with, what are some of the commonalities that you can leverage? How about we start with something that is typically *not* included in all of these laws?

Most of the laws apply to electronic or computerized data, and do not apply to paper records. An example where a case was thrown out because of this technicality is a case from early 2009, *Pinero v. Jackson Hewitt Tax Service Inc.* In this case, the plaintiff's claim was rejected because the data loss (or mishandling) in question was hard copy, paper-based data, not electronic data. Only lawyers and legislators may know why the laws were written this way, but most likely it is because the largest data breaches in the last several years have been computer or electronic based. Dumpster diving still happens, but the mount of data that you can reach via networks and computers far exceeds what might be thrown out with yesterday's lunch in a smelly dumpster. Why get dirty when you can obtain more data in your pajamas while being serenaded by reruns of your favorite sitcom?

Not all states are like this, however. California's SB 1386 and Alaska's legislation specifically protects all personal information, sometimes called personally identifiable information (PII), regardless of the media on which it is stored.

This brings us to the next "UN" commonality, what defines PII? This is a painful question whose answer varies slightly among all the different pieces of legislation by which you may be required to comply. All the different permutations are far outside the scope of this book, but it's a great example of when it's appropriate to bring in your legal team. Make sure that they pay close attention to what kind of data could become PII just based on what is stored near or around it! As an example, look at the scoping section of PCI DSS. If you store the expiration date of a credit card by itself, it is not considered cardholder data. But if you store it "near" the actual card number, it is considered cardholder data, and subject to the same requirements as the card number itself. Once you complete this process, you will realize how scary of a picture this legislation paints, and will take a hard look at the data you do store about your consumers, and the need to store it and ways to protect what you do store.

One commonality shared among several of the states is an "escape hatch" for encrypted data that is lost. Many states say that you do not have to go through the notification process if the only data that was lost was encrypted data. This is another nuance that your legal team should consider, as many states and some of the Federal Banking Inter-Agency Guidance do *not* make that distinction. They consider an encrypted tape the same as they would an unencrypted USB drive, and require notification per their guidelines.

The final commonality that varies between states is the time you have to notify and method by which you must do it. Each state approaches this slightly differently, including some that have an allowance for working with law enforcement before a notification is made, and others that put a specific time limit (usually somewhere in the 30-day range if it is spelled out) by which you must notify consumers. The notification in most cases must be something prominent, and potentially to include multiple communication methods, from posting a bulletin on your Web site, to taking out ad space in a media outlet, to issuing a press release. Again, unfortunately, you will not save on legal fees by reading this book. The best advice you will get is to closely involve your legal team when planning your data breach notification strategy.

How Does It Compare to PCI?

With the commonalities we mentioned earlier, there are several ways that PCI and State Data Breach Notification Laws compliment each other. Looking at the types of media covered, PCI DSS covers *all* types of media (paper and electronic) as do some states and the U.S. Federal Government. From a notification perspective, you may not be required to notify individual cardholders under PCI DSS, but you are required to have an incident response plan (Requirement 12.9) and notify your acquirers, card brands, and potentially law enforcement, depending on the situation. This means that your Public Relations department is probably already involved, so extending a message to consumers is just one step farther than you have to go for PCI DSS.

PCI DSS can have an "escape hatch" if you were found to be compliant at the time of the breach. So far, the card brands maintain that no company was compliant at the time of their breach. Industry pundits argue both sides of the issue, but in reality, companies that are breached are usually doing something dangerous (or *not* doing something security-critical) that leads to that occurring. Since PCI DSS is so wide and sweeping, it's not a far leap to assume that the holes that attackers squeeze through (or in some cases *drive* through) are in fact addressed by some part of PCI DSS. At the very least, PCI DSS evolves to cover modern attack methods as well as modern security technologies; if a breach happens through a method not even remotely covered by PCI DSS, it is highly likely that the next edition of the standard will include a new safeguard or control addressing that vulnerability.

> **NOTE**
>
> PCI DSS changes every 2 years as part of a process you can read about on the PCI Security Standards Council Web site (www.pcisecuritystandards.org), which is really, really slow compared to how the operation of the criminal hacker community changes. Focusing on security and not on checkboxes is what will save the day.

Final Thoughts on State Laws

One thing left out of this book is the numerous state laws that introduce fines and penalties for poor security practices. As of this writing, Minnesota's Plastic Card Security Act, Nevada's new "PCI Law" (which amends NRS 603A), and the new Massachusetts Data Breach Law (Mass. Gen. Laws Ch. 93H) are the first in a growing trend of states providing criminal liability and remedies for the inevitable victims from a data breach. These laws typically lay out a similar set of controls to the high level components of PCI DSS or ISO27002, but leave much to the interpretation and implementation of programs designed to address these laws. Nevada's is the first to specifically call out required compliance to PCI DSS, and actually provides a Safe Harbor exception if you are compromised, but found to be compliant at the time of the breach. Unless Federal legislation is drafted in the near future, expect the confusing and frustrating landscape of state-based data breach legislation to continue, and to be tested in the court system.

PCI AND THE ISO27000 SERIES

As of this writing, the ISO27000 series (www.27000.org) are devoted to Information Security. For those of you who are not new to Information Security, you may remember BS7799 or ISO17799 as security framework standards that you may have assessed against. Those have been updated and are now part of the ISO27000 series of standards. Those standards are as follows:

- ISO 27001: Specification for an information security management system.

- ISO 27002: The 27000 series standard number of what was originally ISO17799.

- ISO 27003: A new standard intended to offer guidance for the implementation of an IS Management System (ISMS).

- ISO 27004: A new standard covering information security system management measurement and metrics.

- ISO 27005: The methodology independent ISO standard for information security risk management.

- ISO 27006: Guidelines for the accreditation of organizations offering ISMS certification.

More standards and documents are still under development, but for the purposes of this book, we will only focus on ISO27002 which most closely represents commonalities with PCI as an information security framework. According to the framers of PCI DSS, they will informally tell you that ISO17799 was a significant consideration when developing PCI DSS, and in fact, if you review the last iteration of Visa's Cardholder Information Security Program (CISP) you will see an even closer relationship with ISO17799.

At a high level, ISO27002 has 12 domains (PCI DSS has six domains, 12 requirements). Those are as follows:

- Risk Assessment and Treatment
- Security Policy
- Organization of Information Security
- Asset Management
- Human Resources Security
- Physical Security
- Communications and Ops Management
- Access Control

- Information Systems Acquisition, Development, Maintenance

- Information Security Incident management

- Business Continuity

- Compliance

At first glance, you will notice several things that are unique to ISO27002 not included in PCI DSS. ISO27002 is an information security standard and framework, where PCI DSS only concerns itself with one specific type of data, cardholder data. Most experts agree, if you have a mature ISO27002 program, PCI is eezy-cheezy.

Let's take a moment to explore what ISO27002 will give you that PCI DSS will not. ISO27002 details a process for risk assessments, while PCI just requires that they are performed in various parts of the standard. ISO27002 gives much more guidance to Asset Management and Human Resources Security, as well as the Organization of Information Security, Communications and Operations Management, and Information Security Incident Management. In some cases, ISO27002 addresses things you don't see at all in PCI like Business Continuity.

While a deep dive of ISO27002 is outside the scope of this book, security professionals will tell you that a mature ISO27002-based information security program will provide better protection than most of the industry or government regulated standards with which merchants and service providers might need to comply. The mere maturity of the program will provide for an easier path to PCI DSS compliance.

PCI AND SARBANES–OXLEY (SOX)

The Sarbanes–Oxley Act of 2002 (SOX) was enacted as a result of the numerous public company accounting scandals of the late 1990s and early 2000s in the United States such as Enron, Tyco International, and Worldcom. Accounting firms defrauded millions of investors, and bankrupted the retirement plans of many employees. These scandals along with the events of September 11 kicked off a market slide and impacted investors globally.

While many IT workers grumble just as loudly when you mention SOX as they do when you mention PCI DSS, SOX is not an IT regulation. In fact, most of the consternation created around SOX comes from one element of Section 404. Although the entire piece of legislation is substantial in size,

Section 404 comprises two subsections (a and b) that kicked off this entire frenzy. The two relevant subsections under Section 404a are as follows:

1. state the responsibility of management for establishing and maintaining an adequate internal control structure and procedures for financial reporting; and

2. contain an assessment, as of the end of the most recent fiscal year of the issuer, of the effectiveness of the internal control structure and procedures of the issuer for financial reporting [2].

Did you realize that it was only these two sections made such a big mess? It's humorous when you think about it. SOX's spending far exceeds that of PCI DSS, yet PCI DSS's requirements take up so much more space than SOX!

Part of the reason for this is that Section 404 does two things that generated a ton of work for large accounting firms. The first part of sub-bullet 1 requires that companies define a control set. PCI DSS does that for you – it's the standard. Where SOX becomes easier to manage from an IT control perspective over PCI DSS is that you are allowed to define your own controls that are sufficient to protect your financial data. PCI DSS does not afford you that luxury. You must comply with their predefined control set. The second part of SOX requires companies to be audited against that control set. That's similar to hiring a Qualified Security Assessor (QSA) to assess and validate your compliance with PCI DSS.

If you are a company subject to SOX, hopefully you are far along in your control framework maturity, and do not have problems passing your audits. If it takes 10 signatures to order a ream of paper, you might have a mature SOX program!

Although the SOX and PCI DSS teams attack different problems, there are things that each can learn from each other. For one, it makes more sense to manage to a common set of company controls, and then map those controls into each standard you might have to follow. For example, if you have password and authentication controls defined, you should be able to map those back into PCI DSS during an assessment of PCI DSS, and if PCI DSS changes, you should be able to go the other direction and make sure your controls are sufficient. Given the choice, most companies would prefer to manage to a common set of controls that address all compliance frameworks versus managing the four to five different compliance frameworks directly. If you can get your company focused on controls instead of requirements, you will have a better chance of maintaining compliance, and spending less with new compliance directives.

REGULATION MATRIX

The matrix below (Table 14.1) illustrates some of the overlap and commonalities between PCI and other major compliance or security initiatives. One of three possible entries is listed in each cell. Cells with the term "Yes" in them

Table 14.1 Detailed Regulation Matrix

PCI Requirement	ISO27002	Common SOX Controls	Mass Data Breach Law
Install and maintain a firewall configuration to protect cardholder data	Yes	Yes	?
Do not use vendor-supplied defaults for system passwords and other security parameters	Yes	?	No
Protect stored [cardholder] data	Yes	Yes	Yes
Encrypt transmission of [cardholder] data across open, public networks	Yes	?	Yes
Use and regularly update antivirus software	Yes	Yes	No
Develop and maintain secure systems and applications	Yes	Yes	No
Restrict access to [cardholder] data by business need-to-know	Yes	Yes	Yes
Assign a unique ID to each person with computer access	Yes	Yes	No
Restrict physical access to [cardholder] data	Yes	Yes	Yes

Continued

Table 14.1 Detailed Regulation Matrix *Continued*

PCI Requirement	ISO27002	Common SOX Controls	Mass Data Breach Law
Track and monitor all access to network resources and [cardholder] data	Yes	Yes	No
Regularly test security systems and processes	Yes	Yes	Yes
Maintain a policy that addresses information security	Yes	Yes	Yes

means that there is a direct correlation, or that most implementations would require a similar control to be put in place. Cells with the marque "?" designate a possible match, but it depends on the implementation or specific control set. Cells with the term "No" in them means there is not a direct match between the initiatives, but depending on other areas (such as a security policy requirement), you may end up with overlap. Instead of comparing the Data Breach Notification Laws, we'll see how the new Massachusetts Data Breach Laws (thought to be the most aggressive today) compare to PCI DSS.

Based on everything we have covered, are you surprised that PCI and ISO27002 are so closely matched? If anything, this graphic could be used as the argument to invest in an ISO27002 program so that you don't have to chase all these individual initiatives!

How Do You Leverage Your Efforts for PCI DSS?

First and foremost, make a partnership with your legal team. Personality issues aside, your legal team should be your best friend during this process as they will be able to help you to lay out all the elements of risk and remedies, so you can justify the quantifiable costs associated with Information Security. Once you have these all laid out for your organization, you will be able to determine what PCI DSS already requires, and address any gaps quickly.

SUMMARY

PCI DSS has much in common with many of the existing security practices or laws and regulations with which your company might have to comply. We explored how PCI DSS shares similarities with State Data Breach Notification Laws, and briefly touched on new data breach related laws that are ever increasing in number and scope. We compared PCI DSS to

ISO27002 and showed you how implementing and maturing something like ISO27002 would most likely exceed the base requirements of PCI DSS (and most other compliance initiatives). We discussed SOX, how it came to cause such a big mess, tips to use when dealing with both, and some of the dangers you might run into if you hand your PCI DSS compliance program over to those teams.

Data breaches are not going away, and as long as companies lag in protecting the information of constituents, expect laws to continue to be drafted and the landscape to become more complicated. The best thing you can do is step back and implement a solid information security program, ensuring that your base control set and framework meets the requirements of PCI DSS (and any other initiative you may be facing), and manage to that.

REFERENCES

[1] National Conference of State Legislators. State Security Breach Notification Laws. www.ncsl.org/IssuesResearch/TelecommunicationsInformationTechnology/ SecurityBreachNotificationLaws/tabid/13489/; 2009 [accessed 30.07.09].

[2] FindLaw.com. HR3763. http://news.findlaw.com/cnn/docs/gwbush/ sarbanesoxley072302.pdf; 2009 [accessed 30.07.09].

Myths and Misconceptions of PCI DSS

As we previously discussed, Payment Card Industry Data Security Standard (PCI DSS) has transformed the way many organizations view information security. While we've heard that something will take information security from the wire closet to the boardroom many times before, PCI actually accomplishes this for many organizations – both large and small. While it should be clear to our readers that following all of the PCI DSS guidance will not magically make your organization secure or prevent all incidents, the standard contains many of the common sense security requirements that are essential for protecting cardholder data.

PCI DSS was unified from card brand individual security mandates such as CISP and SDP and established to increase the security of card-accepting merchants and thus reduce the risk of card transactions and resulting fraud. As of today, "PCI DSS compliance includes merchants and service providers who accept, capture, store, transmit or process credit and debit card data."

The aforementioned quote from the PCI DSS document reminds us that the applicability of PCI DSS is nearly universal.

In this chapter, we look at common PCI DSS myths and misconceptions. We will also dispel those myths and provide a few useful tips on approaching to PCI DSS.

Let's get to the myths.

MYTH #1 PCI DOESN'T APPLY

Myth #1 is pretty simple, but, sadly, very common: "PCI DSS just doesn't apply to us, because we are small, or we are a University, or we don't do e-commerce, or we outsource "everything," or we don't store cards, or we are not a permanent entity, etc." This myth takes over an organization and makes it oblivious to PCI DSS requirements and, almost always, to information security risk in general.

Here is one recent example: a campaign of Norm Coleman for U.S. Senate in 2008 has announced [1] that "If you donated online to Norm Coleman's 2008 Senate campaign, or his recount efforts, you should call and cancel the credit card you used to make that donation." The reason? Attackers compromised the site and stole both the credit cards numbers of donors and other private information. From the circumstances disclosed in the media, one can deduce that the information was stored in violation of PCI DSS rules.

Another example is more blatant: health care providers have been so busy with HIPAA that many became oblivious of PCI DSS arrival. A recent paper in "SC Magazine" called "PCI-DSS: Not on health care provider's radar" [2] reports:

> However, since Medicare reimbursement is not at risk with PCI-DSS compliancy, it has been virtually ignored. It doesn't help that major health care publications are openly misinterpreting the PCI-DSS standards for health care providers, with statements such as: "[Providers] do not have to worry about compliance with PCI standards... they aren't storing any card numbers" [2].

A perfect example of Myth #1 at work! PCI DSS is not about storing data; it is about those who accept payment cards or capture, store, transmit, or process such card data. Want to guess whether most health care providers accept cards? Didn't think so – the number is probably close to 100.00 percent. Indeed, the paper mentioned earlier [2] confirms: "In 2009, virtually all health care providers take credit cards – and virtually none of them are PCI compliant."

> **NOTE**
>
> **Question**: If I only accept cards from June to August each year and I only use a dial-up terminal, I am "safe from PCI," right?
>
> **Answer**: Wrong. Even though your scope of PCI DSS validation is very, very small, you are definitely subject to its rules because you – surprise! – accept payment cards. PCI DSS applies to those who "accept, capture, store, transmit, or process credit and debit card data." If you do, it applies to you – end of the story. No myths can change that.

It is also interesting to note that one of the data elements required to be protected under HIPAA is customer payment information, which often means "credit card data." This means that HIPAA technically preceded PCI DSS when it comes to cardholder data security! However, this doesn't stop the health care provider from ignoring both regulations in one fell swoop.

The reality, as we mentioned earlier is pretty simple: PCI DSS does apply to your organization if you accept payment cards or capture, store, process, or transmit any sensitive payment card data (such as PAN) with no exceptions. Whether you cure, educate, rent, offer, sell, or provide doesn't matter – what matters is whether you charge! If you do, PCI DSS does apply. Hopefully, if you picked up this book whole being unsure whether PCI DSS applies to your organization, reading this book convinced you that becoming compliant and secure is indeed in your future if you deal with payment cards.

Admittedly, different things need to happen at your organization if you have absolutely no electronic processing or storage of digital cardholder data compared to having an Internet-connected payment application system. The scope of compliance validation will be much more limited in the former case and so your PCI project will be much, much simpler. For example, if a small merchant "does not store, process, or transmit any cardholder data on merchant premises but relies entirely on third-party service providers to handle these functions" he is only responsible for validating a small part of PCI DSS. Specifically, he would be responsible for the parts of "Requirement 9: Restrict physical access to cardholder data" as well as a small part of "Requirement 12: Maintain a policy that addresses information security for employees and contractors" via a self-assessment questionnaire (SAQ) Type A (13 questions overall).

Let's explore this example in more detail. As we covered in Chapter 3, "Why Is PCI Here?," payment card brands such as Visa and MasterCard label merchants that process fewer than 20,000 card transactions a year as "Level 4." As you now know, such merchants currently are required to validate their PCI compliance using a SAQ.

In addition, as described in PCI DSS standards, if a merchant matches the criteria below, he is considered to be "validation type 1" and needs to fill the SAQ Type A (the shortest). The criteria are as follows:

- Merchant does not store, process, or transmit any cardholder data on merchant premises but relies entirely on third-party service providers to handle these functions.

- The third-party service providers handling storage, processing, or transmission of cardholder data is confirmed to be PCI DSS compliant.

- Merchant retains only paper reports or receipts with cardholder data, and such documents are not received electronically.

- Merchant does not store any cardholder data in electronic format.

Explained simply, the aforementioned criteria describe a situation where a merchant accepts credit cards as payment, but does not have any electronic storage, processing, or transmission of cardholder data. Think about it for a moment! PCI DSS does apply if you do not store, process, or transmit any card data on your premises at all! This example highlights that fact that card acceptance is sufficient to make the merchant to fall under PCI.

The exact scope of its validation as covered by SAQ Type A is shown in Fig. 15.1.

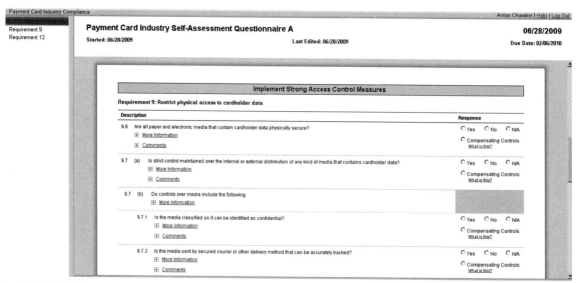

FIGURE 15.1 Self-Assessment Questionnaire (SAQ), Type A

The merchant needs to validate part of Requirement 9 and part of Requirement 12. Specifically, sections of Requirement 9 cover the storage of physical media (printouts, receipts, etc.) that has cardholder data. For example, quoting from PCI DSS SAQ Type A [3]:

- 9.6 Are all paper and electronic media that contain cardholder data physically secure?

- 9.7 Is strict control maintained over the internal or external distribution of any kind of media that contains cardholder data?

- 9.8 Are processes and procedures in place to ensure management approval is obtained prior to moving any and all media containing cardholder data from a secured area (especially when media is distributed to individuals)?

- 9.9 Is strict control maintained over the storage and accessibility of media that contains cardholder data?

- 9.10 Is media containing cardholder data destroyed when it is no longer needed for business or legal reasons?

All of the above deal with the physical media such as printouts that may contain card data. He is also subject to one sections of Requirement 12, which covers the merchant's relationship with service providers that actually handle data (again, see PCI DSS SAQ Type A [3]):

- 12.8 If cardholder data is shared with service providers, are policies and procedures maintained and implemented to manage service providers, and do the policies and procedures include the following?

- 12.8.1 A list of service providers is maintained.

- 12.8.2 A written agreement is maintained that includes an acknowledgement that the service providers are responsible for the security of cardholder data the service providers possess.

- 12.8.3 There is an established process for engaging service providers, including proper due diligence prior to engagement.

- 12.8.4 A program is maintained to monitor service providers' PCI DSS compliance status [3].

All of the above deal with the responsibilities of the third party that handles processing, storage, and transmission of data.

Overall, the choice is pretty simple: either you comprehend PCI DSS now and start working on security and PCI requirements or your acquirer will make it clear to you at some point when you won't have much room to maneuver.

MYTH #2 PCI IS CONFUSING

Myth #2 is just as pervasive: PCI is confusing and not specific. At first, it might seem like it is true: after all, there is a whole book is written about it! However, this is actually a myth, despite the fact that people who didn't invest enough time into learning about PCI compliance might be a little confused about it.

In addition, this myth seems to be purposefully propagated by some people to "muddy the waters" and thus to make PCI DSS seem impossible to achieve and thus not worthy of even trying. For example, when confronted with the need to change their business process to avoid storing the card data (simpler task as you now know) or with the need to secure card data (a harder task compared to not storing it), many smaller organizations go into the "ostrich in the sand" mode and try to pretend the problem is unclear, unsolvable, or confusing, instead of tacking it head on.

Namely, those under its influence often proclaim things such as

- "We don't know what to do, who to ask, what exactly to change."

- "PCI just confuses us – we can't do it."

- "PCI is confusing; until you give us something better, we will not do anything to protect the data"

Sometimes it also devolves into the following:

- "Just give us a task list and we will do it. Promise!"

The reality is quite different: PCI DSS documents explain both what to do and then how to validate it. Apart from people who propagate this myth, you just need to take the time to understand the "why" (the spirit of the standard and cardholder data security), the "what" (the list of PCI DSS requirements), and "how" (common approaches and practices related to PCI).

PCI is actually much easier to understand than other existing security and risk management frameworks and regulatory guidance. Looking at some of the advanced information risk management documents (such as ISO27005 "Information security risk management" or NIST 800-30 "Risk Management Guide for Information Technology Systems"), with their hundreds of pages of sometimes esoteric guidance, is a refreshing reminder that PCI DSS is, in fact, pretty simple and straightforward.

Most of the gray area talk you hear about PCI DSS typically comes from companies that are trying to find creative ways not to do anything to their business or their technology. Most of these can be solved by removing the emotion from the situation, and logically laying out the cost and risk associated with making a change versus staying the same.

Let's compare what PCI says and what some other guidance documents say:

PCI DSS in Requirement 5 states:

"5.1 Deploy antivirus software on all systems commonly affected by malicious software (particularly personal computers and servers).

5.1.1 Ensure that all antivirus programs are capable of detecting, removing, and protecting against all known types of malicious software.

5.2 Ensure that all antivirus mechanisms are current, actively running, and capable of generating audit logs."

ISO17799 (a little outdated but still in wide use) states [4]: "Precautions are required to prevent and detect the introduction of malicious software, such as computer viruses, network worms, Trojan horses, and logic bombs."

NIST 800-53 document "Recommended Security Controls for Federal Information Systems," itself a 174 page tome, states [5] "The information system implements malicious code protection." Additional NIST documents, such as 800-83 "Guide to Malware Incident Prevention and Handling: Recommendations of the National Institute of Standards and Technology," do provide useful additional guidance on malware protection, but that is another 101 pages to read (!).

The aforementioned example demonstrates that even though PCI DSS needs some focused attention from the merchants, it is not confusing, but more specific than other industry security guidance. While historically PCI creators had BS7799/ISO 17799 in mind, their standard ended up being much simpler than its ISO-created inspiration, but lost of few things that people consider important (for example, all the security project management requirements).

Still, there are definitely areas in PCI security guidance that can be made more specific. For example, when PCI DSS document was updated from version 1.1 to version 1.2, the updated document contained several dozen clarifications and explanations, brought up during the review phase. An interested reader can check them in the document "Summary of Changes from PCI DSS Version 1.1 to 1.2" (www.pcisecuritystandards.org/pdfs/pci_dss_summary_of_changes_v1-2.pdf) issued by the PCI Council in

October 2008. The clarifications made provided additional details, such as, for example [6]:

- Throughout Requirement 1, added routers to clarify that the requirement applies to both firewalls and routers.

- Added an example of a network diagram "that shows cardholder data flows over the network."

- Changed the following terms: "specific need" to "legitimate business need", "credit card data" to "PAN." Provided examples of where PAN may be displayed.

As PCI DSS grows up, all the remaining ambiguity should be reduced through the efforts of participating organizations and by adopting to the needs and requirement of the merchants as well as the evolution of the threats.

Finally, security cannot and will not ever be reduced to a simple checklist. Even today some criticize PCI DSS for being a manifestation of "checklist security" which does not account for individual organization's risk profile. PCI guidance is as close to a checklist as we can get without actually leading to increased, not reduced, risk.

MYTH #3 PCI DSS IS TOO ONEROUS

The next myth, Myth #3 is closely related to the above: PCI DSS is too hard. Sometimes, it becomes too expensive, too complicated, too burdensome, just too much for a small business, about too many technologies or even simply "unreasonable."

Sometimes this myth is close to reality, but not for reasons people think. "PCI is too hard" becomes true if merchants are treating their card data in a particularly careless way. For example, we introduced a concept of "flat network" in Chapter 4, "Building and Maintaining a Secure Network." To remind, it means a network that is not segmented by firewalls or filtering routers into zones or segments. Such network design means that if a single system handles card data, the whole network is in-scope for PCI DSS. Yes, that means all servers, all desktops, all network devices and everything else connected to it becomes subject to all PCI DSS requirements! Such situation, even if relatively rare, has been known to happen and thus make PCI DSS compliance very hard as the scope grows from a single system or a handful of systems to possible tens of thousands of systems. Every such system will need to be scanned for vulnerability, have its security configuration verified (these include the password length and complexity, use of encryption, etc.)

In this case, "PCI is hard" will not be a myth, but PCI DSS guidance will not be the reason to blame: the operators of such network will be.

WARNING

If you think PCI is too onerous, please stop and consider this: do you think that wearing a seat belt while driving is too onerous? How about brushing your teeth every day?

Things are new and unusual, the ones you have not been doing are often first seen as onerous. When you were 3 years old, it is very likely that brushing your teeth was seen as a huge task – and an annoying one as well.

So, if you happen to think PCI and data security is too onerous, you simply need to start paying attention to it – and it will stop being onerous after you get good at it.

Similarly, if a simple change in a business process will lead to removal of stored cardholder data, continuing to operate without such change and engaging in attempts to protect such data, rather than remove it will be shortsighted and lead to PCI being indeed "too hard."

On the other hand, the reality is that PCI DSS exemplifies common sense, baseline security practices, which every organization needs to take into account when planning their IT and business operations. PCI only seems hard if you were not doing *anything* for the security of your data before; hopefully this book will help to make PCI DSS easier for you. Still, it might not be easy for a large, distributed organization, but it is clearly much easier than creating and running a well-managed security program based on a good understanding of your risk.

As observed by one of the authors, people who complain about PCI DSS being too hard and emitting loud calls for "Make PCI Easier!!!" are often split into two camps:

- "Please, please make PCI easier by letting us skip the requirements; or, better, they just let us 'JUST SAY YES ON THE SAQ!'" camp.

- "We know that our security program makes us PCI compliant; please make it easier for us to prove it!" camp.

As you can guess, the organizations that fit into the first camp and those that fit into the second camp are very different. While some in the first will miss the joke in *ScanlessPCI* (a joke site set up by a band of security experts to poke fun at some of the organizations that ignore security), the second camp is often concerned with relating their "risk-focused" approach to PCI's mostly "control-focused" approach.

It is possible to make PCI easier even for those in the first camp, those people who just "want it gone": make doing the right thing easier for them (while making doing the wrong thing harder): not storing card data, outsourcing processing, etc. For example, a lot of merchants store card data because they are under the mistaken impression that such data falls under the "Financial Rule of Thumb" of storing financial records for 7 years. Such actions are making PCI DSS much more difficult or, in the case of storing CVV2 or other prohibited data, impossible. Even for chargebacks, which obviously don't go back 7 years, storing the PAN and other sensitive data is not needed.

On the other hand, while in the second camp, one sometimes hears things like "we have a good security program and we manage our risk well! – why should we spend time on that PCI thing? We are probably in good shape already!" These organizations are likely doing a good job with security and want to use all that to quickly "prove compliance." In this case, making PCI easier will include making it easier to assess, validate, and prove compliance and overall make the whole "assessment experience" a little less painful. Still, it will not be harder than building that risk management program that they already have built.

So, as we mentioned, you can make PCI harder for yourself by making the wrong decisions. For example, developing your own Web application complete with credit card processing will increase your PCI scope likely beyond your ability to handle. On the opposite, using a third-party checkout service will do just the opposite and make PCI and data security easier. Review the previous section on Myth #2 and notice that not touching the cards will make your PCI experience so much easier – without going into the application security esoteric such as OWASP guides, SQL injection, cross-site request forgery, and other things better be left to those who enjoy writing books about PCI DSS compliance.

MYTH #4 BREACHES PROVE PCI DSS IRRELEVANT

Myth #4 seems mostly driven by the media: it claims that "Recent card data breaches prove PCI irrelevant." We suspect it stems from the fact that reporting failures and other "bad stuff" typically draws more listeners, readers, and watchers compared to reporting successes and thus attracts more media attention. Note how much press time the catastrophes, corrupt politicians, and various technology failures get; and the bigger the better!

However, it encourages some organizations to develop a negative, destructive mindset and thus to do a bad job with PCI DSS and data security. As a result, they would suffer from a devastating data breach, which is more than a little ironic because they were trying to "focus on the breaches, not on compliance." Breaches of organizations that validated their PCI compliance should get more people to focus on security as well as on maintaining compliant and secure state, not the other way around: if somebody got breached, you now need to do a better job to not end up like his organization. It is worthwhile to mention that QSAs carry part of the blame as well: cases where blatant security mistakes, severe configuration weaknesses, forbidden data storage, and even compromised systems were missed by the "easy grader" assessor who focused much more on writing a report and not enough on actually collecting the data for the report.

WARNING

It is often assumed by security professionals that people outside of security industry will not take advice to protect data from mainstream media. Sadly, people often do. In light of this, the author team would make this into an explicit warning.

Dear reader! Newspapers, magazines, and even IT "trader rags" and information security press are NOT a reliable source of security guidance, whether for technology or for policy security guidance. Read them to know the news, but go to experts for detailed guidance on how to secure your data.

Again, the reality is exactly the opposite: data breaches remind us that basic security, mandated by PCI DSS, is necessary, not sufficient, but you have to start from the basics before you can advance in your security education. As you learn more about security, you usually come to realize that nothing guarantees breach free operation. Let's pick a few examples from PCI DSS and check whether they are a good idea as well as whether they guarantee the absence of breaches. Table 15.1 shows

Table 15.1 PCI DSS Requirements for Data Security

Requirement Number	PCI DSS Requirement	Important for Data Security?	Guarantee Lack of Card Data Loss?
2.1	"Always change vendor-supplied defaults before installing a system on the network – for example, include passwords…"	Yes, default password is a frequent avenue for attackers	No
2.2.4	"Remove all unnecessary functionality, such as scripts, drivers…"	Yes, sample scripts, etc are often abused to get access to systems	No
2.3	"Encrypt all non-console administrative access"	Yes, guessing an admin password exposes the entire systems to attackers	No
3.2	"Do not store sensitive authentication data after authorization"	Yes, theft of such key data allows account abuse	Yes! No data means no data breach
5.1	"Deploy anti-virus software on all systems commonly affected by malicious software"	Yes, viruses, spyware and other malware leads to theft of card data	No, despite anti-virus tools, the malware can still spread to the systems

Continued

Table 15.1 PCI DSS Requirements for Data Security *Continued*

Requirement Number	PCI DSS Requirement	Important for Data Security?	Guarantee Lack of Card Data Loss?
7.1	"Limit access to system components and cardholder data to only those individuals whose job requires such access"	Yes, stolen access credentials makes "hacking" the system very easy	No, as other means of breaking in can be used by attackers
8.5.11	"Use passwords containing both numeric and alphabetic characters"	Yes, such passwords are much harder to guess and then to be used to steal the data	No, even complex passwords can be guessed or systems compromised without the passwords

excerpts from PCI DSS as well as their relation to data protection and data breach prevention.

Table 15.1 allows us to conclude that PCI DSS controls are necessary to prevent card data loss and theft, but few of them can be considered sufficient.

NOTE

Recent breaches remind us that PCI DSS is insufficient – and it is. Only ongoing and adaptable risk management program with quality strategy and execution can be considered an end-state.

Finally, one of the authors' colleagues likes to say that every breach proves that PCI DSS is even more necessary. PCI DSS is a great start for security, but a really bad finish, as we discover in the next myth.

MYTH #5 PCI IS ALL WE NEED FOR SECURITY

Myth #5 is probably the scariest one of all: PCI is all we ever need to do for security. People in the grasp of this myth would proclaim things that will shock every security professional; for example:

- "We have handled PCI – we are secure now."

- "We worked hard and we passed an 'assessment'; now we are secure!"

Or even, in its more extreme form,

- "I filed my PCI compliance documents; now I am compliant and secure."

The above maxims remind the authors of how in the 1990s many executives proudly proclaimed, "I have a firewall, I'm secure" and then refused to pay attention to "overblown" security concerns. At the very least, a firewall might block some suspicious connections, while filed report on compliance paperwork on its own does not provide any protection – and in fact only introduces additional risk of fire.

Recently, one of the authors was shocked to read the following on what purports to be a security blog post that talked about the now-infamous Heartland Payment Systems data breach: "Is complying to PCI not enough anymore?" It seems that even security professionals can somehow fall victim to this myth. Another common manifestation is an organization that doesn't pay much, if any, attention to data security is being suddenly jabbed by PCI DSS requirements. More often than not senior management will "make" IT do "that PCI security thing."

It often leads organizations to focus on "pleasing the assessor" and then forgetting that a happy assessor does not mean that your organization is protected from information risks.

Moreover, this myth is actually wrong on multiple levels! First, validating PCI DSS via an assessment or self-assessment does not mean that you are done with PCI DSS as you now need to maintain compliance. Also, it certainly does not mean that you are done with security. In addition, it also doesn't mean that you are secure, just that you validated PCI compliance and hopefully made an honest step towards reducing your risk; now you need to maintain your compliant status and data security!

Again:

Validating PCI compliance via onsite assessment or self-assessment does NOT mean that:

- You are "done with PCI" and now can ignore it.

- You are "done with security" and now cannot do anything to protect your data.

- You are "secure" or as even secure as you need to be.

The reality is again different: PCI just mandates minimum security, not maximum or optimal.

PCI is basic security; it is a necessary baseline, a lower watermark, which was never meant to be the "end state" of guaranteed secure data. No external guidance document, even well-written and followed with utmost diligence, can guarantee that – just as excellent police work can never guarantee "crime-free" environment. People don't expect police, prosecutors, and laws to "end crime" – so why do some people think that QSAs, approved scanning vendors (ASVs), card brands, and PCI DSS document will end cybercrime?" This is a useful thought to keep in your head as you are finishing that PCI validation.

WARNING

If you hear somebody lament the fact that he was PCI compliant and then got breached and had all card data stolen, please pause before bashing PCI DSS for this unfortunate course of events. It is hard to say for sure without having the details, but in most case the authors have seen in the field, such breach was the fault of the merchant and not of PCI DSS, PCI Council, or any other regulatory entity.

Finally, PCI is about cardholder data security, not the rest of your private or regulated information, not your organization intellectual property, not identity information such as SSNs, etc. It also covers confidentiality, and not availability of such data. These quick examples show that there is a lot more to data security than PCI DSS, and there are clear areas where PCI does not focus.

Specifically, perfect PCI DSS compliance and validation will not:

- Make your "out of scope," non-cardholder data such as SSNs secure.
- Make your trade secrets and other intellectual property secure.
- Make your "out of scope" systems and networks secure.
- Make your card data and other data more reliably available for its users.
- Make you automatically compliant with any other international, national, state or industry regulation.

It might only minimally affect:

- Security of your other data – the implemented network safeguard might help and so might the change of organization culture due to security
- Your readiness to address other regulations

Thus, you are certainly not "done with security" even if you maintain ongoing PCI compliance. For example, one of notable PCI QSAs likes to say that you likely need "PCI+" or even "PCI++" to deal with risks to your data today.

MYTH #6 PCI DSS IS REALLY EASY

The next myth, #6, is the opposite of myth #4: PCI is easy: we just have to "say Yes" on a questionnaire and "get scanned." As merchants become more familiar with PCI DSS, some start to feel that PCI is not that scary – it is about getting a mysterious "scan" from an entity called "an ASV," then answering "Yes" to a bunch of lengthy questions and paying an "outrageous" fee of $8.95 with their monthly merchant account bill. Given the above view of PCI DSS as "annoying but tolerable" such merchants have fully succumbed to this myth. Their misconceptions are expressed in claims that PCI is about getting a scan and answering some questions or that it is a paperwork exercise or even that it can be bought for $8.95 monthly compliance fee.

For merchants and service providers that don't have to go through an on-site QSA assessment, PCI DSS compliance is indeed validated via external vulnerability scanning by an ASV and SAQ. However, it is worthwhile to mention that there is some work involved before many of the merchants can truthfully answer "yes" to those question and would be able to prove this, if requested.

WARNING

PCI DSS is not easy. It is definitely not easy for a large company that needs to collect all the evidence for compliance validation from different systems. However, these activities, if not easy, are actually useful for security and overall manageability in that company.

PCI DSS is pretty easy if all card processing is outsourced to a reliable and secure processing provider, who allows you to not touch the data.

Here is an example: Requirement 1.1.2 mandates a "current network diagram with all connections to cardholder data, including any wireless networks." We show a few examples of such diagrams in Chapter 4, "Building and Maintaining a Secure Network." What would answering "Yes" to this question entail:

1. Having a diagram available

2. Making sure that the diagram is indeed current and all network connections are reflected on it

3. Knowing the locations of cardholder data (itself a massive project at many organizations!)

4. Confirming that it shows all connections to all locations of cardholder data

5. Knowing which wireless networks are deployed and where, including those deployed by divisions and other business units (and possibly rogue as well)

Clearly, this takes more than checking a book or clicking "Y" on a computer. This is what turns minutes into months.

A slightly simplified reality is that a typical small merchant who processes cards online would at least need to do the following:

a. Get a network vulnerability scan of the external systems from an ASV, resolve the vulnerabilities found, and then rescan to verify that.

b. Do the things that the SAQ questions refer to and maintain evidence that they were performed; then answer the questions affirmatively and retain proof of that validation.

c. Keep up with periodic maintenance and other requirements until you no longer wish to accept credit cards, in other words: maintain compliance.

In other words, achieve PCI DSS validation and then maintain PCI DSS compliance for as long as you plan to accept cards. You can only answer 'yes' if you have ground for saying 'yes' on the questionnaire and can prove it, even with no assessors or acquiring banks looking over your shoulder.

NOTE

Question: My management told me to ignore everything, including security hardening of my servers and even response to an ongoing hacking incident and go focus on "pleasing the QSA." What should I do?
Answer: Apart from changing a job, you mean? Sorry, bad joke. What you need to do is try to tie all the key security things you know you need to do (we are assuming here that you actually know what those things are) and tie them to PCI DSS requirement. Under such PCI umbrella, the management should be more accepting of what you actually need to do for security. Result: achieve both security and PCI DSS compliance.

Specifically, even on the vulnerability scanning side, the typical perception that "get a PCI scan and you are done" is essentially misguided. PCI DSS requires you to run both internal and external network vulnerability scans at least quarterly (in reality, twice a quarter since you'd need to fix the vulnerabilities and then rescan to confirm it!) as well as after every major network change. Internal scans can be run by in-house security staff, while the external scans must be performed by an ASV, and these are then used to satisfy your PCI Validation Requirements and are submitted to your acquiring bank. By default, all Internet-facing IP addresses are "in-scope."

NOTE

It is a common misconception that the PCI DSS scanning validation requirement applies only to systems that process card data. If you are subject to PCI DSS scanning requirements (which happens when you have systems connected to the Internet), all of your externally visible systems are subject to security scanning (by an ASV) as well as those systems involved in processing, storing, and transmitting the data and the ones "directly connected" to them (by an internal team or a consultant).

MYTH #7 MY TOOL IS PCI COMPLIANT

Myth #7 is in believing that your network, application, tool is PCI compliant with the resulting conclusion that this achieves compliance for your organization. This myth manifests itself in statements from merchants such as "My payment application vendor said his tool is 'PCI compliant'" or "They put together a network and it is PCI compliant." However, no tool can make you compliant. In fact, people often confuse PA-DSS certified application with PCI DSS compliant organization, which literally have little to do with each other, even though both come from PCI Council.

Just to remind, PCI DSS is a "multifaceted security standard that includes requirements for security management, policies, procedures, network architecture, software design, and other critical protective measures. This comprehensive standard is intended to help organizations proactively protect customer account data." (PCI Council website [7]) On the other hand, PA-DSS is "to help software vendors and others develop secure payment applications that do not store prohibited data, such as full magnetic stripe, CVV2 or PIN data, and ensure their payment applications support compliance with the PCI DSS." (PCI Council Web site [7]) The former applies to an entire organization while the latter applies to a payment application only.

TOOLS

PA-DSS list contains all of the validated payment applications that need to be used by the merchants. It is not uncommon for an acquirer to refuse to board merchants that use applications which are not on the list or even the versions of the applications which are not on the list.

However, using this list will get you a list of tools, but you still need to deploy the tools in the manner prescribed by the DSS document.

In reality, there is no such thing as "PCI compliant tool, application, configuration or network," PCI DSS compliance applies to organizations only. You can struggle toward, achieve, and validate PCI DSS compliance only as an organization. Using PA-DSS-compliant, application is only a small piece of the whole puzzle.

Despite that, the authors have been asked multiple times by various industry colleagues about certain pieces of IT infrastructure being PCI compliant. Here is one recent example – Fig. 15.2.

Figure 15.2 was shown to one of the authors with the question of "Is this PCI compliant?" Even though some people will start debating this with crafty arguments for "yes" and "no," the immediate response was "no way to tell." There are simply too many things that can make or break PCI DSS compliant status of an organization. For example:

- What are the password policies on these servers? Are the compliant with the whole host of requirements 8.5, such as "8.5.5 Remove/disable inactive user accounts at least every 90 days" or "8.5.9 Change user passwords at least every 90 days."

- Is there logging performed? Is such logging as good as requirement 10.2 mandates. Namely, is logging sufficient to reconstruct the prescribed events.

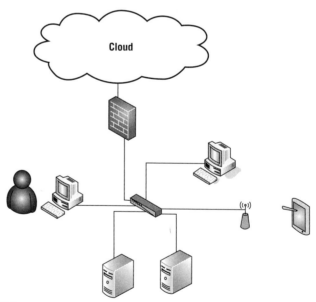

FIGURE 15.2 *Is This Network PCI Compliant?*

- Is vulnerability scanning done? Are scans "run [..] at least quarterly and after any significant change in the network?" Are discovered vulnerabilities remediated?

- Is file-integrity monitoring software deployed to "alert personnel to unauthorized modification of critical system files" (requirement 11.5 in PCI DSS)?

- Moreover, are the security policies "established, published, maintained, and disseminated" (Requirement 12.1 in PCI DSS)? Even, is there "a formal security awareness program to make all employees aware of the importance of cardholder data security" prescribed by PCI DSS Requirement 12.6?

WARNING

Security policy is pretty darn important for your PCI DSS compliance program (since it is mandated in Requirement 12 which we cover in Chapter 6, "Protecting Cardholder Data") as well as for data security. However, here is the dirty truth about policy: it does nada, none, zero to secure the data unless it is actually followed in reality and enforced by security technology and process.

Further, the authors hypothesize that this is exactly why policy development is listed in Phase 6 of "PCI DSS Prioritized Approach" [8]. Security professionals say "policy comes first," but policy needs to be actually implemented have ANY impact on data security and risk.

The above lists only a few of the reason for why the above pictures environment might or might not be part of a PCI DSS compliant organization.

Thus, "no way to tell" is the only genuine response. There is no way to judge PCI compliance on just isolated servers.

NOTE

Your network, application, tool are not PCI compliant, even though the payment application can be PA-DSS compliant. PCI DSS compliance, however, applies to the entire organization.

Answering the question is only possible "in bulk," considering all the conditions, criteria, and requirement. And the way to achieve this is to follow your own path through PCI DSS requirement. You can also be assisted by "PCI DSS Prioritized Approach" which lists the recommended, risk-derived order for following the requirements. The document can be found on the PCI Council Web site [6]. Figure 15.3 shows an example from the PCI Council document called "Prioritized Approach to PCI" [8].

Milestone	Goals
1	**Remove sensitive authentication data and limit data retention.** This milestone targets a key area of risk for entities that have been compromised. Remember – if sensitive authentication data and other cardholder data are not stored, the effects of a compromise will be greatly reduced. If you don't need it, don't store it.
2	**Protect the perimeter, internal, and wireless networks.** This milestone targets controls for points of access to most compromises – the network or a wireless access point.
3	**Secure payment card applications.** This milestone targets controls for applications, application processes, and application servers. Weaknesses in these areas offer easy prey for compromising systems and obtaining access to cardholder data.
4	**Monitor and control access to your systems.** Controls for this milestone allow you to detect the who, what, when, and how concerning who is accessing your network and cardholder data environment.
5	**Protect stored cardholder data.** For those organizations that have analyzed their business processes and determined that they must store Primary Account Numbers, Milestone Five targets key protections mechanisms for that stored data.
6	**Finalize remaining compliance efforts, and ensure all controls are in place.** The intent of Milestone Six is to complete PCI DSS requirements and finalize all remaining related policies, procedures, and processes needed to protect the cardholder data environment.

FIGURE 15.3   *PCI DSS Prioritized Approach*

As we mentioned, PCI DSS combines technology, process, policy, awareness, and practices as well. For example, Requirement 12 covers security policy, incident response practices, security awareness, and other nontechnical safeguards and controls. Don't focus on isolated pieces; rather, build the big picture, track a path, and move ahead towards PCI DCC compliance and data security.

MYTH #8 PCI IS TOOTHLESS

Myth #8 is simply a view that "PCI DSS Is Toothless." This myth shows a completely wrong worldview of PCI DSS and security; a dangerous delusion that is also wrong on several levels.

First, it embodies the view that data security measures are only deployed due to regulatory pressure, such as from PCI DSS, and not from genuine need to reduce risk to information. This myth is often used to justify not doing anything about data security with merchants believing – erroneously that if even they are breached and then also found noncompliant, their business will not suffer[1]. Similarly, people read the popular media and then ignorantly claim that companies are breached and then continue being profitable so they should not care about PCI and security. Finally, they claim that compliance costs most than noncompliance without doing any research into this subject, which then leads to faulty decision making.

Honestly, such views are often held by merchants who are used to just accepting the risk of card data theft. In fact, in the pre-PCI era it made good sense to accept such risk because it was not the merchant's loss, but the issuing banks that would need to reissue the stolen cards. Here is a commonly utilized conceptual risk formula[2]:

Risk = Threat × Vulnerability × Value of Loss

If we apply it to this situation, we'd realize that before PCI the merchant's risk was indeed exactly 0 and absolutely didn't depend on threats that the merchant faced, as well as vulnerabilities his environment had. PCI DSS transferred the risk back to where it should belong – wherever the data is lost or stolen. Thus, one can say that PCI DSS created the risk for merchants to motivate them to protect the data.

Second, in addition to being a wrong mindset, it is also simply wrong. PCI DSS noncompliance and resulting loss of cardholder data packs a lot of bite which includes fines, possible lawsuits, mandatory breach disclosure costs, investigation costs, possible card processing rate increases, cost of additional security measures, and cost of victim credit monitoring. It is really not only about the fines; among the above "teeth" the following were actually frequently observed:

- Breach disclosure costs: Although it is not the direct consequence of PCI DSS noncompliance, these costs always result from the breaches, frequently caused by blatant disregard for both data security and PCI compliance.

- Legal costs: In case of suffering a breach and then being found noncompliant, the chance of a lawsuit mentioning negligence is higher.

- Fines: The card brands are not very vocal about fines, but public reporting of recent large breaches did mention fines ranging all the way up to $10 m.

---

[1] Just ask CardSystems, sold for peanuts after a massive breach
[2] As this formula is conceptual and not strictly mathematical, it is often written with many different variations.

- Publicity: The experts can debate how the negative publicity maps into actually dollar losses, there is no denying that the name "Heartland Payment Systems" was not known outside of a narrow segment of payment professionals and now the query on Google for its name finds more than 240,000 pages related to the massive breach. Do you really want your company name to become a synonym for "data breaches?" Exactly, neither did they!

To top it off, a victim merchant can be labeled "Level 1" and thus subjected to an annual QSA assessment – at their own expense. Admittedly, not every breach will incur all of the above, but some are simply unavoidable.

NOTE

If breached and then found noncompliant, your business will suffer. The exact amount of loss that you will take cannot really be predicted up front, but it will be there. In the very worst case, your business name will become synonymous with "data breach," just as Heartland Payment Systems did. And even though TJ Maxx, the victim of the second largest breach before Heartland, is doing better now than they were doing before the breach, the documented losses, included court settlements of $9.75 million [9], were significant.

Overall, it is much more useful to think of customer and cardholder data protection as your "social responsibility" and not as something you do because of some scary "PCI teeth" somewhere! The companies talk about corporate social responsibility (CSR)[3], but often forget that caring for the private data of their customers that was entrusted it to them due to the current predominant paradigm – use of a payment card with a magnetic stripe – is the simplest form of corporate social responsibility. What more fits the definition of "embracing responsibility for the impact of their activities on the environment, consumers, employees, communities, stakeholders, and all other members of the public sphere," than caring for those precious bits and bytes from the magnetic stripe?

---

[3] Sometimes corporate social responsibility (CSR) is defined by stating that the business must accept all responsibility for the results of its activities on the nature, environment, customers, employees, and even public at large. Moreover, commercial orgs must actually work in the public interest by encouraging community and choosing to discontinue practices that harm the public sphere or can be seen as unethical. CSR concept is surely controversial but evidences suggests that business are more often pushed to focus on things other than profit, whether it is good or bad.

CASE STUDY

Next, we present a case study that illustrates what is covered in this chapter.

The Case of the Cardless Merchant

Sometimes, merchants unknowingly accept PCI-related risk and can be left facing substantial fines.

Payton's "P-Funk All Stars" Party Palace is a recent startup company attacking the ever-popular children's birthday party celebration location market. Payton recently left her position at a retailer to start her company, and her previous experience included a basic understanding of PCI and that compliance was important and mandatory. When Payton was looking for the ability to accept major credit and debit cards, she made sure to find an Independent Sales Organization (ISO) that offered management of her POS devices.

Upon receiving the contract from her ISO, she noticed that she would still be filing for her own Merchant ID, but one of the ISO's divisions, PayProcess Express, would be leasing and managing her POS equipment. For an extra fee, they also agreed to perform settlement services and reconciliation reports. Payton's funding was not substantial, and preferred the transactional-based fees instead of hiring someone part time to perform this function.

Six months into her venture, her business was booming. She received a peculiar call from someone in the fraud department of her ISO asking very odd questions about her setup. She learned that her business was identified as the possible source of a cardholder data breach. After explaining that she outsourced all of her maintenance and upkeep to PayProcess Express, she was informed the business unit was sold to another company, and that the merchant ID was still issued to her directly, therefore she was responsible for paying for fines and the forensic investigation.

Payton was crushed. How did she end up in this situation? She was now facing significant fines that could affect her ability to meet her creditors and payroll.

Payton made one critical error. While her knowledge of PCI was critical to how she set up her payment processing environment, she mistakenly thought that having a third party manage her systems would cover her in the case a breach occurred. In reality, Payton was responsible for keeping up with her compliance, and she failed to ensure that Requirement 12.8 was met with respect to her outsourcer.

Had Payton processed under PayProcess Express's merchant ID, she may only be facing lost business due to consumer confidence versus facing fines and fees associated with the breach.

SUMMARY

Here are all the myths again:

- PCI just doesn't apply to us, because…we are special.

- PCI is confusing and not specific!

- PCI is too hard.

- Recent breaches prove PCI irrelevant.

- PCI is easy: we just have to "say Yes" on SAQ and "get scanned."

- My network, application, tool is PCI compliant.

- PCI is all we need to do for security!

- Even if breached and then found noncompliant, our business will not suffer.

Now that you know what the myths are and what the reality is, you are one step closer to painless, effective PCI DSS program as well as to secure and compliant organization that cares about its customers by protecting their data.

Remember that PCI is common sense, basic security; stop complaining about it – start doing it! By focusing on immediately useful parts of PCI DSS, you can start towards a full-scale risk management program. Then, after validating that you are compliant, don't stop: continuous compliance and security is your goal, not "passing an assessment." For example, remember that compensating controls are usually temporary controls, not excuses to never do the right thing.

Overall, it is much more useful to develop "security and risk" mindset, not "compliance and assessment" mindset. Just as there is no true guaranteed "job security" today, there is no "guaranteed information security"; there is only one thing: doing the best you can do and being above average, so that attackers leave for greener pastures.

REFERENCES

[1] Web site www.kare11.com/news/news_article.aspx?storyid=542102 [accessed 12.07.2009].

[2] "PCI-DSS: Not on health care provider's radar" in "SC Magazine" online. www.scmagazineus.com/PCI-DSS-Not-on-health-care-providers-radar/article/138783/ [accessed 12.07.2009].

[3] PCI DSS SAQ. www.pcisecuritystandards.org/saq/index.shtml [accessed 12.07.2009].

[4] ISO/IEC 17799:2005. www.iso.org/iso/iso_catalogue/catalogue_tc/catalogue_detail.htm?csnumber=39612 [accessed 12.07.2009].

[5] NIST 800-53. Recommended Security Controls for Federal Information Systems and Organizations. http://csrc.nist.gov/publications/drafts/800-53/800-53-rev3-FPD-clean.pdf [accessed 12.07.2009].

[6] Summary of Changes from PCI DSS Version 1.1 to 1.2. www.pcisecuritystandards.org/pdfs/pci_dss_summary_of_changes_v1-2.pdf [accessed 12.07.2009].

[7] PCI Council. Website www.pcisecuritystandards.org [accessed 12.07.2009].

[8] The Prioritized Approach to Pursue PCI DSS Compliance. www.pcisecuritystandards.org/education/docs/Prioritized_Approach_PCI_DSS_1_2.pdf [accessed 12.07.2009].

[9] TJ Maxx Settles Data Breach Charges. www.consumeraffairs.com/news04/2009/06/tjx_settlement.html [accessed 2.08.2009].

Index

343